SOMEONE ELSE'S SAINT

How a Scottish Pilgrimage Led to Nova Scotia

MATTHEW R. ANDERSON

POTTERSFIELD PRESS
Lawrencetown Beach, Nova Scotia, Canada

Library and Archives Canada Cataloguing in Publication
Title: Someone else's saint : how a Scottish pilgrimage led to Nova Scotia / Matthew R. Anderson.
Names: Anderson, Matthew R. (Matthew Robert), author
Description: Includes bibliographical references.
Identifiers: Canadiana (print) 20250102021 | Canadiana (ebook) 20250104970 | ISBN 9781990770692 (softcover) | ISBN 9781990770708 (EPUB)
Subjects: LCSH: Pilgrims and pilgrimages—Scotland. | LCSH: Pilgrims and pilgrimages—Nova Scotia. | LCSH: Trails—Scotland. | LCSH: Trails—Nova Scotia. | LCSH: Hiking—Scotland. | LCSH: Hiking—Nova Scotia. | LCSH: Scotland—Description and travel. | LCSH: Nova Scotia—Description and travel. | LCSH: Ninian, Saint, -432? | LCGFT: Travel writing.
Classification: LCC DA867.5 .A53 2025 | DDC 914.14—dc23

Cover photo: iStock/background image: 2089131771, footprints: iStock-1131769507

Cover design: Gail LeBlanc

Pottersfield Press gratefully acknowledges the financial support of the Government of Canada for our publishing activities through the Canada Book Fund. We also acknowledge the support of the Canada Council for the Arts and the Province of Nova Scotia which has assisted us to develop and promote our creative industries for the benefit of all Nova Scotians.

Pottersfield Press
248 Leslie Road
East Lawrencetown, Nova Scotia, Canada, B2Z 1T4
Website: www.pottersfieldpress.com
To order, phone 1-800-NIMBUS9 (1-800-646-2879) www.nimbus.ca

Conseil des arts du Canada | Canada Council for the Arts | Funded by the Government of Canada | Financé par le gouvernement du Canada | Canada

Arts Nova Scotia Nouvelle-Écosse | Nova Scotia

Printed in Canada on recycled paper.

For Sara:

Because I was following you,
I found my way to Ninian.

TABLE OF CONTENTS

WALKING

"I am driven to the riverbank by habit and history and temperament."
(Ariel Gordon 2024)

When there's always so much to do, to simply "go for a walk" becomes an act of defiance. As a pastime, walking seems almost too ordinary and simple to mention. It's just step after step, repeated, again and again. Our dopamine-addicted brains have learned to clamour for the distracting shock and applause of social media. What you're choosing when walking any distance is not entertainment or pleasure in any typical sense. It's choosing – at first – to be bored.

Paradoxically, the unhurried pace turns out to be fulfilling. As one walks for the sake of walking, the mind settles down. If we're paying attention, we notice things. In the monotony, our breath. In the aching ankle or the blistered toe, the presence of our bodies, so often neglected in front of screens. Step by step, before us, we begin to see more sharply: not only hill, tree, rock, flower, sidewalk, fence, wall, overpass, or garbage, but also, and whether or not we always want to – memories, people, regrets, ideas, and hopes.

Unbidden, our inner lives and our imaginations join us, stepping between and around the landscape. If we're fortunate, we also begin to sense nature anew. The quiver of a stem of dewy morning grass, the light reflecting off the windows of an old building, the smile of a passer-by, the erratic blue flit of a damselfly, or a scurrying in the underbrush. Revelations sometimes fall into rhythm beside us. Resolutions to some problem sidle up alongside, although they often stay no longer than the next step or the next breath, before diverging from our path again, gone too soon to be recognized.

Keep going. Long-distance walking is not primarily an instrument for exercise or pleasure, although both will likely arrive with us at the end of our trail. First and foremost, walking is meditation. For those with the good fortune of mobility, walking is a spell our feet cast over us, quieting our brains while, step by step by step, the rhythm bonds us for good to our bodies and to the body of the world.

This is a story of two walks. If you've never been to southwest Scotland or northeast Nova Scotia, you may not know the places described in this book's two long-distance pilgrimages to the mysterious St. Ninian. That's okay: even locals may not have seen, or noticed, all of what's in these pages. Noticing is part of the beauty and benefit of walking. Once the only way most people travelled, in an age of mindfulness walking has come back into its own as a way to pay attention, to remember, to learn, to protest, to heal, and to laugh and share company.

As a pilgrim and a pilgrimage scholar, I've witnessed many of my colleagues focussing on one particular pilgrimage – the Camino de Santiago. It's hard to argue with what Spain offers: views, infrastructure, Rioja, churros, paella, and an international community of fellow travellers that sets out in waves on the Camino each day from France.

But wherever you might be, I guarantee that the land *where you are* is also full of stories, and maybe even some miracles to match Santiago's. Your trails may not be as developed as Spain's, but perhaps your walk will begin to change that. Walking the much less well-known Whithorn Way in Scotland in 2019, or the Nova Scotia Ninian Way (my own invention) in 2024, wasn't easy. But by walking where we are, we summon the past from the land we're in relationship with and bind ourselves to it in a small way. We bear witness to communities, dreams, injustices, memories, and interesting little spots that a driver, speeding past, may never notice.

In North America, walking means learning about Indigenous pasts and futures, and about Indigenous presence and sovereignty. Here in Nova Scotia, we honour first the Mi'kmaq whose land it remains, and after them the Acadians, the Gaels, the Black Nova Scotians, and others, the generations whose lives intertwined with these specific fields, woods, towns, and streams.

Dr. Sara Parks and I moved to Pomquet, Nova Scotia, in 2022. For two years, I had the good fortune to lead pilgrimages for Camino Nova Scotia, a guided spiritual walking program of the Atlantic School of Theology in Halifax (with support from the Oifis Iomairtean na Gàidhlig – the Office of Gaelic Affairs). I slept in community centres and church halls. I swept dusty basement floors and blew up air mattresses only to deflate them all eight hours later for the next leg of the journey. I learned where the bakeries, fish coops, coffee stops, grocery stores, and emergency clinics were all over mainland Nova Scotia and the Island of Cape Breton. The province of Nova Scotia became "real" to me in those walks – no longer just spots on a map, but *places* alive with store clerks and trail managers, guitarists and community volunteers, folk songs and pharmacists and farmers' markets.

This "making real" is what pilgrimage can accomplish. Antigonish was somewhat abstract when Sara applied for the job that brought us here from her work in the U.K. But through walking the hills and marshes of Pomquet, South River, and Antigonish, the waters of St. George's Bay and the people who live here have become real to me. Quite unexpectedly, so has St. Ninian – a figure I'd often told my pilgrimage students was probably mythical. This book is a bit of giving back to this place and honouring its stories (from both sides of the Atlantic), in the hopes of making them more real for you as well.

THE HEADS OF AYR

"Like any new experience, so much about starting out on a walking pilgrimage begins as a mystery."

"Tide's out at the Heads already?" shouted a woman in a flapping yellow windbreaker as she strode toward us over the wet rocks, trailing a man and a dog.

"Heads?" I called back. A Scot could say my name and I wouldn't understand it.

"Heads!" she repeated, as if I were daft. She pointed over my shoulder: "The Heads of Ayr. Brave to pass so soon on such a dreich day!"

I turned to look at the cliff whose wet footings we four Canadian pilgrims had just circumvented. So that was why our feet had been slipping into the surf where the map had shown a path. Born and raised in land-lubber Saskatchewan, I am not exactly a connoisseur of tides.

The Whithorn Way is a twenty-first-century trek superimposed over the approximate route of a medieval pilgrimage path in Scotland. Its set-up was fuelled by temporary grants and undertaken by a hopeful conglomeration of tourist, government, and religious groups. Its purpose is to take the hardy – and the foolhardy – the 143 miles, or 233 kilometres, from Glasgow to the southwest tip of Scotland. There, on the Machars peninsula, lie the remains of the *Candida Casa*, or White House, the resting place of St. Ninian, an obscure fifth- or sixth-century bishop.

Because the full walk would take about nine days, and we Canadians only had a week of vacation, we'd skipped the initial, urban sections of the trail, and taken the train straight from Glasgow's central station to Ayr and the coast. From there, we'd walked through Alloway Village with a stop at Robbie Burns' farmstead (turned) shrine, then followed a short path to the beach.

Already in our first hours we four pilgrims had learned several facts. Not all were connected, nor were they of equal worth: 1/ Robbie Burns hadn't been much of a farmer, which was perhaps how he'd had time to sire children by seemingly every woman in the neighbourhood. 2/ Some of the best seafront in Ayr is inhabited by caravan parks you can't cut straight through to the coastal paths. 3/ Scottish Heritage sells tasty rhubarb-custard candies whose ingredients unexpectedly include pork gelatine (important to know with a vegetarian in the group). 4/ The well of St. Mungo we passed on the path to the sea contained votive pebbles predating Christianity, and so, logically, the saint. And perhaps most importantly for travellers from away: 5/ because local volunteers are responsible for the signage of the Whithorn Way and associated paths such as the Ayrshire Coastal Path, the upkeep of those signs – even their existence – varies widely. Sometimes leading unwary hikers, more or less, into the sea.

Peter Ross of the Scottish Outdoor Trust would later tell us: "Use is the cure." This seemed to be true of just about everything about the Whithorn Way. The few signs we found turned out to be more confirmation than direction. Fortunately, my friend Ken Wilson, a writer and an avid long-distance walking enthusiast, had come with Ordnance Survey (OS) maps. These are a prerequisite for any U.K. rambling, even when the maps remain folded in your pocket. Once, when I was lost on a trail in the Peaks district, a Brit wouldn't even give me directions until she'd seen that I at least had had the sense to bring an OS map along.

I'd be remiss not to mention that it's now possible to get better maps to all sections of the Whithorn Way than we had back in 2019. Not only that, but we had the poor fortune to be promised trail maps and guidance we never received. In short: our trip isn't indicative.

Like any new experience, so much about starting out on a walking pilgrimage begins as a mystery. What might seem obvious later is far from clear at the outset of a journey. Christine Ramsay had only just arrived from Western Canada and was still suffering badly from jet lag. She was doubly fatigued by the constant retracing of our steps. Sara Parks, the only one of us who'd grown up beside the ocean, looked at the surf and announced matter-of-factly that the tide was going out. Having grown up on the prairies, myself, an expanse of heaving saltwater is something I find beautiful, but ominous, and certainly beyond understanding. I admit that when planning the route, I hadn't thought of tides having an effect on our timing.

The day before our departure we'd visited Glasgow Cathedral. There, we'd seen the brightly saturated work of Herbert Hendrie, perhaps Scotland's best-known stained-glass artist. One of the windows features St. Mungo (the pet name for St. Kentigern, founder of the cathedral). Mungo is standing between a king and queen, holding a ring triumphantly. Beside him, a boy clutches a large fish. The story is that King Riderch accused his queen, Languoreth, of infidelity. He had her ring thrown into the water, and publicly accused her of giving it to her lover. If she could not find it, he threatened to put her to death. St. Mungo came to her rescue with a miracle. He ordered that a fish be caught. When its mouth was opened, there was the ring.

One doesn't have to read much Scottish history to realize that what might be most miraculous about this story isn't the fish and ring but the fact that for once there happened to be a saint available to step between a powerful man and his murderous intent. As we walked, the sea never yielded any rings to us – unless you counted the lids from plastic water bottles left by the tides. But it gave us a Mungo-style gift, nonetheless. Sara, the Maritimer, was walking with her head down, scanning the beach. "Look at this!" she hollered. She held up a piece of beach glass. Etched on its green surface was, inexplicably, a single scallop shell. As the ocean receded, it had left us one of the most globally recognizable emblems of pilgrimage, the scallop shell of the Camino de Santiago. It was hard not to take it as a sign that, despite our confusion, we were on the right path.

The instructions we'd been given never mentioned the fact that parts of the trail only existed at low tide. And despite a half hour of searching, there'd been no sign of the trail head our verbal instructions indicated should be there. With Sara's advice, we decided to brave the sliver of rocks that allowed us to squeeze around the headland, anxious to begin our trek to Ninian.

Poor St. Ninian. If you've never heard of him, you're not alone. He's the underdog saint of Scotland, an historical footnote and a half-transparent wisp of a story compared to bold and brawny Columba up the coast. Southwest Scotland hosts two saints, and ostensibly, two competing narratives. Yet in the polite, but firmly fought, "battle of the saints" that has been roiling in Scotland for over a millennium, there is no question as to winner and loser (Towill 1978, 195). Even in the twenty-first century, when Scottish pilgrimage is a tourism exercise where village councils share some of the same goals as local churches, sleepy little Whithorn has to work ten times as hard as the folks at Iona to get any respect – even notice – for its St. Ninian.

Ninian might not have it so bad were it not for St. Columba, warrior-monk, being more charismatic and more historically authenticated (Bradley 1996, 24). Iona is a small island about three miles long with a permanent population of fewer than 150. But Columba makes it a significant pilgrim magnet. The wee place attracts a tourist influx of about 130,000 a year. The Iona Abbey was rebuilt in the 1930s and has since been the home of a lively ecumenical monastic community. The winning combination of a contemporary Iona community, good stories, and a fascinating, rebuilt historic site in a stunning location draws crowds. In his book *The Quest for Celtic Christianity*, Donald Meek remarks dryly that "The location of Iona, as an island once isolated on the western edge of Scotland, was, and remains, a primitivist's dream" (57).

Our destination – Whithorn and its Ninian – doesn't lack for rugged, rocky headlands and ocean views. But the village itself is in a quiet valley, not the kind of windswept Scottish isle on which our post-Romantic-era imaginations prefer to situate saints. Nor does Whithorn boast a permanent monastic community putting out best-selling devotional literature. Whithorn's abbey is quietly well maintained. But like almost all medieval abbeys in the Isles, it consists of a few explanatory plaques and the ruins left by a scavenging Reformation. Whithorn does have a fine museum featuring remarkable, early medieval stone crosses, and a new Welcome Centre. But where the hum of the curious and faithful is rarely far from you in Iona, in Whithorn you're more likely to hear farm tractors ferrying hay than the sounds of pilgrims hurrying to their saint.

Both Iona's website and the Whithorn Trust website claim to represent "the site of the earliest Christian community in Scotland." These statements can't both be true. Despite the popular vote stacked so strongly against it, Whithorn staunchly maintains its pride of place. Whoever Ninian was, and whenever he may have lived, the Whithorn Priory Church of Scotland bearing his name wants you to know at least one thing: Christianity was there before Columba came along.

THE HEADS OF POMQUET

"Pomquet became famous for its ship carpenters who ranked among the best in Nova Scotia ...."

(Stanley-Blackwell and MacLean 2004)

Pomquet Beach is glorious for a swim or a walk, a jewel of Nova Scotia's North Shore. The locals pronounce Pomquet as "Pawm-kit" in both English and French. From the Beach to Saint Ninian's Cathedral in Antigonish, Nova Scotia, is about twenty-three kilometres. The cathedral was consecrated in 1874 – almost 150 years to the day from the arrival of our inaugural group pilgrimage that took place on September 14 and 15, 2024.

Compared to the Scottish route, the Nova Scotia Ninian Way is a breezy stroll. It's just a day's outing, unless you do what we did, and spread the walk over two days to allow for a Sunday morning arrival at the cathedral. The Nova Scotia Ninian Way is far from a nature hike on a dedicated recreational trail. (To discover examples of those, see Michael Haynes' 2015 guide, *Hiking Trails of Mainland Nova Scotia*). Rather, it's a pilgrimage along the edges of streets and secondary highways.

In any case, you won't want to rush. Since you start on a beach, if the weather is nice, take your shoes off and dig your toes into the sand. Walk the surf barefoot. The Heads you see here are Cape George to the west and, rising in front of that, almost as if from the beach, the triangular outcrop of Monk's Head, topped by the former farmhouse known as Chez Deslauriers. The comment I've heard most frequently from those seeing the cropped green of Monk's Head is "Can you imagine mowing that?" (Only recently, my wife and I ran into one of the volunteer grass-cutters at an Acadian dinner. He casually dispensed tips on how to manoeuvre a lawn tractor "if it starts skidding sideways downhill.")

Now turn and look east. The land you see there is the shoreline of Cape Breton Island. The Mabou Highlands rise, hazy, to the northeast. The western and eastern promontories bracket the waters of St. George's Bay, a twenty-six-kilometre divot out of Nova Scotia's north shore, featuring relatively shallow, warm waters from the Northumberland Strait.

Straight ahead and slightly left, just past Cape George, lies Prince Edward Island. To your right and much closer stands Pomquet Island together with its lighthouse. Despite its name, Pomquet Island is connected by an underwater ridge not to Pomquet, but to the Bayfield side of the harbour channel.

There's no one reason to begin a pilgrimage to the Nova Scotian Ninian here at the waters of St. George's Bay. I suggest it because it's so pretty, because Ninian almost certainly arrived at Whithorn in Scotland by sea, because the Atlantic connects our two pilgrim destinations, and because the Nova Scotia Ninian Way intersects the communities that make the northeast of Nova Scotia's mainland what it is.

Besides, the route has a few advantages over other possible walks. One is relative safety: in this land of few footpaths, by starting at Pomquet Beach, a trekker to Antigonish can make the trip by secondary roads and avoid the main highway, the 104. Undoubtedly, another advantage is that a slight detour will bring you by our home. There, we can sit under the gazebo and contemplate a tiny finger of the same Pomquet Harbour that helped form the beach area, and reflect on the Mi'kmaq who have fought back against the loss of their land and rights, the Acadians who hung on (and came back) despite *Le Grand Dérangement*, the Black Loyalists whose early settlement further to the east represent such an important but under-recognized part of Canadian history, the Gaels whose immigration marked this land but whose language and culture were so stigmatized as to be almost lost, the New Englanders who arrived to take over massive land grants, and the more recent immigrants and come from aways like myself, each with their own stories.

The Mi'kmaq were always here. Everyone else came later. While the Mi'kmaq camps in and around Antigonish Harbour were seasonal and focussed on fishing, what is now Tracadie, further east, comes from the

Mi'kmaw word for "the settlement." Any place called "the settlement" was certainly permanent, as archaeological evidence confirms. Our walk to Ninian takes place in the most northeastern area of mainland Nova Scotia, once known as Agg Piktuk, or "the explosive place," one of the seven districts of the Mi'kmaq homeland (Paul 2022, 14-15). Agg Piktuk was perhaps given that name because of the coal and lignite deposits so close to the surface in places like Pictou. In the long view, Indigenous presence in Nova Scotia goes back over ten thousand years.

As elsewhere in North America, the first Europeans to this place describe the land as an almost-uninhabited Eden, teeming with wildlife, clouds of birds that blotted out the sun, and schools of fish that made the water seem almost solid with life. We now know that at least some of that wildlife, and certainly much of that emptiness, represents the aftereffects of an earlier apocalypse (Grenz 2024, 152-156). Thanks to evidence as varied as archaeological remains and ice-bound records of global carbon sequestration (Flyn 2021, 84-87), estimates are now that up to 90 percent of Indigenous populations in the Americas lost their lives in the largely unrecorded plagues of smallpox, scarlet fever, measles, chicken pox, and other previously unknown diseases that ripped through Indigenous societies after first contact with Europeans (MacKinnon 2014, 52-55).

Mi'kmaki would have been no different. It was a post-contact, post-apocalyptic Indigenous society that saw the first French colonists arrive in the Bay of Fundy area, and then develop villages further north and east. Because the Mi'kmaq and the Acadians cooperated and grew close, the name of the Acadian community established in 1774, Pomquet, is likely related to that of the local First Nation, Paqtnkek (pronounced Bug-nuh-geg). Locals believe the term means sand, or sandy beach (Landry 1990, 20), or perhaps "hitting bumps in the water while landing on shore," a reference to the underwater ridges at Pomquet Beach Provincial Park, a pristine stretch of sand.

The Mi'kmaq were first. The land is theirs. But well before there was a New Brunswick, Nova Scotia, Prince Edward Island, or state of Maine, there was "Acadie," an important swath of historic French settlement along the Atlantic coast. Antigonish County has long been known for its predominance of "Mc" and "Mac" prefix surnames, its tartans, its kilts, its Gaelic singers and dancers and Highland Games. However, Acadians have pride of place among the European arrivals, despite the historic effort to eradicate them from the whole of the region.

The date 1755 has become justly infamous for "*Le Grand Dérangement*," known in English as "The Great Deportation" or "The Expulsion of the Acadians." (1755 is also the name of an Acadian band formed in the 1970s, performing mainly in the Chiac French dialect of New Brunswick.) There had been rumblings of trouble for the French settlers in years prior, as the English wrested control from France of the Maritime areas of the so-called "new world." New Englanders like the future surveyor general of Nova Scotia, Charles Morris, had begun surveying Acadian settlements in 1748, strategizing their rapacity.

The year 1755 marks the beginning of the forced removal from Acadie at the hands of the British of over eleven thousand French-speaking inhabitants, most of the estimated population of fourteen thousand. Many of the deportees died in the overcrowded ships taking them to unknown lands, more died as prisoners and exiles in those places, and remarkably, some made it back to the fields, forests, tidal marshes, and rivers of the only homeland they had ever known.

The villain most often associated with the Expulsion was the then-Lieutenant Governor Charles Lawrence, and he has much for which to answer. But it was surveyor Charles Morris who was behind the plan to capture Acadian men while they were at Sunday morning mass, threatening their families with bayonets until the men acquiesced and went to the ships (Marsh 2015). Robert Monckton, for whom the New Brunswick city is still named, and ironically, the francophone Université de Moncton, was in charge of the initial round-up of men and boys. Monckton was the commander at Fort Beauséjour, which had been renamed Fort Cumberland by the British in honour of the Duke of Cumberland, "also known as Butcher Cumberland for his role in suppressing a Jacobite uprising in the Scottish Highlands in 1746" (Leblanc 2020, 41). The Jacobites were royalists who wanted to return a Catholic monarch to the thrones of England and Scotland. Cumberland's 1746 victory over their army at the Battle of Culloden led to the Highland clearances, which in turn occasioned the waves of Catholic Gaelic exiles filling overcrowded ships to Nova Scotia.

If nothing else, the two walks featured in this book show how Nova Scotia and Scotland have been linked in many ways, British imperialism and its hunger for land being among the most obvious.

The violent and murderous "clearing" of Acadie and its effects on families, on political systems, and on colonial relations with Indigenous peoples is too complex a narrative to tell here in every detail. But it's a story of betrayal, of farm and fishing village emissaries imprisoned by casually deceitful governors, of British troops setting fire to churches, homes, barns, and boats so that anyone who escaped the initial round-ups of prisoners would have no home to return to, of broken promises, pillaged livestock and possessions, and harvest-ready crops left to rot in the fields.

Troops descended on Acadian villages, loaded entire families on to hardly seaworthy chartered ships, and destroyed whatever they couldn't carry away. Officially, the plan was to "resettle" Acadians in the American colonies, England, and, eventually, western France. But it's now known that large numbers of the imprisoned Acadians perished in the brutal transport. In January 1759, five ships started out from Île Saint-Jean (now Prince Edward Island), with a thousand Acadian exiles. When they arrived in Saint-Malo, France, nearly half had died on the voyage (Leblanc 2020, 146). This is the pre-history behind my home, a history not evident in the 250th anniversary float the community recently built for the Antigonish Highland Games, and the colourful peasant costumes worn by Pomquet's smartphone-checking teens. But it's a story known by every Acadian just the same.

It turns out that oppression and exile are pretty much constant throughlines in telling the stories of these trails, no matter whether Mi'kmaq, Acadian, Gael, or Scot, and no matter which side of the Atlantic we're on. British military and colonial action, and later, the "soft threat" of English cultural pervasiveness, are threads running through *both* the Scottish and the Nova Scotian Ninian walks.

In the Nova Scotian case, there are stories of Acadians lowering their family dishes and meagre savings into wells as soldiers arrived under the Union Jack, and of whole families fleeing into woods or marshes to hide, sometimes finding refuge among sympathetic Mi'kmaq. In *We Were Not the Savages*, Daniel N. Paul describes the Expulsion within the larger context of Mi'kmaq relations with colonists. He describes how Mi'kmaq honoured their partnerships with the Acadians during the Expulsion, because the Acadian settlers had achieved a markedly more amicable and mutually enriching relationship with the Mi'kmaq than the British ever seemed to consider (Paul 2022, 174-175). The Acadians and Mi'kmaq for the most part shared food and knowledge; the British looked down on the locals. Paul doesn't mince words: "In hindsight, it's fair to say that the majority of British military men and English colonists who died in conflicts with Amerindians during England's colonizing days were victims of the pompous white supremacist beliefs of their leadership" (Paul 2022, 97).

The six families who first founded Pomquet in 1774 and officially requested land grants in 1789 were returned deportees (Leonard 2007, 80). They include the ancestors of our neighbours, the Deons and Doirons. They were among those deported via Virginia (which wouldn't take them), then imprisoned in England, then shipped to Saint-Malo, France, only to immediately begin saving money to return to Acadie, this time to Pomquet, about twenty years after their forced exile. They paid their return fare, booking passage with Jersey Island merchant vessels (Leonard 2007, 74; Leblanc 2020, 23). That they were so anxious to return says much about them and their deep ties to this land.

Sara and I suspect that the swampy and sloped piece of land where we live near the border of Upper Pomquet was braced against sliding into our little salt-marsh inlet by long-ago Acadians. The solid ridge running diagonally across the waterside edge of our property, parallel to an old stream, looks suspiciously like one of the dikes for which Acadians (who always seemed to tackle – or be relegated to – the most miserable land for farming) are famous. By some trick of zoning we don't quite understand, when we purchased our place, we were also required to purchase an adjacent mini lot, which made us the caretakers for a small rectangle that once contained Upper Pomquet Acadian school #24. Its foundation is all that remains. The crumbling concrete rectangle sits, hidden, among our aspen and hawthorns.

For decades during the early twentieth century, this little one-room schoolhouse welcomed the children of Pomquet. There's a badly overgrown apple tree not far from the foundation, and the broken-down remains of small wooden bridges over the stream that borders our land. I sometimes imagine the tree in its youth, providing September apples for the children in their best back-to-school outfits. A photo of the school in an old Pomquet history book shows the hills remarkably bare of the alders, dogwood, and hawthorn that threaten annually to overwhelm our driveway. The slightly blurry black and white image shows the school standing majestically alone among cropped fields.

Each spring, Sara and I head to Antigonish's Five-Cent-To-A-Dollar general store to buy fresh Acadian flags for the simple wooden sign that stands on the edge of the property to commemorate the once schoolhouse. We mow its narrow rectangle of grass and plant begonias and daffodils under the sign. (Red, white, blue, and yellow, if possible, to match the Acadian flag.) It's a small bit of thanks, but the least we can do. We suspect it's only because of the Acadians that we enjoy whatever footing we have in this marshy area, where underground streams and high water tables can turn a yard gelatinous when it rains.

The British became the permanent colonial presence throughout the Maritimes. But most were not content, as the Acadians had been, to learn from the Mi'kmaq and achieve at least some kind of harmony with existing, Indigenous society. The British weren't interested in the Acadians, either, except for their land. Nor were they that interested in the Gaels, except when Scots passed for English, or could afford to buy the land confiscated from Acadian and Mi'kmaq at a premium. So perhaps it's fitting that recent cultural celebrations tend to favour the other groups.

Acadians in greater numbers than ever mark "*quinze août*" (the Acadian national holiday on August fifteenth). In August 2024 we celebrated the 250th anniversary of Pomquet. The Scots have an annual Gaels' Day in Iona, Cape Breton, host Highland Games not far from St. Ninian Cathedral in Antigonish, and recently celebrated the 250th anniversary of the arrival of the *Hector*, the first ship to officially carry Scottish Highland settlers to Pictou Harbour. The *Hector* colonists were the start of an influx: between about 1775 and 1850, roughly sixty thousand Scottish settlers landed in Nova Scotia. At Confederation, Gaelic was the third most-often-spoken language of Canada, behind only English and French. The Oifis Iomairtean na Gàidhlig – the Office of Gaelic Affairs – is an official arm of the Government of Nova Scotia's Tourism office. And, of course, Nova Scotia has its own tartan, gracing everything from neckties to jars of blueberry jam.

There are some interesting similarities between Antigonish, Nova Scotia, and Whithorn, Scotland. Geologists will point out that the vast movement of geological plates connects the landscapes of both Nova Scotia and Scotland. They note that, despite the ocean now between them, the Cape Breton and Scottish Highlands were once of a single piece, rubbing shoulders as part of the same chain. Sometimes, Antigonish seems to suffer from being on the doorstep of its photogenic sibling, Cape Breton, just as the lowlands of Ayrshire, Dumfries, and Galloway that host the Whithorn Way suffer from not being the scenic spots north and west. Yet the histories of Ayrshire and Galloway are no less interesting than their neighbours, and the same is true of the history of Antigonish and its regions.

Both Dumfries and Galloway in Scotland, and Antigonish County, Nova Scotia, are primarily rural areas. Both have seen cycles of rapid settlement alternating with sudden and severe depopulation. Most of all, it's the people that connect the two places. Even though so many of the Scots who came to Nova Scotia came from the Highlands rather than places like Dumfries and Galloway, there is a pronounced Scottish flavour to Nova Scotia's entire North Shore; many street signs in Antigonish are in both English and Gaelic. Although northeast Nova Scotia never suffered the bloody sectarian wars of Scotland, Peter Ludlow, an academic who has imbibed the town and county's history from early childhood, noted that it took a "canny Scot" to "navigate the factional waters of Antigonish" (Ludlow 2015, 64).

Perhaps it's not surprising there should be a cathedral to St. Ninian in a place whose name, translated, means New Scotland. Ten years after it was built in Antigonish, a local newspaper declared about Saint Ninian Cathedral that it was the new *Candida Casa* – (Ninian's Shrine in Galloway), and that Nova Scotia now provided the home for "a noble Celtic bishop who inherits the faith and speaks the language of Ninian" (*Antigonish Aurora*, Feb. 13, 1884, "St. Ninian and the Early Scottish Church," p. 2. (A5-1884-110-2)).

Yet nothing about the Saint Ninian Cathedral in Antigonish was fated to happen the way it did. Fittingly, the story of *Antigonish's* St. Ninian is wrapped up with a convoluted story of immigration, and with the history of the Acadians, the Gaels, the Mi'kmaq, and the British. In fact, Ninian of Antigonish owes his existence not to the Scots, but rather to someone whose mother tongue was not the Gaelic of the Highlands, nor even the English of the occupiers, but rather, like our Pomquet Acadians, the language of Molière.

DUNURE CASTLE

"This is nowhere, I guess, in the grand scheme of things. But it's nice enough."

(Customer in the Harbour View Coffee Shop, Dunure, Scotland)

Even as a rank amateur, I know that the trick to effective beach-walking (on sand) is to find the sweet spot. Don't walk in the thick sand higher up, where your boots sink in too deep. And avoid the muck and water closer to the surf, where the going is slippery and wet. There's often a ridge of hard sand somewhere in between. Find that, and you can make some speed. But as the Scottish Ayrshire Coastal Path proceeded south, more often than not, there was no sand; we were forced to go over long beds of fist-sized stones or navigate thick curtains of stinking black goo left by the tides.

Like any good story, a pilgrim walk possesses a narrative arc and plotlines that sometimes overlap. For a medieval walker, setting out on a pilgrimage usually started with a "summons," perhaps a dream or penance. Our call to Scotland was not particularly spiritual: an idea hatched over wine and laughter in Canada. Once pilgrimages are started, however – and they start well before the first step – they contain both movement and direction. There is, inevitably, hardship. Sometimes, if one is lucky, there are visions and miracles.

Like most contemporary pilgrims, we set out with a light step and hope in our hearts: after all, the Whithorn Way was ancient enough to be interesting, new enough not to be crowded with other pilgrims, and related enough to our various histories and areas of scholarly study that we hoped we might discover something interesting in its stories and paths.

It is a truism from pilgrimage studies that a pilgrim group both requires, and creates, relationships. Sara and I had come up to Scotland from the English Midlands and had met Ken (whose PhD research was in walking as performance) transiting from a walk in Ireland. Christine had just arrived by air in Glasgow. Sara, unfortunately, could only take the weekend away from her post at the University of Nottingham, so had just one full day on the trail. Ken, Christine, and I were starting out knowing we had over one hundred miles ahead of us. Within an hour of setting out, we had already shared the magical experience of walking, sun-dappled, through a leafy green tunnel of deciduous forest that opened from the village of Alloway towards the sea. That first afternoon, I felt I could already agree with what Catriona McMillan wrote in 2013 in her *Whithorn Pilgrimage: A Report*: "On a pleasant day, walking along secluded pathways searching for caves, chapel ruins, and wells is almost surreal" (46).

The route south from Ayr consisted of a series of beach walks between headlands gradually opening up as the tides receded. How many headlands did we have to traverse? One of us remembered two, but after we rounded the second, we faced only another beach. Someone else was certain it was three. We passed the third headland and saw still more sand and another set of cliffs.

We kept up hope: Dunure, the village we were supposed to come to, must be just around the next headland. Only it never was.

By the time the next bend actually did yield a view of something other than more coastline, much more of the day had passed than expected. Our lengthy stops at the Robbie Burns site, and our delay at the Heads of Ayr had set us back. Dunure was our first major destination, the spot where we were supposed to turn inland from the coast. We were surprised at how tired we were from scrambling over rocks and slipping along banks of kelp. Apparently, we still had almost half of the fourteen-mile walk ahead of us, even though Ken's pedometre said we'd walked twelve miles already. Clearly, something was out of whack. It was already three o'clock in the afternoon.

We stepped gratefully into the Harbour View Coffee Shop, a hobbit-y spot framed by flowers and snuggled into the earth. True to its name, its windows faced the little harbour. The place was cheery and warm, but nearly empty except for a server and two women enjoying tea and coffee cake. I was anxious to order the same. When they heard our accents, we got talking.

"From Canada, are ye?" said one. "Canada's beautiful. I've been to Ottawa." We traded reminiscences about Canada's capital. I mentioned that many of the historic buildings in both Ottawa and Montreal are Scottish, their design heavily influenced by nineteenth-century Scottish architects, businessmen, and investment.

Perhaps I should have stopped there, but I didn't. I mentioned that Scots helped build Canada's settlements. And that fourteen of our Prime Ministers were of Scottish heritage. As the two women's eyes began to glaze, I tacked on fact after fact about Scottish influence on Canada (McGoogan 2011). And, of course, I said, as a kind of finale, one of Canada's provinces is actually called "New Scotland" (Nova Scotia).

"Well, Canada's a beautiful place," one of the two repeated, by way of ending my monologue. "You folks are lucky." That made her the second person we'd met, in as many conversations, who'd said we Canadians were "lucky." It was a phrase I'd hear again and again.

I opened my mouth, but she lifted a finger: "We're just locals," she said quickly, before I could regale her with more trivia. "From here." She shrugged, then smiled again: "It's nowhere, I guess, in the grand scheme of things. But nice enough."

Looking out at the dark ruins of Dunure Castle, rising without a seam from the rock of the Carrick coast behind the café, her words seemed quite the understatement. Dunure Castle is haunting. That day it looked particularly romantic against the threatening skies, with the island Craig Ailsa behind it.

Julia Muir Watt's detailed historical guide to the trail, *Walk the Whithorn Way*, mentions Dunure in connection with a story called the "roasting of the Abbott" (57). In 1560, the Scottish Parliament abolished the Catholic mass in Scotland, effectively pushing out Rome and dissolving monastic communities. In an irony of history, this official act also had the effect of forcing generations of the Scottish Catholics who would end up in Nova Scotia to practice their faith in secret, thereby setting the austere tone of their worship for over two centuries to come.

The newly Protestant Scottish Parliament abolished monasteries along with "official" Catholicism. For some years, the abbeys had already been waning, turning from Rome to the support of wealthy and powerful local aristocrats. The year 1560 sounded their death-knell, and their former protectors were the first to feed on the carcasses. The decommissioned monasteries became the sites of violent squabbles between "nobles" over land and money (Murray 1995, 44).

Quintin Kennedy, the last abbott of Crossraguel Abbey, happened to be the uncle of Gilbert Kennedy, the Earl of Cassilis, a powerful and ruthless aristocrat known locally as "The King of Carrick" (Brown 1996, 168). While the abbeys were being torn down and dissolved, Gilbert at first defied the Parliament, and encouraged his uncle to continue to celebrate masses in Carrick. Quintin continued as abbot, or at least living on the grounds with a small group of monks, until his death in August 1564 (Lawson 1883, 39).

But well before his uncle's passing, the lands and rents of Crossraguel Abbey were targeted by the Earl, who was sure he had them in his pocket. Then, in 1570, during the Marion civil war, the Scottish Crown granted control of the abbey to a commendator. That person, to everyone's surprise, turned out *not* to be Earl Kennedy.

Instead, Crossraguel Abbey was granted to Allan Stewart, a Kennedy rival.

The trouble began immediately. In addition to the family connection, Kennedy had historic rights as "bailie" of the place. At first, he tried to purchase the benefice, or at least its profits, from Stewart. When this was refused, he acted quickly. He hid with armed men – accounts call them "rough retainers" – in the Crossraguel woods. They kidnapped Stewart and took him to Dunure Castle. When Stewart refused to sign over the land and income, Kennedy up and slow-roasted the poor soul over a brazier of coals in Dunure Castle's Black Vault. Eventually, one of Stewart's relatives hid in the castle's chapel, let in helpers, and successfully stormed the stronghold to rescue him (Brown 1996, 171). There was a financial settlement levied against the Earl, rapping his knuckles for the misdeed. Allan Stewart was released, but he never walked again.

All this mayhem and murder, intrigue and history breathed from the walls and soil around Dunure Castle, and we could still have our tea and cake and discuss how lovely Ottawa is during the summer. That, we were discovering, was what happened in places that the woman we'd met called "nowhere in the grand scheme of things."

BROKEN PROMISES

"The feast of St. Anne was a fascinating spectacle — both reverent and lively — attended by crowds of worshippers. It was accompanied by waving flags, bell ringing, intoned psalms and chants, bonfires, banqueting, and firing guns, all symbols of joy."

(Stanley-Blackwell and MacLean 2004)

Across from Pomquet Beach, on the east side of the mouth of Pomquet Harbour, is a dirt road referred to on maps as "Old Ferry Road." There, you can join others casting a fishing line out into the small, fast-running channel. Your line will pull hard, either left or right, depending on which way the tide is flowing. Apparently, the fishing is not bad. But despite the road's name, the ferry service is non-existent.

In the early part of the last century, the Pomquet ferry was run by the province and allowed folks from the Pomquet side to get across and do their shopping at one of Bayfield's three stores on the east shore. It delivered many women of the Acadian community to their jobs in the lobster and fish canning plants built in Bayfield in the 1920s, which along with Bayfield's cheese factory, carriage works, mills, and tanneries were major sources of employment at the time. Local Pomquet historian Alfred Benoit told me his mother-in-law was one of those who took the ferry to work in the cannery. It was run at first by a Joe Atwater from the Bayfield side (perhaps related to the first Keeper of the Island lighthouse, John Atwater), and from the Pomquet side, Henry Doiron, one of the descendants of the original families.

These days, there's no real road on the Pomquet Beach side. The ferry docked at a long-disappeared bridge between Pomquet Point and the beach that wasn't rebuilt after it was destroyed repeatedly by storms (Google maps' satellite view still shows the underwater footings). On the Bayfield side, the canning plant has also disappeared. No one seems to remember when the last ferry ran. However, if it were still in service, walkers toward Saint Ninian Cathedral, Antigonish, would have the option of starting further east than the beach, at St. Anne's (sometimes spelled St. Ann's) Church in Paqtnkek First Nation.

St. Anne's, sometimes called Summerside Church, has always been a Mi'kmaq place of worship. Despite its humble appearance, it holds pride of place as being on the site of the first building for Christian worship in the area. In fact, the Mi'kmaq were the first Christians along the North Shore. The first chapel at the Mi'kmaw community was founded in 1717, well before the major influx of Highland Scots that gave Nova Scotia so much of its identity, before the founding of Pomquet as an Acadian community, and before the influx of Loyalists whom the British rewarded by kicking out the Acadians and disowning the Mi'kmaq. St. Anne's was the name given to the church when the cornerstone for the present building was laid on July 26, 1867, on the feast day of St. Anne, the mother of Mary and grandmother of Jesus.

St. Anne's is a Mi'kmaw Catholic church. Sara recently offered a pouch of tobacco in thanks to local elder John R. Prosper for speaking to her undergraduate class, and he accepted it, but made sure to tell her, "I'm Catholic. I'm Christian." Fewer Mi'kmaq are now practicing Catholics, partly in response to the damage done by the government's unholy alliance with churches to create Canada's genocidal "Indian Residential School" system (Methot 2019, 45). Nonetheless, for many years there was a celebratory Catholicism amongst many Indigenous populations. Not unlike village processionals in rural Brittany and Normandy, St. Anne's Paqtnkek historically had its own solemn processions, when women "outfitted in their pointed caps and jackets embellished with ribbon trim [and] men [in] broadcloth coats with beaded epaulettes and woven belts" accompanied a statue of St. Anne carried in procession to the church (Stanley-Blackwell and MacLean 2004, 139). Peggy Thompson's

2022 volume *Antigonish: A History in Pictures* reprints a photo of one such procession in 1920 (49).

In the early days of settlement, the Mi'kmaq were so Catholic that according to South River local historian Fraser Dunn, Catholics all over Nova Scotia can thank them for the easing of the restrictive Penal Laws in this province, laws that once kept Catholic children from schools, kept Catholic families from buying and owning land, forbade "popish priests," and prescribed jail terms for those who harboured them. According to Dunn, it was the Mi'kmaq who were fed up with the British religious restrictions. Wanting a priest, they attacked the garrison in Halifax in protest. Under pressure from the irate Mi'kmaq, the governor finally allowed them a priest, whose presence quieted the troubles so effectively that the cleric ended up on the British payroll and even eventually enjoyed a pension, leading the way for the gradual relaxation of the laws for all Catholics.

While some Indigenous people in Canada understandably reject anything to do with settler religion, many others have embraced and adapted different forms of Christianity. Patty Krawec, in her book *Becoming Kin: An Indigenous Call to Unforgetting the Past and Reimagining our Future* (2022) discusses this, as does Dr. Ray Aldred of the Vancouver School of Theology, a friend and co-author of mine, in our book *Our Home and Treaty Land* (2024b).

It has always struck me as fitting that Anne is such a popular saint among Indigenous Catholics: stories about her come not from the canonical New Testament, but from apocryphal literature like the Proto-Gospel of James. Like the apocryphal Gospels, Indigenous expressions of the faith have had a long, traditional, and powerful – but not necessarily official – status. Indigenous Christians increasingly exercise mentorship toward other expressions of the church in this land (e.g., Aldred and Anderson 2024; Krawec 2022), just as Anne as a mother might have been expected to do with Mary. Somehow, the association makes sense.

Typical of other early Indigenous Catholic churches, the missionaries did not seek official title for the land on which the first Paqtnkek church was built. Perhaps they felt it was obvious it belonged to the Mi'kmaq. Perhaps it *was* obvious, until the British came along.

Fresh from victory in the Seven Years' War, the new British colonizers "granted" huge tracts of (Mi'kmaw) land, including the Indigenous church, right out from under the feet of the original inhabitants. Much of it was "given" to United Empire Loyalists fleeing the American Revolution. A party of Loyalists under a man named Timothy Hierlihy landed at Town Point in Antigonish Harbour about this time, taking up the "soldier's grant" that once spanned both sides of Antigonish Harbour. They established the townsite there, before Antigonish was established further inland (MacGillivray 1935).

When the British started granting land away around what is now eastern Pomquet Harbour, the Mi'kmaq quite rightly protested that the land was theirs, that it had always been theirs, and that they had the church to prove it. In 1783, George Henry Monk, the newly appointed "Superintendent of Indian Affairs" travelled to Antigonish in response to settler "dread of the Indians" (Upton 1975, 5). He discovered that it was in fact the Mi'kmaq who had reason to fear. The influx of settlers into Antigonish Harbour, they told Monk, was already causing them to lose their seasonal fishing grounds. Monk "agreed" to the setting aside for perpetual Mi'kmaq use of the lands of their church and their burial grounds along what became Pomquet Harbour, just to the east.

Unfortunately, Monk's promises were not translated into law, and three years later his office and authority ceased to exist when Britain ceased to fund the Superintendent, and the young colony of Nova Scotia refused to take on the post and its costs. Loyalist settlers were happy to profit from the gap (Upton 1975, 6). After another fifty years, perhaps because of the undeniable material evidence of a building, and perhaps because of a certain Bishop Joseph-Octave Plessis from Quebec, whom we shall soon meet, Nova Scotia confirmed Monk's initial land "grant" more officially. In 1824, it recognized that one hundred acres, including the church, were set aside for Mi'kmaq use and the colony again confirmed Mi'kmaw ownership of the area (Paul 2022, 264-268).

But local non-Indigenous farmers and fishers would have none of it. For just over a half-century, they'd exercised tenure illegally, and now they completely ignored the 1824 correction. They continued to sell and resell the land despite Mi'kmaq possession. They ignored protests even to the point of threatening Mi'kmaw worshippers.

Whatever the law said, the land had been taken over. Yet the Mi'kmaq were determined to hold on. In 1842, a survey commissioned by the Imperial government in Britain and carried out throughout the colony under Lieutenant Governor Lord Falkland, found that the Mi'kmaq settlement "at Pomquet [Harbour]" was "one of the [province's] healthiest" and comprised at least twenty-six families (Upton 1975, 18). Falkland was scathing when he wrote to London that "Most Colonies have done something for the relief of this class [the Indigenous] of their people ... but the records of Nova Scotia hardly shew any intention of that kind" (Upton 1975, 18).

Despite such blows, the Indigenous community along the North Shore thrived and grew. It was only due to sustained legal efforts exercised over two centuries that in 1990, the land which had always been Mi'kmaq by heredity, by fact, by history, and even by British recognition, was finally and officially recognized as such by the government and local non-Indigenous landholders in a way that could be enforced.

Not many years ago, St. Anne's was damaged by the hurricane-force winds that increasingly afflict Nova Scotia. Funds were raised and the church repaired so that it is still in use by Paqtnkek worshippers. If the Pomquet ferry still ran, our pilgrimage to the Antigonish Ninian could perhaps start there, with a gift to the people who were here first, and if we were fortunate, a blessing for our journey. We would then proceed north to the Old Ferry Road, somehow cross the small, fast-flowing strait, and land on the sands of the beach that has given this whole area its name.

MEETING LOKI

"No. You don't want that one."

(Scottish pub owner to me, prodding
me away from the Guinness tap)

Full disclosure: as far as I know, unlike my wife, none of my ancestors was Scottish. Even so, like many other Canadians, I find the sound of bagpipes haunting and single malt Scotch a fine drink. For good and ill, we Canadians owe much of our history to the Scots. Scots staffed the Hudson's Bay Company posts that stretched out across northern North America. They were often the first Europeans trading with central and western First Nations. Importantly, among their descendants are the Michif (Métis), an Indigenous post-contact nation who were instrumental in the history of the prairies, from which I hail (Anderson 2024).

At the same time as I appreciate these facts about Scots, I find tartans confusing, and haggis only mildly interesting. To my untrained palate, Irn-Bru is just cream soda dressed up in Protestant orange. As an outsider I tend to find older Presbyterians starchy and gruffly righteous, especially around alcohol and dancing. Nova Scotia's Catholic Scots seem more free – so free that the history of Antigonish is wrapped up with various Temperance movements which tried to the curb the social ills alcohol can cause.

Sometimes, Scots are downright scary. I had a professor from Edinburgh for undergraduate Greek: she had a frighteningly sharp intellect and brooked no failure. Ever since, I've had a bit of a knee-jerk reaction to an Edinburgh accent, fearing I am being judged. Beautiful as the country is, I've never been one to fantasize about visiting it.

But furnished with a grant from the Concordia University Part-Time Faculty Association to research pilgrimage and common land access (Anderson 2018), I knew that Scotland would be one of the best places to do so. Scots and Canadians share similar social structures, with comparable cultural outlooks. The Scottish law allowing limited public access to trails on private lands is relatively new. We Canadians could learn a lot from how it's being implemented. Also, I teach and research the history of pilgrimage. The track to St. Ninian is so ancient, and Ninian himself so enigmatic, that these factors combined to bring me to Glasgow in the summer of 2019. My reasons to visit the country were not sentimental, but practical. Yet, if you're not careful, Scotland grows on you like moss on a stone fence.

Our next stopping point was Maybole. It turned out to be a town so deceptively bland you wouldn't know how steeped in history it is. The Gardenrose B&B sits on a hill on the north side of the burgh. The house is preserved in Charles Rennie Mackintosh Arts and Crafts style. The grounds – as the name indicates – were similarly beautiful. The owners of the B&B told us how the designer of their house built two similar Arts and Crafts-style homes, and then moved to Canada, "where he died."

Both Sara and Ken immediately quipped, at the same time and without pause, "Probably froze to death." We four Canadians laughed. Our hosts didn't break a smile.

There was one other slightly jarring moment. We asked the owner where we should eat. She seemed hesitant. "The Maybole Arms is probably the safest place," she finally said.

Safest?

A short walk downhill took us by the stone apse of the petite and pretty English-style St. Oswald's Episcopal Church, through a wrought iron art deco walking bridge over the train tracks, and down the middle of a small park leading to the shuttered and extremely quiet village centre. A sign indicated that the "John Knox Street" we were on was named for a debate on the Mass held there in 1562 (Lawson 1883, 41). It took place between the great Scottish Reformer and the same scholarly abbot, Quintin Kennedy, whose nephew roasted his secular competition for the abbey eight years later at Dunure. At the time of the debate, both sides claimed victory. But the street is named after Knox.

We came across another interesting plaque. Once upon a time, it announced, Maybole was known as a cobblers' town. The boot and shoe industry had been a major employer. The posting indicated that when the footwear industry collapsed in Scotland, many Maybolers moved to Hamilton, Ontario, Canada. There is still an area in Hamilton called "Little Maybole," the plaque said. I've been in Hamilton several times, but I've never noticed Little Maybole.

If the town centre was preternaturally quiet, Maybole's Main Street was the opposite: a horror story turned up to high volume. It turned out Main Street was a terrifyingly narrow two-lane boulevard that doubled as Motorway A77. We would learn to loathe the A77; it's the main road from the ferry terminal at Cairnryan to Glasgow and Edinburgh to the north. Traffic on it runs far too quickly, especially through villages like Maybole.

As we edged along the minuscule pavement (sidewalk, in North American English), semi-trailer trucks (lorries, to the locals) roared past, their human-height tires only inches from us. Our bodies were pulled slightly, packs-first, by the wash of their passing, then released again into backdrafts of diesel. I was surprised how many trucks carried heavy loads of lumber. Long trailers of logs are a sight I tend to equate with Canada, and in fact, with our gravel road near Pomquet. I was later to learn from Peter Ross that Scotland had begun to cultivate Douglas fir and lodgepole pine, many of the initial seedlings imported decades ago from British Columbia. While the tree-cropping has sometimes been successful, in his opinion the foreign species and the diseases that accompany monocultures of farmed trees have not made forestry in Scotland any easier. Or local economies any better.

Maybole is just north of the Galloway Forest. Galloway, according to Peter, produces most of Scotland's lumber exports. Within Scotland, itself in uneasy relationship with England, Galloway has always been a region on its own, with a unique geography, political history, and culture, itself in an uneasy relationship with Scotland.

The major roadway through the middle of Maybole didn't make our trek to supper easy. At the south end of town, we reached the Maybole Arms, a two-story brown brick building trimmed in red, with a sign announcing: "Meals now served." We stepped inside and asked for menus. The owner, Callum McKelvie, came out from behind the bar. He crossed his arms over his chest and apologized: we had arrived on the one night of the week the kitchen was closed. There was a chippy just up the street: why not try there? At the sound of our voices, a dog stirred, looking from McKelvie to us.

We negotiated that Christine would buy fish and chips, and I'd buy the beer. When I went to the taps, McKelvie showed me, with barely a word, what he thought of my taste. He clucked his tongue and sighed loudly when I tried pointing to the Guinness. Suitably chastened, I ordered McEwan, at which there was the briefest hint of a smile, then a nod. There was a selection of Ayr Brewing Company ales and pouring these seemed to make him the happiest – a twinkle of his eyes with a "You'll like that, then."

He and his dog Loki, who had trotted over from his spot near the bar, disappeared for a few minutes and returned from the idle kitchen with plates, ketchup, salt, vinegar, and cutlery just as Christine also returned, bearing our supper in greasy paper bags. The batter was so hot it burnt our fingers. But it was delicious, and the chips crisp and brown. (North Americans tend to find U.K. chips, or french fries, undercooked. I suppose the opposite is likely true as well.)

We ordered another round and congratulated ourselves and our hosts on a wonderful meal even if the food wasn't quite from the Maybole Arms. Folks chatted with us, while, with the help of a few morsels of fish, we made friends with Loki. The evening gradually suffused with a gentle glow of conviviality. The town "on an eminence" had put on a warm welcome for us pilgrims. I'd go back to the Maybole Arms, although I admit I might plan it again for the kitchen's night off.

ANTIGONISH GETS ITS SAINT

Antigonish's first Roman Catholic church was a small chapel erected between Church and College Streets, close to the present-day Bank of Nova Scotia ... Five years later, the small structure was built as a "mission" of Arisaig parish and given the name "St. John's."

(From the website for St. Ninian Parish Cemetery)

If you must choose a saint's name for your new building, it's hard to be more respectable than St. John's. But it's also hard to be duller. There are so many schools, hospitals, churches, and even knightly orders named St. John's that the title has become commonplace. There's little to distinguish the moniker as Scottish, or Maritime, or even Catholic. A community that needs to assert its uniqueness could do better.

Perhaps that's why on his pastoral visit to the Maritimes in 1812, Bishop Joseph-Octave Plessis made the suggestion to the parishioners of the young parish of Antigonish that they change the name of their new building from St. John's to "St. Ninian" (Walsh 1989, 35; St. Ninian Parish Cemetery website).

Some of the history books I've consulted make Bishop Plessis' remark sound like it was almost off-the-cuff. I doubt that. Although I'm not Catholic, I've had occasion to spend many hours in meetings with Catholic bishops. I can confidently say that at least on official business, they do not make remarks of *any* sort lightly. The level of thought – some might say, strategizing – that goes into even the most mundane changes to a policy statement or a memorandum has on occasion left my ad hoc Protestant mind reeling.

Add to this the fact that Plessis had been the secretary to four bishops before finally being ordained to the office himself. He was renowned for his political and ecclesiastical acumen. Plessis not only survived the beginnings of British oversight over New France and its Church, but he also confirmed the official position of Catholics and ensured their importance going forward in Canadian society. There is every reason to believe that Bishop Plessis' "suggestion" of St. Ninian as a name was one small chess move in a very long game with the British authorities, a move that the bishop felt might help set the course for Catholics in northern Nova Scotia for decades.

The *Dictionary of Canadian Biography* notes that Plessis was born only three weeks after the British conquest of New France had been recognized by the Treaty of Paris. In the new political realities brought about by their overlordship, the Bishop of Quebec became the de facto archbishop of all Catholics in the land, whatever their ethnicity. Plessis smartly cultivated amicable, but not intimate, relations with the British authorities and with his ecumenical counterparts.

Bishop Plessis was, in fact, *Arch*bishop Plessis in everything but title. Responsible by default for most of what had become British North America, he tried to ensure that Catholics in places like Antigonish, so far from the creature comforts and the seminaries of Quebec City and of Montreal, were still cared for spiritually. In return, he was criticized within Quebec for diverting much-needed priests to the Maritimes. For instance, in July 1815 he appointed Father Remi Gaulin, a twenty-eight-year-old who was only four years a priest, as the first resident pastor to St. Ninian. To Gaulin fell the responsibility for a vast area including not only the town and areas south, but Cape Breton as well.

Records show that one winter, Father Gaulin walked the one hundred miles return trip to Cheticamp, Cape Breton, across St. George's Bay ice, rather than to be slowed by taking the longer, and safer, way around by land (Walsh 1989, 35). (In February 1844 another priest, Père Louis Modeste Anssart, fell through the ice together with his horse while making the same crossing. His body was only recovered three months later during spring break-up and buried at Pomquet.)

While sending young priests to the Maritimes and appointing others as teachers, Plessis negotiated with Rome for support, with London for recognition, and with his own priests for help in setting up educational institutions that might guarantee the long-term survival of Catholicism. The War of 1812 was a gift to Plessis and his struggling Catholics. In exchange for his active support of the British against the Americans, Bishop Plessis was finally given the official appointments that equalled at least tacit recognition of his North American ecclesiastical authority.

Plessis frequently visited poor Catholics in the regions. These trips could turn adventurous. In his journals, he describes hearing confessions in cowsheds. He writes of how, once, the ship that took him from Prince Edward Island (then Île Saint Jean) to Cape Breton was mistaken for an American privateer. He was forced to stand at the bow in full ecclesiastical regalia to keep the Catholic fishers from cutting their lines and bolting. Meanwhile a farmer, seeing the ship from shore, had already fled with his family into the woods before realizing it was not American pirates or British soldiers, but the Catholic prelate who was visiting (Johnston 1960, 233).

The *Dictionary of Canadian Biography* underlines that on his eastward tours, Plessis also took detailed and sympathetic notes concerning the state of "his" people among the Acadians, the Scots, and the Mi'kmaq (in other words, the very groups certain to be disadvantaged by British colonialism). From our twenty-first century vantage point, where Indigenous peoples have to go to court to prove every right already guaranteed to them in Treaty, it's interesting to read Plessis' empathy for the Mi'kmaq who, in his words in 1812, "see the English establish themselves among them, pillage their lands, steal their hay, take over their salmon fishing, without making any effort to obtain justice."

As for Nova Scotia's Scottish Catholics, there was work to be done there, too. Because Catholicism had been persecuted so long in Scotland, Catholics there had spent years in hiding, celebrating spartan masses without the benefit of buildings and vestments. They transported these oppression-hardened habits with them to "New Scotland."

In his visits, Plessis urged Catholics to sing, to get together publicly, and to build churches, now that the Penal Laws had been repealed in Nova Scotia. But the secretive habits developed under persecution died hard. More than once, the bishop so used to the grand churches of Quebec celebrated mass in Nova Scotia in barns and meadows, with few, if any, creature comforts.

It seems likely that Plessis' suggestion to Antigonish Catholics that they should rename their building Saint Ninian was something deeper than a casual recognition of the Scottish Catholic influx. Even though Ninian predated the Protestant Reformation by nearly a thousand years, for many in Scotland, Ninian had become a symbol of Catholicism, of episcopal regularity, and what's more, of Scottish independence from English control.

"His name has ever been held in benediction by the Catholics of Scotland," opined the editor of one of the local newspapers in 1884 (*Antigonish Aurora*, Feb. 13, 1884, "St. Ninian and the Early Scottish Church," p. 2. (A5-1884-110-2)). Perhaps the people of Antigonish appreciated the fact that by picking up on the bishop's suggestion, they were grafting themselves onto a long narrative. They became part of a story of underdog Catholicism, of a recognition of papal authority, and not least, of standing up to the English, even while living alongside them.

ALWAYS SOMEONE ELSE'S SAINT

"It may be doubted whether all this welter of confusion, conflation, misunderstanding, and at times, one must suspect, deliberate deception [about Ninian] will ever be convincingly elucidated."

(Barrow 2004)

So, what made Ninian of Scotland the name Bishop Plessis suggested for the young parish's building in Antigonish? Who was this saint?

The problem is: no one really knows. In fact, for most of my life, I joined the majority of my colleagues in pilgrimage studies and early Christian studies in the belief that he never existed.

This is because, to get to Ninian, there's no way around a bit of a historical knot, tightly tangled and confusing. Some threads we can unravel. Some may go nowhere. Of the little we know of Ninian, almost all of it originates with an English monk known as the Venerable Bede, who mentioned the saint in 731. You might think the year 731 was ancient, and it was. But 731 was already over three hundred years later than Ninian was supposed to have lived. In fact, there are not one, but two eighth-century bits of writing about Ninian: Bede's mention, and another piece related to it, called *Miracula Nynie Episcopi*, or *The Miracles of Bishop Ninian.* That anonymous hagiography (saint story) was perhaps penned by Bede's friend, the English Bishop Pehthelm, a bishop who had just gone to Whithorn and to Ninian's shrine there (Clancy 2001, 3; MacQueen 1961, 23). The *Miracula* was in turn used in the 1100s by Ailred of Rievaulx to compose a much longer hagiography for Ninian. But by this time, it had been over five hundred years since the saint had supposedly been alive.

Since we think the *Miracula* is somehow related to Bede's source (whether Pehthelm or not), everything we know about Ninian these days, more or less, goes back to those two items: especially Bede's eight-century parenthetical comment, "Oh, by the way, there was a saint named Nynia …." Without Bede, Ninian would be another person lost to history. But because of Bede, we have a saint, a story, a centuries-old pilgrimage destination, the devotion of royalty and recluses, and numerous St. Ninian's churches around the world, including in Antigonish.

In other words, what is now an immense tree of Ninian tradition grew largely from a single paragraph penned in the year 731 for which no one any longer knows the origins. We do know that Bede was a conscientious historian. He generally relied on sources. But we don't know much else.

For the record, here's what Bede wrote:

> "The southern Picts who live on this side of the mountains had, so it is said, long ago given up the errors of idolatry and received the true faith through the preaching of the Word by that revered and holy man Bishop Ninian, a Briton who had received orthodox instruction at Rome in the faith and the mysteries of the truth. His episcopal see is celebrated for its church, dedicated to St. Martin where his body rests, together with those of many other saints. The see is now under English rule. The place which is in the kingdom of Bernicia is commonly called Whithorn, the White House, because Ninian built a church of stone there, using a method unusual among the Britons." (*The Ecclesiastical History of the English People* (III: 4, 115))

Notice Bede's careful use of two phrases: "so it is said" and "long ago."

Bede allows that Ninian was a Briton, that is, a pre-English inhabitant of the British Isles. That would make him a Celt who spoke a language something like modern Welsh. According to Bede, "long ago" Ninian converted the southern Picts "on this side of the mountains," which from Bede's perspective would be the Scottish Lowlands, where we walked in 2019.

Something here is already odd, since any Picts we know of lived in northern Scotland, far to the north of Whithorn (MacQueen 1961, 42-43; see also Bradley 1996, 38). Mind you, who the Picts actually were, and where they lived and had their kingdoms, is an academic debate that rages on and may never be answered. For the Romans, the "Picts" were the indigenous Britons who painted and tattooed their bodies, especially before battles. Pict seems to have been a flexible term: a Pict was simply any non-Romanized Briton anywhere in the isles.

Despite such vagueness, Whithorn was not and could not have been Pictish: the entire region between Hadrian's Wall and the Antonine Wall had long been "Romanized" (Towill 1983, 201). Or maybe – and here's the first confusion – Romanization is exactly what Bede is referring to.

It doesn't help that Bede's description of Ninian isn't even the main point of what he's saying. This section on Ninian is a bit of a tangent, and Bede seems to imply that he's dealing with a lack of data. The details about the stone building and the education in Rome are clear enough. They must reflect something Bede heard from a source. The stone church, or at least some of its remains, exist to this day: I spent a lovely afternoon in the crypt there. But Bede doesn't seem willing to say that his source is reliable in every detail, given his words "so it is said."

It's not much to build a saintly life on. Then again, stories have been built on less.

As Bede would have known in 731, Christianity had existed in southern Scotland for centuries. These days, we've discovered hard evidence to back that up, including the so-called Latinus Stone, a marker now on display in Whithorn, dateable to the late 400s. This is less than a century from the very earliest window of dates for Ninian (Forsyth 2009, 19-41). The stone's Latin inscription seems to be a quote from the *Te Deum*: "We praise you, O Lord" (Forsyth 2009, 25). So when Bede discusses Christianity in Scotland, he knows it's been around a long time, over three centuries before his day.

In my university classes I often ask students to put on their metaphorical "detective hats" when looking at historical sources. Then I ask them to set aside, for a bit, the question of whether a story is true, and instead ask themselves what a story *accomplishes*. What does a story *do*? That will often give us clues as to its possible origins.

Let's do that with Bede.

When he wrote his *Ecclesiastical History of the English People* in 731, the Northumbrian kingdom of which Bede was a part had recently extended its control into the area around Whithorn. Bede says as much: "The see [or Bishopric area] is now under English rule" (no doubt a nod to his friend Pehthelm). Practically, in light of the fairly new linkage between where he lived and Whithorn, and the history of contestation over southern Scotland, Bede had every reason to emphasize, adapt, or perhaps even invent, a connection in the past that would give a lineage to his diocese's control of the area.

The one thing Bede couldn't do was to have Ninian be an English saint. Why not? Because the story is set "long ago." There were no Angles or Saxons in the British Isles at the time. The English didn't exist yet as a people.

Several Bede scholars believe that Bede would have promoted Ninian as an Irish saint if he could have, because of his English antipathy toward the holdover Celtic Briton Christians (Wood 2009, 79). I'm not so sure. The Irish were monastic and insular, while Bede wanted to promote an ecclesiastical structure based on diocese and synod. So perhaps it was less that he tried to *negate* an *Irish* background to Scottish Christianity than that he wanted to portray St. Ninian *as a Roman*, even if he had to be a Celtic, Briton Roman. In other words, Bede may have been happy to promote the idea that a Romanized bishop got to the Scots before an Irish Celt like Columba did (Wooding 2009, 15; Wood 2009, 72, and Meek 2000, 130). Perhaps *this* was the whole point of his comment.

It's also interesting that Bede calls this Ninian he refers to a "bishop" and not a monk – yet another reason *Bishop* Plessis might have suggested the name for Antigonish. Irish Christianity was known for its *monks*. Back then, Irish Christianity was unusual for being monastically based and having different liturgical customs and even dates for Easter from other Catholics. Although Bede himself was a monk, his whole church upbringing would have made him more sympathetic to a Ninian than to a Columba – that is, to a late Roman or sub-Roman missionary bishop than to an entrepreneurial Irish monastic.

Interestingly, centuries later this Scottish-Irish competition would play out again in a different form in Nova Scotia. In 1844, Rome recognized the de facto split between Irish Halifax and Scottish Antigonish by creating two dioceses in Nova Scotia and assigning a Scot, Bishop Fraser, to one and an Irishman, Bishop Walsh, to the other (Walsh 1989, 61). Some folks feel that the establishment of the Diocese and of Saint Ninian Cathedral in Antigonish rather than Cape Breton was a stratagem designed to keep at least some northeastern parts of the mainland away from the Irish and in Gaelic hands (Ludlow 2015, 48).

In an 1884 opinion piece in the *Antigonish Aurora*, the editor enthused that the local Catholics had not only preserved Gaelic tradition in Nova Scotia with their Ninian Cathedral, but that the Nova Scotians had also managed to recover the venerable saint's history for Scotland itself: "Galloway again, after a convulsion which made a wreck and ruin of its Catholic institutions, rejoices in a true episcopal successor of Ninian [here in Antigonish]" (*Antigonish Aurora*, Feb. 13, 1884, "St. Ninian and the Early Scottish Church," p. 2. (A5-1884-110-2)).

But back to Durham, to England, and to Bede:

Bede's identification of Ninian as a bishop implied a Church that was exercising control in the hinterlands even in the fourth or fifth century. Some have proposed that Ninian was an "orthodox" Christian (orthodox being another word Bede emphasizes), sent north to correct some kind of "heresy" amongst Christians who were already there because of being part of the Roman Empire. There is another, early piece of evidence from St. Patrick that doesn't mention Ninian, but notes something about Picts becoming "apostate," which of course implies that they must have been Christian before that (you can't be apostate from a belief you never had). Perhaps the Whithorn group were Pelagian Christians who had taken beliefs condemned as heretical with them into the north (Wood 2009, 74). From the fourth to the sixth centuries, during the church's convulsions over what was heresy and what was orthodoxy, bishops often travelled to "correct" communities (McCarthy 2009, 64-67).

What language did the semi-mythical saint speak? Bede presents Ninian's mother-tongue as what we now call Brythonic, a Welsh-related language that at the time would have been widely spoken across Briton (Moffat 2005, 306). Undoubtedly, as a churchman he would also have spoken Latin.

So Bede seems to present Ninian as a Celtic Briton bishop who went or returned north a long time ago, perhaps to set straight and bring back into the orthodox fold the already-Christianized people of what was to become southern Scotland.

There's not much on which to build a story.

But the truth is that almost all hagiographies are more fabulation than fact. As I teach my students of early Christian literature, we need to look at saints' stories as *stories* – as "sacred fictions" – rather than focus on the little bits of highly interpreted history that underlie them. In fact, stories about saints tell us less about the saints themselves than they tell us about the needs and concerns of the storytellers. Ninian represents the opening volley in a very, very long battle between two sacred sites – Whithorn and Iona – and over the meaning of Scottish history (Bradley 1996, 43).

What I mean is that whoever he was, St. Ninian was turned into a story, and soon a highly *political* story, volleyed between Catholics and Protestants, and between the English and the Scots. In the end, Ninian turned out to be far more important to history and to political strategists like Bishop Plessis (and perhaps Bede) as a symbol, rather than as a real person.

Columba, about whom we know so much more, came to symbolize the *Irish* influence on Scotland. But Ninian could be claimed as a hometown boy. In fact, this is exactly how he was portrayed in Antigonish in the late nineteenth century: "The Picts among whom Ninian laboured were Gaels [like us]" (Antigonish, Feb. 13, 1884, *St. Ninian and the Early Scottish Church*, p. 2. (A5-1884-110-2).

In terms of much later Scottish church politics – never easy for foreigners to decipher – Columba the independent missionary was sometimes claimed by later Protestants (Bradley 2013, 14), while Ninian the Bishop sometimes stood in for Catholics, and sometimes for Scottish Episcopalians: in any case, for the more "traditional" church. All this even though Ninian predated the Protestant Reformation by nearly a thousand years!

The longer the historical distance, the harder it is for us to separate *any* early Christian saint from the cult that revered him or her. This problem is especially troublesome in Ninian's case, for which we have the combination of a very weak history and a very strong medieval cult.

If Ninian were real, he was responsible for southwest Scotland only, the area of present Galloway, and certainly not the Highlands and lowlands of the north from which most of the settlers to Nova Scotia came. The historical Ninian may have come from Galloway originally, as the *Miracula* suggests, or he may have had ties to the area around Hadrian's Wall, and to Northumbria, as Bede seems to suggest.

In 397, the earliest possible date of Ninian's arrival, Whithorn lay in the region between Hadrian's Wall to the south and the Antonine Wall to the north. Whithorn was what academics call "sub-Roman." This means it was Roman some of the time, but not always (depending on the most recent battles), and it was Roman culturally in most but not all ways. If Ninian had been Irish, he would have had less Roman influence and would have likely come from what is now Northern Ireland, a similar distance across the water from Whithorn (MacQueen 2007, 14).

One last wrinkle to this story: There is a small but intense group of scholars – mostly Scots, and mostly men – who passionately debate Ninian and his history. Scholars often differ from the general public. Among Ninian scholars there has been a growing consensus based on the work of Thomas Owen Clancy (2001) in Glasgow, who adapted the earlier work of others, that the name Ninian may in the end represent nothing other than a scribal error. Let me repeat: perhaps the majority scholarly opinion these days is that Ninian didn't even *exist*, at least by that name. According to Clancy and his sources, the name Ninian comes from a miswriting of the word *Uinniau*, meaning "Finnian."

According to this theory, from ancient Roman times *many* early Christians were active in Whithorn. But the only name we have is a corruption of Finnian of Moville, an Irish monastic who came to Whithorn later and who was the teacher of none other than Columba. Bede (or perhaps Bishop Pehthelm) simply made up the story of Ninian and set him in the fourth and early fifth century. All of history's long attempt to get behind Bede's references amount to little more than our desire, in Clancy's words, to find the "pleasing dove-tail joint ... between the end of Roman Britain and the beginning of Scotland's new, Christian story" (Clancy 2001, 1-28).

Are you still with me? I know it's confusing! In the end, we're left with three broad options:

1: Ninian was an ancient Roman Briton. This is the traditional story, as known throughout Catholic history and repeated by Bishop Wayne Joseph Kirkpatrick at the 150th anniversary mass of Saint Ninian Cathedral in September 2024 when our group of walkers arrived to be blessed and share in the celebration. According to this story, St. Ninian lived and worked in the dying days of Roman Britain, from around 360 to around the year 432, just as the Roman legions sailed away from Briton's white cliffs never to return. Ninian was a Celtic bishop trained in Rome and "the earliest Christian missionary to spread the Gospel message on Scottish soil." In 397 he established his church in Whithorn, where perhaps he had been born and grew up. It was the first Christian settlement north of Hadrian's Wall. His feast day is September sixteenth.

There's something quite romantic about this option. It sounds precise, even though the dates are all guesses. It makes Ninian a kind of ecclesiastical King Arthur, a late-Empire local leader. Ninian represents order, certainty, and continuity with an idealized past. His life, conveniently, also roughly coincides with the dates for St. Patrick in Ireland. And this story explains the unusual term *Candida Casa*, or White House, which was made of stone and supposedly uncommon among the Britons, since *Casa* was an early word for a simple monastic building in Roman times (MacQueen 1961, 17).

But there's also a second option:

2: Ninian, still as a Celtic Briton, but a century later in a chaotic dark-age world. Here, St. Ninian lived and worked in the late 400s or very early 500s, as Celtic and powerful new Anglo-Saxon settler kingdoms jockeyed for control of a post-Roman Britain. Instead of going to Whithorn to evangelize Picts who were pagans, in this scenario Ninian was sent north to correct a form of heretical Christianity that still hung on from the earlier Roman days.

This option coheres nicely with some of the archaeological evidence, especially the so-called Latinus Stone. In this option, Christianity likely existed in Whithorn for at least a century before Ninian arrived, since Christianity was part of a package of Roman military presence. But the church at Whithorn became associated with Ninian because of his importance.

Finally, there's a third option, preferred by many academics but unsatisfying to others, including me:

3: Ninian was not Ninian at all. In fact, St. Ninian was St. Finnian, likely St. Finnian of Movilla, Ireland, misnamed as Ninian only because of a scribal error. And Finnian didn't actually *found* Whithorn, although his name transformed to Ninian and became associated with the establishment of the shrine. Instead, there was already a late-Roman monastery started in the early 400s by folks whose names have been lost, but some of whom we have inscriptions for on stones at Whithorn, people with names like Latinus, Viventius, Floris, and others.

A century or so later, Finnian (not Ninian) of Movilla went to Whithorn from just across the sea in what is now Northern Ireland, to study in Whithorn in the mid 500s (Clancy 2001, 1-28). Finnian was relatively famous, so his name got attached to the place, and then garbled in Bede's sources. What's more, once he was back in Ireland at Movilla, Finnian's most famous student was St. Columba, who later fled to Iona and become the *other* missionary to the Scots.

The problem with this approach is that it would have taken some major disruption in the life of the Whithorn Abbey for Finnian's name to be mixed up into Ninian by locals who had always known and repeated the traditions of the place. The archaeological evidence at Whithorn indicates no such disruption. So why would there be such a forgetting (Wooding 2009, 13)?

Confusing? Good. The truth is, while having so many possibilities seems unsatisfying for a saint's story, this kind of confusion, rhetoric, uncertainty, and plain old embellishment is far more common in almost all hagiographies than most of us realize.

While there's some kind of back-story behind Bede's references, it's the narratives that developed later that have become far more influential. Interestingly, this may be true of our more recent stories as well, the ones we tell about Ninian of Nova Scotia.

A GOOD PLACE FOR LANDING

"For many years after [the shipwreck] a phantom ship is often seen in St. George's Bay. I have seen it once and it looks like a long lighted-up train travelling at night. All of a sudden, it disappeared and the next few days there was a big windstorm. When people would see this flaming or phantom ship, it was always a sure sign of a storm."

(Landry 1990)

On our Nova Scotian walk, we began with the pleasure of strolling a much more pleasant beach than the treacherous rocks and seaweed we started on in Scotland. Pomquet Beach has been a provincial park since 1970. Even on a blustery day such as met our inaugural group walk of the Nova Scotia Ninian Way in September 2024, this stretch of tawny sand and wide ocean is so beautiful that it makes for an extremely pleasant introduction to a local pilgrimage.

The reminiscences of the old folks of Pomquet, recorded in the mid-twentieth century, note that the beach and Pomquet Point were the sites of occasional shipwrecks – which explains the lighthouse on Pomquet Island. Stand on the beach facing the water, and to your right you'll see the island, which at just over a half kilometre long and 250 metres wide doesn't even show on Google maps unless you take the satellite view. Look carefully and you can see the small white tip of a building on the north side. That's the lighthouse, set on the Strait side to warn boats. The lighthouse has quite a history – it was built in 1867 for a full-time lighthouse keeper, with attached home. It had six "Keepers" over the years until its demolition in 1960 and replacement with an automated beacon.

Just as the islands off the Ayr coastline in Scotland have a rich history, so does this one in St. George's Bay. The longest-serving lighthouse keeper was George E. Millar, who with his wife Ruth raised six children and "generations of cattle" on the tiny bit of real estate. George's granddaughter, Ruth Edgett, wove the reminiscences of her aunts and uncles into a novel about the lighthouse, titled *A Watch in the Night*.

One story recorded in interviews with Pomquet old-timers speaks of a phantom ship, ghost tales, and fire in the sky after a deadly shipwreck from which only bodies were recovered. Somewhat more historical solidity lies behind the account of another wreck, this time around 1885, when a brig carrying coal mistook a Pomquet yard light for a lighthouse and ran aground. Because it was beached over a Sunday, the event brought out the entire community, who worked to coax the schooner back into deeper waters. The Pomquet priest arrived and led prayers for the stranded ship, with most of the women of the community praying the rosary. Meanwhile the rest of the community struggled to push the stranded vessel back off the sands and into St. George's Bay (Landry 1990, 25). The story is that eventually, "buoyed by prayers" the small schooner sailed back out into the bay. Perhaps, in addition to the prayers, the fact that the community had lightened the vessel by relieving it of most of its coal might have aided the effort.

In his recollections of early life in Pomquet, Simon Landry tells the story of a poor family on one of the islands of Pomquet Harbour who had completely run out of food. In the moment of their greatest desperation, they prayed that the Lord would provide a miracle for them. A day later, on Pomquet Beach they discovered barrels of flour, presumably from yet another shipwreck. Disaster for one meant answered prayers for others.

Pomquet Beach is a couple of kilometres long, and perhaps fifty paces wide at mid-tide. In any case, here you can't roam quite as freely as you can in Scotland. Certain sections are fenced off, and the dunes and forest form a solid embankment, cut through only by the boardwalks from the parking area.

The location is one of the few refuges in Nova Scotia of the endangered piping plover, of which fewer than fifty mating pairs survive in the province. A significant number meet and match on Pomquet Beach, so there's joy all around when a little fluff-ball with long legs pops up during fledgling season. Thankfully for them, plovers have the advantage of being cutely photogenic.

About halfway down the beach headed west, you're faced with a decision. You can turn left and take a pleasant boardwalk over fields of moss, lichen, and by mid-July, blueberries, to the parking lot. There you'll find toilets, a few interpretive trails on other boardwalks, and the main road leading away from the Provincial Park and toward the village of Pomquet. It's a bumpy, and not overly scenic, route.

But if you're like our group of walkers, you will be enjoying the beach so much that it's better to continue straight west. Follow the edge of the ocean for over a kilometre more as it gradually curves to the right toward the raised headland at Monk's Head. After some maneuvering on tracks across a marshy lowland on Monk's Head Road, frequently full of puddles, you'll see a track leading uphill to Chez Deslauriers, the Acadian cultural centre on Monk's Head.

Chez Deslauriers has been renovated with new faux cedar-shingle vinyl siding after the damage done by storms in the fall of 2022. There are Adirondack chairs gathered in a semi-circle under a snapping Acadian flag, and more seating on the deck of the renovated farmhouse. If you can, go visit it, and lean back and enjoy the extraordinary views back toward the beach and over Monk's Head Harbour to your right. Or let your eyes fall on the mesmerising wavelets of the sparkling strait to the north. It's a grand location. If you arrive on a Friday lunchtime during the summer, you may be lucky enough to be able to order fishcakes, pâté (meat pie), or fricôt, an Acadian soup. All three are superb and served by local volunteers. And, as someone said to me recently: "There isn't a better view in Antigonish County."

THE WAY IS – MOSTLY – MADE BY WALKING[1]

"To Phil from Andrew: the day I found the green track."

(Dedication found inside the front cover of a used copy of the guidebook *A Way to Whithorn,* by Andrew Patterson)

In the middle of my research on Ninian a slim, worn guidebook came across my desk. It was written by Andrew Patterson, titled *A Way to Whithorn,* and published by Saint Andrew Press. On the cover was a photo of a rich, green forest. The back cover was filled with psychedelic, pseudo-Celtic interlacing.

I flipped the book open; it was published in 1993. That's a surprising date for a publication about pilgrimage. Hape Kirkeling's formative *I'm Off Then: Losing and Finding Myself on the Camino de Santiago* came out thirteen years later in 2006. Kirkeling's book went on to sell millions of copies in German and English and was perhaps the match that lit the fire which is the contemporary walking pilgrimage movement. The movie *The Way,* directed by Emilio Estevez and starring Martin Sheen as a man who grieves his son on the Camino, came out in 2010.

Although well over a half-million walkers now annually walk the Camino de Santiago, in the early 1990s there were relatively few. Patterson's book about the Whithorn Way in Scotland predates the revival of walking pilgrimage in Europe by at least a decade. Patterson was very

[1] I have heard it repeated that the quote "The way is made by walking" comes from the Camino de Santiago. In fact, it appears to originate with the *Zhuangzi,* one of the foundational texts of Daoism.

much at the front edge of what he could not have known would become a movement.

Patterson wrote passionately about local industry and agriculture, and importantly, identified work and unemployment as justice issues for southwest Scotland. His opposition to mono-cropping trees and his interest in the environmental changes to the Whithorn Route continued to be echoed by later environmentalism. At the dawn of the 1990s, he was already greatly concerned about the climate crisis. His book is also intensely interested in the transition from specific religious affiliation to a generalized "spirituality," and how this might play out in Scotland.

On top of everything else, Patterson is just a fun writer. His descriptions of his homeland are lush and loving: "The glittering horizon of Luce Bay beckons," he writes. "Beyond woodlands and the wild headlands, the Pilgrim Way weaves to its destination – and the wilderness can be felt, banging in the blood of life" (Patterson 1993, 10).

Patterson was a minister in the Church of Scotland. He was one of that increasingly rare breed of clergy who combined his piety with a keen intellectual interest in a wide range of subjects. Reading his book, I began to get a feel for the person. I decided I would look him up and send an email introducing myself. My web search found a photo of him looking quintessentially Scottish to my Canadian eyes: wearing a backpack over a corduroy suit-jacket, ready for the Trail. I could imagine the elbow patches and pipe.

On a closer look, however, the photo turned out to be from an obituary in *The Scotsman*, dated January 11, 2016. Patterson had died in 2015 at the age of sixty-six. The obituary referred to him as a "quixotic radical environmentalist who was a minister of the people and a teacher." He had finished out his life on a houseboat, it said. Somewhat in shock, I found myself hoping he got to walk the Whithorn Way one last time before he died.

We started the trail further north than Patterson did. I think – I *hope* – he would have approved of the Whithorn Way beginning at the cathedral in Glasgow and running the whole of southwest Scotland. Reading his guide, with its descriptions of rough camping, I don't know what the Scot in the walking jacket would have thought of us Canadians, holed up in a fancy B&B in Maybole, drinking wine.

There may have been another reason we pilgrims were so warmly welcomed in that town. Patterson's early guidebook had traced a route further south, from New Luce. It was the Maybole historical society that lobbied for the route to run from further north than Patterson's, through their town. With financial assistance from the EU, the Scottish government, and the North and South Ayrshire Councils, they concluded: "The feasibility study identifies a broad trail through Ayrshire following the likely routes taken by pilgrims to the shrine of St. Ninian ... highlighting the economic potential for rural communities (Ayrshire Green Network Consultancy Study for Ayrshire Joint Planning Unit, Forestry Commission Scotland and Scottish National Heritage" (June 2011): 2.0/12).

It's indicative of the non-religious aims of contemporary pilgrimage that it wasn't a priest or minister like Andrew Patterson who headed up the Maybole proposal. It was a marketing expert. In an interview in the April 28, 2011, *The Scotsman*, he admitted the group's initiative was inspired by other pilgrimages working "as [economic] revitalizations."

The route to Whithorn we followed in 2019 was the so-called westerly route. It begins under the Romanesque arches of Glasgow Cathedral, then traces the River Clyde before turning south through Paisley, Kilwinning, and Ayr. This is where we joined it, just in time to hug the coast (sometimes literally) until Dunure, where the path jogs inland to Maybole and then back through Kirkoswald to the coast at Girvan.

The first sections of the trail are more urban and populated; once into South Ayrshire and Wigtownshire, it becomes quite rural, and settlement more and more sparse. From Girvan, the way proceeds southward onto the Machars peninsula. From there, with a jog to Barrhill, it continues roughly south through New Luce, past Glenluce Abbey and on to Luce Bay. By this point, villages – even houses – can be few and far between. Cell coverage ranges from spotty to nonexistent. Although this may be problematic, it's also true that from here, ocean views abound. After another short section on the moors, the trail more or less follows an inland path parallel to the coast, until it reaches the places associated with St. Ninian.

In 2012 and 2013, on the 850th anniversary of Paisley Cathedral, a Christian group followed this route in stages from the cathedral to Whithorn, on what was called the "Paisley 850 pilgrimage." This walk was almost certainly a stimulus for setting the more permanent Whithorn Way along the same path. In the autumn of 2013, Catriona McMillan at the Solway Institute of the University of Glasgow produced *The Whithorn Pilgrimage: A Report*, which was also influential in solidifying the route.

It made sense, then, that this was the trajectory we followed. It had been chosen by the "Scottish Pilgrim Routes Forum," a loose and (it appears) sometimes fractious amalgam of community, heritage, touristic, religious, and walking interests that came together to make the Whithorn Way happen. The trail they decided on sits more or less atop the same medieval route that McMillan and the Maybole group studied, and that the Paisley group walked (Bold 2018, 153).

Is this the "original" route? In the end, that's not a valid question. A better one might be "what does original mean?" Especially when travelling over the kind of open moorland we encountered in the final days, medieval pilgrims followed general tracks that could change from year to year depending on rainfall or a particularly nasty earl with "rough retainers" in wait. Likely, there were as many ways to Whithorn as there were pilgrims. To top it off, the majority of medieval pilgrims likely arrived at the shrine by boat. For much of history, water travel has been safer and faster than across land.

Historically, the westerly route we followed was the "royal route" once popularized by Scotland's Catholic royalty. James IV, the great Renaissance King of Scotland, was an ardent Whithorn pilgrim, and he travelled the route we did (although quite a bit more comfortably). He was a pilgrim king if ever there was one, a devout pilgrim in the fullest sense of medieval Christian practice (Bold 2018, 157). One of his biographers went so far as to state that the King was "addicted" to the Whithorn pilgrimage (Macdougall 1997, 197).

I'd like to travel as he did, at least once. His journeys sound like a pilgrim's Cirque de Soleil: James' usual pilgrim retinue could number in the hundreds. It included priests, jugglers, jesters, chefs, sommeliers, diplomats, and hangers-on. Notwithstanding the carnival feel, James was known to have spent hours on his knees alone before the Shrine of St. Ninian, perhaps making up for some less than pious activities on the way there.

Mary, Queen of Scots, also followed this royal road to Whithorn. On her way, she was hosted by the same Earl Kennedy who played such a role in crippling the Commendator of Crossraguel Abbey (Muir Watt, no date, 56). Kennedy apparently behaved himself much better with the Queen than he had with his rival for the abbey.

These days, there is no royal procession to tag along with, and precious little evidence of the route's one-time popularity. The way felt rather lonely at times. In any case, to walk to Ninian in the twenty-first century is to be part of a movement of generally secularized pilgrimage more focussed on steps than saintliness (Margry 2008, 13-46; Anderson 2019b). Such non-religious pilgrimages find their model in the revitalized Camino de Santiago in Spain. Ever since, similar routes, with similar hopes of gaining adherents, are increasingly attaching themselves to historic trails everywhere, especially in Europe. There were Camino-like touristic and economic hopes for the Whithorn Way when it was "revived," hopes that have not yet materialized. It's no mistake the framers of the route chose a trajectory passing through some of the least economically active parts of Scotland.

Medieval Christian pilgrims, especially kings like James IV, expected to worship at a shrine at the end of their voyage. That would be a problem now, on a route where there's a debate over whether the saint even existed! Fortunately for Whithorn, the absence of a saint's body at the end of a pilgrimage route is no longer a problem; most twenty-first century European pilgrims are busy concentrating on their own bodies, especially the state of their feet (Anderson 2019a). For many contemporary walking pilgrims, it's the path that's important – the endurance, the testing of personal limits, and the landscapes encountered along the way. Such postmodern pilgrims may harbour vague hopes of personal or relational transformation, or of some kind of discovery of worth or meaning, maybe even of illumination or healing. But these hopes usually don't attach to a shrine at the end of the journey.

However, endings are still important, and it's best if a twenty-first-century pilgrimage can either start or end near a transportation hub. One of the many ironies of walking pilgrimage, and an increasingly glaring problem in an age of climate crisis, is that in order to walk such a long and low-tech trail, the international traveller usually arrives by air.

"The Whithorn Way" can be found on several different websites, although in 2019 it was difficult for an outsider to get a read on the level of cooperation amongst different groups, and which, if any, officially represented the path. From our experience, the first step I'd suggest now would be to contact the Whithorn Trust at https://www.whithorn.com/walk-the-whithorn-way/.

Sara was leaving for England the next morning, so I was up early to walk with her to the train station. Maybole's station is charming, but small. When the three-car train putted in, she got on for the Glasgow airport, and I headed back uphill to see how our hosts interpreted the term "full Scottish breakfast."

It turned out we had more food than we could eat: eggs, toast, haggis, black sausage (blood pudding), a potato tatty, pork sausage or "streaky" bacon (simply bacon, to us Canadians), brown beans, and fried tomatoes and mushrooms. If it all sounds like a full day's calorie intake, you're right. After Maybole, we realized that if we were to eat like this at the start of the day, we didn't need lunch. After that, we never bothered to pack one.

On our way out of town we saw a familiar tawny tail – Loki, the mascot of the Maybole Arms. Ken and Christine had befriended both dog and master, and Callum and Loki sent us off with a wave. We set out toward our second abbey (third, if you counted Paisley): Crossraguel. We were passing fields of yellow-bloomed canola. The sky was grey, but the field edges we passed were bright with wildflowers: vetch, spearwort, and, being Scotland, purple thistle. We mugged for photos just outside the town, under a sign that read: "Haste Ye Back." We were on track for Ninian.

THE ACADIAN WAY

Bordering on the seashore, with its harbors and small islands, [Pomquet] rivals in beauty and picturesqueness the fairest spot in "La Belle France" itself.

(MacLean 1976)

The road to Pomquet Beach Provincial Park is unpaved. Depending on the weather and the vagaries of county maintenance, every few months it disintegrates into an unbearable stretch of potholes, a bone-jarring fact of country life. It also tends to be walled in by brush, and much less picturesque than the route past Chez Deslauriers. By contrast, the latter offers lovely views of the western arm of Pomquet Harbour. Either way, once you're on to Pomquet-Monk's Head Road, you're back on asphalt, with both its ease of footing and its faster traffic.

In the fall of 1773 and into 1774, the first recognized European settlement of Pomquet took place when six families returned from their exile in Saint-Malo, France. They returned first to Arichat, then moved to the area around Pomquet Harbour. Their names are still common in our area: Lamarre (a Frenchman who had married an Acadian), Duon/Deon (the eldest of the group), Doiron, Broussard, and Vincent. A sixth family – the Leblancs – stayed in the area only a short time before relocating again to points west of Nova Scotia (Alfred Benoit; Stanley-Blackwell and MacLean 2004, 19).

Those families settled where you are now walking. It's interesting that on a 1784 map of Antigonish Harbour and its new lots, surveyor Charles Morris II made the notation "French" at the drawn but unnamed Pomquet Harbour, along with five small squares indicating homes (Walsh 1989,

27). These would be the five founding families, as they became known. The small settlement quickly grew into a vibrant community. Pomquet developed a lasting reputation not only for prosperous small farms but also for fine carpenters, dating back to the shipbuilding the area was once known for.

Like southwestern Scotland, Nova Scotia's north shore is largely rural. However, while the area of Dumfries and Galloway has yet to recover from its marked depopulation, Nova Scotia's Pomquet and Lower South River, which lost so many residents to Boston and other New England sites at the turn of the last century, have lately seen an increase in density. This is likely due to come from aways like Sara and myself, seeking lower house prices and commuting distance to Antigonish.

However, easy access to town and highway exacts its own costs. The train through Pomquet still sounds its lonely and lovely horn twice an evening. It's an ethereal pleasure to hear it pass, especially on dark and foggy nights. But there was a time when you could catch that train into Antigonish from Upper Pomquet Station (built in 1879) for ten cents. The station was closed and torn down in 1972. On the spot where women, men, and children in their going-to-town clothes once waited impatiently for the ride into Antigonish, lawn tractors now mulch grass and neighbouring cows gaze from behind fencing. The sagging remains of the nearby Co-op store that was once so crucial to the community were finally demolished and removed the year after we moved to the area. Those who paved Pomquet's roads in 1962 didn't foresee that when it's only fifteen minutes by car into town, local community pays the price of convenience.

Pomquet does its best to fight the pull of Antigonish. It's helped by the presence of the Pomquet Fire Hall, the Société acadienne Sainte-Croix (which also operates the Musée de Pomquet behind the school), Sainte Croix Catholic Church, a large and very active French school complex (the École Acadienne de Pomquet), and all the regular social events taking place at the Pierre J. Baccardax Hall. The hall was named for an extremely long-serving and popular Catholic priest who, for years, placed himself at the centre of village life. Father Peter owned a succession of Goldwing motorcycles, gardened, attended AA meetings, and fished from his own boat in Pomquet Harbour. He reportedly "never met a bishop he liked," and told one foolish enough to try to move him that if he succeeded, he would have a very unhappy and relapsed priest on his hands, and almost certainly a local uprising.

By keeping Pomquet Harbour on your left as you walk Pomquet-Monk's Head Road toward the church, you get some beautiful views of the village. In the dip in the road just before the short uphill to the church, note the house to your right that was once the Pomquet post office.

If you have time, meander through the cemetery at Église Ste-Croix. The inscription on the gravestone for Father Louis Arthur Venedam is unusual for being in three languages: French, English, and Chinese, the last because of Fr. Venedam's time as a missionary. According to local historian Alfred Benoit, unfortunately, the engraver (who didn't know Mandarin) put the Chinese letters upside down. For years, no one noticed. Beside Venedam's tombstone sits another priest's, interesting for its art deco design.

Some of the priests assigned to the parish were Irish, and eventually, some Scottish or English. Benoit related the story of one English priest who had instructed his housekeeper to welcome English-speakers at the front door of the manse, but to tell any Francophones to enter the home by the rear. One of this priest's French colleagues got wind of the practice and decided to visit himself. When the poor housekeeper, not knowing him, requested that he go to the rear door, he unveiled his collar and demanded to see the offending priest immediately. "That solved that," Benoit concluded with a smile. "From then on, Pomquet's parishioners all had access to their manse by the front door."

After Ste-Croix church, turn right on Taylors Road. Just before you turn, look down Pomquet Point Road past Baccardax Hall: at the bottom of the hill is a small bridge over a creek. The creek flows from a freshwater lake (Pomquet Lake), into Pomquet Harbour. It was here a man named Taylor set up a grist mill and a lumber mill in the 1800s. His large home was sold to a Monsieur Landry. The old home across from Baccardax Hall is the much-renovated Taylor-Landry home. The Taylor name continues in the road you're now walking as you turn right toward Lower South River.

After a short downhill stretch, you'll arrive at the École Acadienne de Pomquet (our group of pilgrims was welcomed to the Musée de Pomquet behind the school complex in September 2024). There's no missing the school, which was built in 2000, and enlarged in 2020. Every day, fleets of school busses, vans, and taxis bring students from a large catchment area.

If you're fortunate, you might hear music from one of the classrooms. Mary-Beth Carty, who was awarded traditional singer of the year at the 2024 Canadian Folk Music Awards, is one of the teachers. The liner notes for her album *Crossing the Causeway* (a reference to the nearby Canso causeway and bridge link to Cape Breton) tell how she wanted to sing in all "four of the strong language traditions in Eastern Nova Scotia: Mi'kmaq, Gaelic, French, and English."

So, if you happen upon *un concert* or a *ceilidh* (the Gaelic word for a party or concert), either at Pomquet School, or at Baccardax Hall, then *santé*! or *slàinte mhath* (cheers). Perhaps it will be Mary-Beth, and that will be a happy ending to your day. If not, continue down Chemin Taylor. Take note of the massive lawns that locals spend hours keeping trimmed. If it's summer and not raining, you're likely to see lawn tractors out mowing. Don't be tempted by the two enterprising homes that have set up their own golf courses. Despite the French names on the mailboxes and the Acadian flags flying near the houses, the lots here do not subscribe to the old seigneurial system where a house sits close by the road and the field stretches behind it. Instead, what's most striking is the sheer size of most of the yards.

Following a stretch of scrubby brush to your left with homes hidden at the end of access lanes, the road curves south. Some of the trees you see farthest to your right sit on the backside of lots originally purchased by Lauchy McDonald, whom you'll meet in connection with the Lower South River settlement. Just before the tracks, to your right, the older shingled house slightly uphill is the "homestead" of the LaCoste family. Raymond LaCoste, who was born in that home, kindly told me about the area when I interrupted his mowing of one of the "golf" lawns. Keep walking, and a few kilometres later you'll cross the train tracks.

Are you still in Pomquet, or is it now Lower South River? I've heard both from locals. This kind of indeterminacy is part of the problem of history, storytelling, and direction-following. Truth is, whether Pomquet or Lower South River, the asphalt you're walking is no different and the pun on the milk company billboard will be just as bad. Example: "If a cow doesn't produce milk, is it a milk dud, or an udder failure?" My wife shook her head: "That one is a dad joke worthy of you!"

Borders have always been porous, especially when there's alcohol, lower taxes, or safety on one or the other side. It was the same with the Romans. Much of what is now southern Scotland was south of the Antonine Wall, and in a satellite area of empire if not always under direct occupation (Moffat 2005, 277-280). The heroic stories of Ninian and Columba, and of St. Patrick and St. George converting the locals by fighting dragons, facing down local chieftains, and subduing the Loch Ness monster are colourful and inspiring. But for years, historians have known that Christianity in Ireland, northern England, and Scotland did not arise as the result of some kind of heroic age of saints. It almost always arose more organically, through gradual infiltration of beliefs and customs.

The Imperial presence brought with it the diversity of empire, including this new faith from the east called Christianity. For instance, we know of a Syrian trader named Barates who was buried by Hadrian's Wall (Eckardt, Müldner, and Lewis 2014, 536). As I was leaving for the Scottish pilgrimage, my friend Dr. Meredith Warren, at the University of Sheffield, told me to make sure to see the "Salaman Stone" on display at the Glasgow Museum (Warren 2022, 1-20). This tomb marker, placed by a father in memory of a son who died at age fifteen, was found in Kirkintilloch, northeast of Glasgow. It's very old, and it's probably Jewish, but it could be Christian. Unfortunately, distinguishing between ancient Christian and Jewish epigraphs can be difficult. The museum only identifies the stone as "Semitic." But the combination of the Latin inscription, palm branch carvings, and the name Solomon, according to Warren, show that there was likely a Jewish community near the Antonine Wall.

Christianity would have arrived in Galloway in the same way, piggybacking Roman influence. Like other Imperial customs, at first the new faith was centred in the towns (Radford 1967, 105-106). Like Roman glass, wine, weaponry, enslaved persons, manners, and hairstyles, Christianity diffused like the goldenrod in the ditches you're passing in Pomquet, spreading from inside the Roman walls to adjoining territories in southwest Scotland, including those not officially under Roman control (Wooding 2009, 10).

SUNK-COST FALLACIES

"Here have I stood for three hundred years in ruins.
The people who lived within my walls had, doubtless, their own
share of sins and frailties. They had, also, their own share of worth,
and goodness. All are now hushed in the silence of death.
When, therefore, you look at my mouldering walls ... and the ferns
sprouting out of the crevices, and the green turf covering the
very pavement which the bare feet of the old monks had worn –
can you not learn from the hand of nature itself, to throw the
mantle of charity over the failures of the past?"

(Lawson 1883)

When our Gardenrose B&B hosts waved goodbye from their rose garden, they told us it was "about a mile" to the abbey. We should have known not to trust such casual estimates; Crossraguel turned out to be twice that far, all of it along the frantic A77. The meagre walking path by the highway gave out altogether as we reached the ancient stones. We were able to duck away from traffic into the abbey grounds just as a light rain started up. We didn't yet know that rain would harden throughout the day.

The internet had said Crossraguel Abbey was open, but the sign at the gate said, "Closed for Renovations." We stood, wondering what to do. By peering on tiptoes, we could just make out the cloister walk and some of the buildings. Ken and I were still deciding our course of action when we realized Christine had disappeared. Seconds later, we saw her inside the barrier, placidly reading information placards. We hesitated a bit longer: should we join in?

Our temerity was probably fortuitous: just as we decided to jump the gate, a middle-aged man in some kind of official parks jacket came ambling up the road from the direction of Maybole. He stopped not far away, looked Ken and me over, turned, and left again without seeing Christine. A few minutes later she hopped back over the barrier, and we headed down the country road our instructions said was next.

Christine was a wonderful travel companion: good-hearted, positive, resolute no matter the weather, and always with something interesting to say. As a professor of film, she had an eye for the landscape. I don't know how many times she'd bring my gaze up from the asphalt by remarking: "Do you see how many shades of green there are in that hill?" Or: "Look at those stunning cinquefoil ... Ken, did you see those?" And Ken and I would look, and of course, she'd be right. I was struck by the fact that often, she didn't seem to know or care which town we were in. But then, if Ken or I were talking about yet another historical detail of a torture or murder or martyrdom, she would discuss René Girard's theories of violence and how they applied to the early history of Ayr and Galloway.

Crossraguel was founded in 1244. It was one of the smallest, and perhaps the poorest, of the abbeys strung along the pilgrimage route from Glasgow to Whithorn. It's the only one that survived intact.

Behind this fact is the long history of the rich behaving poorly and getting away with it. Gilbert Kennedy, the nasty Earl of Cassillis (the one from the roasting), doesn't seem the type to have felt conflicted in his role as a "bailie" – a protector of the abbeys. But he was most definitely in a conflict of interest. He'd been tasked by the government with maintaining the ecclesiastical institutions. At the same time, he (like others of the nobility), was busy draining them of their wealth. Despite his reputation as a pious Catholic, the Earl got his hands on Glenluce Abbey, further south, by having a false will drawn up and then murdering the monk who forged it for him so that there were no witnesses (Lawson 1883, 34). Earl Kennedy went on to unceremoniously strip that abbey of everything, including the stones of its walls and chapels (Brown 1996, 170). For some reason Crossraguel was left alone, perhaps out of respect for his uncle the abbott, perhaps because Maybole's was a poorer abbey that had less to steal in the first place.

Like Paisley, its motherhouse, Crossragruel was a Benedictine abbey of the Cluniac movement. Originally, the abbeys had been part of a social reform in Scotland. When they were built in the 900s they'd helped lift the daily life in rural areas. But by the time of the Reformation six centuries later, they'd become opulent and decadent. The nobles didn't have to fear any popular backlash taking them over – it was tenant farmers and poor peasants who rushed in to tear down the magnificent structures, including the abbey at Whithorn (Cox, Gall, and Yeoman, undated, 32-33). The final destruction of these pearls of medieval monasticism was the end to a long – sometimes glorious, but ultimately tragic – history.

As we proceeded south, we were rediscovering a fact of walking pilgrimage: a trail begins to take on more meaning as one becomes familiar with its stories (Wilson 2020, 6). There are always contested narratives about even the most straightforward of sites along a pilgrimage route. In one version of the story the aristocratic theologian Quintin Kennedy was still alive when Crossraguel Abbey was closed, in another he'd gone to his grave.

Similarly, the "Roasting of the Abbot" story may be well known, but its details seem fluid, even in the hands of locals. Donald Smith's 2015 *Pilgrim Guide to Scotland* has the earl roasting his own uncle, and Muir Watt's guidebook to the Whithorn Way also differs in its particulars. Knox debated Kennedy either at the abbey or in the burgh. Hume's 2009 *Sacred South-West Scotland* (x) places the debate in the abbey, while local signage says it happened in the village of Maybole. Who won, who lost, who was hero and who the villain – the stories are as layered as the stones we were looking at under construction tarps. The histories don't all line up. So why should we expect accuracy from the story of St. Ninian, set so much earlier in history and memory?

Meanwhile, our walk took us up and over emerald hills, past whitewashed farm cottages with madly barking dogs on chains, and through the same forest where centuries ago Earl Kennedy lay in ambush with his sixteen "rough men." At the top of the last hill a stand of beeches formed a peaceable lookout over a green vista. We paused to take in the view of the countryside. Four miles after Maybole, as if crossing a final barrier before leaving, we forded water through a "burn," or depression. On the far side of the moat, the backroads delivered us into the village of Kirkoswald. It seemed a pleasant place to dry off and take a break.

We stopped by Kirkoswald's bright and cheery café and had tea and scones to reward ourselves for our morning's trek. Kirkoswald was the home of Robbie Burns' maternal ancestors. Several of his characters – among them, Tam O'Shanter – were based on people he knew in Kirkoswald, folks now buried in the village cemetery. There were some Burns historical signs. But after learning more than enough the day before about his exploits, we decided to head uphill toward the Kirk after which the village is named.

This "new" church dates from 1777. I noticed stone carvings of swans on the roof and discovered yet again that they indicated the ever-present Kennedys. The swans were the symbol of the Earls of Cassilis. The story is that the famous eighteenth-century architect, Robert Adam, while working with one of the Lords of Cassilis on Calzean Castle, assisted with the church at the same time. The swans were his nod to his sponsors (Hume 2009, 50).

Politics and religion have always been close to Ninian's trail – in Scotland *and* in Nova Scotia (where an Irish architect put a Scottish thistle on the façade of the cathedral). Robert the Bruce was baptized in Kirkoswald. I took a quick walk through "bishop's weed" (elder), ash, and cedar of the Kirk Wood, a small trail opposite the church. For a while, I stood beside Robert the Bruce's baptismal font (dating from an earlier church on the site) and gazed out over the village.

It was in Kirkoswald's church that Abbot Quintin, the Earl's uncle, upon hearing that the Reformer John Knox was in the area, thundered out his 1562 sermon against Reformation doctrines, and personally challenged Knox from the pulpit. Being a Kennedy, the abbot must have felt safe. Perhaps Quintin also felt some nationalist pride: although in some ways the ultimate Scot, Knox's "slipping accent" and time in Geneva had caused him to be mistaken for an Englishman in Ayr (Gribbon 2006, 49).

Knox caught word of the abbot's sermon and showed up the next Sunday with twenty friends, ready for debate. But Abbot Kennedy had wisely decided to stay home, so Knox took the pulpit and preached the sermon for him (Lawson 1883, 39). After some careful negotiation, the two arranged the debate that took place that fall in Maybole on the street where we'd patted Loki that morning.

We left the stone swans and continued on our way. The rain didn't debate at all: it settled in decisively. We meandered damply along a low, white-stone barn following a path that surprisingly, after a small bridge, completely disappeared. Flummoxed, we looked out over a lush, parcelled landscape of low hills and cultivated fields. Nary a trail was in sight. Fortunately, we had Ken's OS maps and my compass. I'd discovered that my U.K. phone could track us in real-time. This was invaluable – we knew where we were, at least. But as Ken later wrote to me, the instructions we'd been given in Glasgow "were cryptic, intended to accompany route maps we didn't have. They often referred to places that weren't on the OS map, which was a problem." (The route maps we'd been promised, which matched the verbal directions dispensed in a Glasgow café, arrived by mail at our Canadian addresses several weeks after the pilgrimage.) The online directions are better now and linked to several apps. Back in 2019, in the walk's early development, we didn't have that luxury.

Our explorations finally revealed a riotously overgrown country track that the compass indicated was the right direction. By ascending it and checking against the moving dot on my phone, we confirmed our route toward the sea. Occasionally, the clouds would lift, raising a grey curtain on a magnificent view of Ailsa Craig, the island just off the coast. Ailsa Craig is an almost unnaturally symmetrical, domed one hundred-hectare plug of volcanic blue-green granite sitting in the middle of the Firth of Clyde. The island was a hiding place for Scottish Catholics, who continued to practice their faith during the Reformation. Locals have nicknamed it everything from "Paddy's Milestone" to "the current bun."

From the shore, Ailsa Craig looks empty. Our hosts later that evening swore it was uninhabitable, proof that locals don't always know better. In fact, Ailsa Craig once boasted two railways, a castle, a tea-room, quarries, and several chapels. Its position midway between Scotland and Ireland meant it was a staging point in the smuggling that included not only those two countries but also the Isle of Man and northwest England. Like everything else in the area, Ailsa Craig was once the property of the Kennedys. When the island held hog farms, rent was paid to the Earl in pigs. In the last century, one of the Craig's notable contributions – and yet another connection to Canada – is that quarries on the island produce a particular form of granite, "Ailsite," which turns out to be the material that's used to make the majority of the world's curling stones (Owen 2018, 31).

Passing between deep green stands of ash and pine, and down burns lined by lichen-covered stone fences, our sodden walk allowed us only occasional views of sea and isle. But we had front-row access to another attraction. On July 20, 2019, just weeks before we set out, the *Independent* reported that Scotland's wind turbines had for the first time produced enough electricity in the first six months of the year to supply the country's needs twice over. We were walking past more and more of the massive turbines. The pervasive "wooosjjh-wooosjjh" as three-storey blades cut through the air above us was a physical presence, a bit like the feeling of being close to the speakers at an outdoor rock concert. From a distance, the blades seemed to move slowly. Up close, you marvel at how something so giant can pass through space so quickly.

Later, I asked one of the locals if Scotland built these great towers. "Unfortunately," she answered, "we import them from Denmark. It's just the Scottish wind we export." As I was to learn, in this part of Scotland the turbines don't just power the lights. Through strategic donations to everything from football teams to village revitalization to church bulletins, the wind turbines help keep the lights on in this part of Scotland in every sense. I reflected on the notion that the wind farms are the new, and one hopes, more benevolent Kennedys of southwest Scotland.

We reached a point where a farmer had installed a tubular steel gate to close the lane to traffic. The OS map showed the path continuing straight ahead. Our instructions didn't mention the spot at all. We debated briefly, then went through the gate, eager to push ahead. Girvan wasn't far; its warm dot on my OS phone app beckoned. The rain had stiffened. We were anxious to get somewhere dry.

Unfortunately, our guess and the OS map were wrong. Pushing past the gate turned out to be an error that cost us. We walked about a kilometre between hedgerows on one side and cropped fields on the other. Soon the path became the mere suggestion of a track. Then it petered out completely, dwindling to non-existence in the middle of a sea of very wet green barley. The OS app told us that Girvan's industrial park was only two fields further south; peering through the mist we could see earth-moving machines working alongside a warehouse-looking building.

"I think this must the way," I said to Ken and Christine. "Anyway," I shrugged, "there's got to be some way through up there by the industrial park." Famous last words.

No path materialized. Eventually, even the trench-line through the grain disappeared. Ahead was only more crop, and in the distance, the diesel roaring of the diggers and scrapers. We conferred again and decided that since we'd walked so close, we should continue.

As Ken later remarked, our decision was a classic example of a "sunk-cost fallacy." We'd put so much time and effort into coming this far, we couldn't bear the thought of backtracking, even though by this point we knew the real path must have been behind us. I've spent years walking and writing about walking's benefits. But to be honest, one of walking's drawbacks is that, when you make a mistake, it can often take an hour to reverse what, in a car, would take five minutes.

Ken resolutely took the lead in his lemon-yellow rain poncho, an ice-breaker plowing a route Christine and I followed. Cold rain pelted down. The waist-high grain soaked us completely, right through to our underwear. I've never been so wet when not actually in water.

Our first mistake may have been a universal result of bad decision-making, but our second was purely because of being Canadian. We were all three strangers to Scottish farming. I've walked hundreds of kilometres along cropped fields in Canada. I grew up around farms. In Canada, at the edge of planted fields, there's a road or another field, usually with nothing in between. If there does happen to be a fence, it's usually three strings of barbed wire, which are easy to lift and step through.

At the south end of the Scottish barley field there was a barbed wire fence, all right. But it was industrial strength: tight, high, and topped with razor wire. What? I thought. Do Scots steal barley at night? (No beer in the fridge, honey, so I'll just step out and nip some of that barley.)

Stymied, we turned to follow the fence at a right angle, now headed west. Finally, where the fence ended, a riotous hedge took over. We could hear the traffic close by on the A77. If we could at least get to the highway, we thought, there'd be some access back to the Ayrshire Coastal Path and into Girvan.

What we hadn't counted on was what Scottish hedgerows are really like. Not having taken "Hedgerows 101" turned out to be our second or third cultural misunderstanding that day. If you're British or Scottish and reading this, you're probably shaking your head right now.

"I'll check it out." Ever responsible, Ken began fighting his way through the patch of brambles and wild rose bushes the size of small trees. He disappeared down a gulley in the direction of the traffic. Christine and I followed. With the various thorns grabbing at us, I was nervous about going down the burn. It was muddy, and slipping would mean ripping skin all the way down. At least Christine and I were wearing long trousers. Ken was trailblazing in hiking shorts.

Up ahead we heard crashing through the brush, then silence. Then, for the first and only time in the years I've known Ken, a string of curses. "Go back!" he shouted angrily over the sounds of the highway. "Go back! We can't get through!"

I'd been protecting the bare skin on my hands by pulling them inside my wet sleeves. Christine had long sleeves and her rain cape. Ken had no such protection. There were not only brambles and spiny roses, but also thick mats of stinging nettle. By this time, Ken was covered from head to toe in abrasions.

Perhaps we should have blamed the saint. Nettles were brought to the British Isles by the same Romans who brought Christianity and, indirectly, Ninian. According to Sara Maitland, the Dumfries and Galloway author of *Gossip from the Forest*, the Roman occupiers of Scotland scourged themselves with nettles, brought from Italy, to treat against the rheumatism brought on by Britain's damp climate (Maitland 2019, 17). Covered with welts from pushing through the nettles, Ken suffered angry skin lacerations and a burning pain that wouldn't disappear for days.

In knife-edged silence we turned our backs on the hedgerow and walked back the direction we had come. We were now circling on the *third* side of the field. Eventually, we'd backtracked completely.

Finally, where we'd passed the steel gate so long before, we found a break in the hedge and a service road that led more or less toward the highway and ocean. We crossed the A77 to the Irish Sea, hours later than planned. Here there was no traffic, but neither could we find shelter. A gale had picked up and was aimed straight at our faces. Frenzied waves spat frigid spray, while gulls hung motionless over the whitecaps, fighting the wind.

I noticed several swans treading water placidly, heads into the storm. The Kennedys.

The shoreline was empty save for a few battened-down buildings and some colourful caravans, stoically bundled against the elements. The gale-force rain made talking difficult. I could feel the wetness of every inch of my skin, and I began to mentally calculate how long hypothermia takes. The tips of my cold fingers were sultana wrinkled. Ken, still in the lead, had even more bare skin exposed to the elements. But as he later admitted, the stinging from the nettles was keeping him warm.

We turned our backs on the frothing Irish Sea and pulled ourselves from the wet cobbles up onto the coastal walk. Dairy farms gave way to an empty golf course, but in our stupor, it took us some time to realize we had somehow managed to reach the outskirts of Girvan.

Within a few blocks of our inn, across from a boat jetty and some kind of ferry terminal, we stumbled by the Harbour Bar. It was open. It was a pub. It was warm. Our sore feet forced us in. Our minds were no longer working.

As in Maybole the day before, the sign promised "Bar meals served." A diminutive Chihuahua held by a man sitting at the bar strained her leash at us, yapping. We shrugged off our wet jackets and fell into chairs. I went to the counter. When asked about food, the barkeep shrugged. "No kitchen." Moral of the story: if you're walking or barhopping in southwest Scotland, don't believe the signs.

"You can get something across the street at Graziano's," the barkeep suggested. "It's good. Isn't that right, Ian?" The man with the Chihuahua nodded. His little dog, bulging eyes and all snout, showed her teeth. I wasn't sure which was Ian. Perhaps I shouldn't have been surprised that, despite the Italian name, Graziano's sold fish and chips.

WHAT LIES WAITING

"I don't believe that. It's a story."

"Still. Would you go walking up there alone at night?"

"Maybe not."

"Maybe not?"

"Okay. I definitely wouldn't."

(A fellow walker as we passed Dagger Woods)

There's something about local history that seems to bring out spry, elderly men with a sparkle in their eyes and a correction to some detail you had counted on as bankable fact. I suspected that if anyone in Antigonish would know of such a figure, who could help me learn the history of Lower South River before my Nova Scotia walk, it would be historian Dr. Barry MacKenzie of the Antigonish Heritage Museum. Sure enough, Barry told me that I needed to talk to Fraser Dunn. "He's what you're looking for," Barry urged. "If Fraser doesn't know it, no one will."

The day of our appointment, Fraser was waiting for me at the museum, ramrod straight, historic maps rolled and ready under his arm. We set up a table in the middle of the main room, right in front of a cabinet of wonderfully intricate Mi'kmaq baskets and under several historic photographs and Antigonish tartans. We had two hours before the museum had to be prepared for the Thursday evening ceilidh. "Take your time. Tourists can just mill around you," Barry joked as he set out chairs. "You'll be one of the displays."

We'd been going over land allotments, Mi'kmaq history, early settler surveys, and local geographical features for almost an hour when

Fraser pointed to a spot on the map and described how the improvement of the Dunmore route led to the abandonment of a portion of the old Manchester Road through Beech Hill. "There's also, of course ..." He stopped. Glanced at me with an unreadable expression, and started again: "Since you're interested in this area, have you heard the stories of the Bauchan?"

"Baccan?" I hadn't.

"Bauchan," he corrected. "It's a ..." He was looking for a word and never quite found it. But something about the way he said it gave me the clue.

"The ghost stories?"

"Yes, those," he answered with a smile.

It turns out that another similarity between our Ninian walks is that both feature stories frightening enough to make a pilgrim's hair curl. In Scotland, the tales mostly concern the areas around Glenluce and Kirkcowan in the south. In Nova Scotia, lucky you: you're about to graze the edge of a neighbourhood known since the first Gaelic settlements as a place not to travel alone by night.

As you cross the train tracks and then ascend the overpass at Highway 104, sweep your eyes to the east and the south. This is roughly an area that since the earliest European settlement has been called Dagger Woods. There doesn't seem to be a single historic event explaining why the woods were given that name. I asked Barry about Dagger Woods. He assured me that "Dagger" was almost certainly a botched translation from Gaelic for something that had nothing to do with anything pointy. "Once the English word became 'dagger,'" he said, "then came the stories."

Well, yes and no, according to Fraser. He agreed that Dagger is probably a mistranslation of a Gaelic word. But the stories are older than that. And they abound, most of the moody, "something is in the fog" variety. Many seem to be variations on some form of haunting, whether by ghost, forest-protecting prankster spirit, fire-causing ghoul, or worse. When one of the local walkers on our inaugural pilgrimage, Peter MacKenzie, overheard me talking about the ghost stories as we stepped along the overpass, he exclaimed, "Oh, the faery woods!" as if everyone knew about them. He had owned some land in the area and while we walked, added to the stories.

Websites mention this little corner of the county in hushed tones, fabricating increasingly unlikely tales of midnight encounters with a panic-causing unseen creature known variously as a bauchan (hobgoblin) or as the "Hidey Hinder." Despite the Gaelic flavouring of the websites, the stories I read actually reminded me of Indigenous traditions of a ravenous, maddening, never-satiated creature such as the Anishinaabe and others call the W∗ndigo,[2] and perhaps the Welistoquay and Mi'kmaq the Chenoo, a creature who terrifies especially those who are themselves lost or otherwise isolating themselves from community support and love. Many of these tales predate settlement.

"Whatever's behind the stories of Manchester Road," Fraser's long finger traced the line on the old map, "the fact is, you couldn't get a team of horses through that stretch for years without them spooking. It happened consistently. People avoided the route at night. It never lost the reputation of being haunted. Eventually, that section was abandoned."

I was about to say that it all seems a bit hard to reconcile with the present-day development in the area, where you're more likely to see a jogger than anything more sinister. To be sure, I've only ever seen joggers on Dagger Woods Road during daytime hours. The nights in rural Atlantic Canada can be black as tar, and the rustlings of every porcupine or skunk, or the ghastly screams of foxes, are magnified by shadow and imagination.

Increasingly, contemporary Indigenous authors identify the W∗ndigo less with some gaunt forest apparition than with the insatiable greed of settler society, even with capitalism overall and its destructive effects on Indigenous society and on our natural world (Methot 2019, 24; Rice 2018). So perhaps the development I tend to find so reassuring is in fact the best evidence of the monster. In any case, on the Ninian pilgrimage you're lucky: it's still daylight. And you're not crossing Dagger Woods to the east or finding the historic and now abandoned section of Manchester Road through Beech Hill to the south. You're staying safe on Taylors Road as you reach the end of the overpass and descend into Lower South River. Good thing.

I came across a delightfully subtle nod to these old ghost stories in Linden MacIntyre's 2009 best-seller *The Bishop's Man.* MacIntyre has his protagonist passing the turnoff for Dagger Woods Road late at night, on

[2] On the advice and according to the practice of Indigenous friends, I do not write the full name of the creature.

his drive back from Antigonish to Cape Breton. At the corner of Dagger Woods Road and the highway (an intersection I pass almost daily), MacIntyre's protagonist sees a solitary elderly hitchhiker. The young priest passes, then thinks better of leaving the poor fellow stranded in such a lonely spot and pulls over. He backs the car up, only to discover that the ancient hitchhiker has disappeared.

Perhaps the constantly reinvented tales of the Dagger Woods bauchan now contain a new moral for this Anthropocene age of climate destruction and anxiety: perhaps the forest spirits have been driven mad by the damage that unchecked greed and resource extraction have caused. Perhaps they travel in search of other forest-minded souls while haunting the sacred trees and streams they are trying so hard to protect.

THE VOLUNTARY ASCETICISM OF WALKING

"You're from Canada? You're lucky, then.
You should be happy."
(Beach squatter near Dunure, Scotland)

Thankfully, ghosts are not the first danger most walking pilgrims need to keep top of mind. Walking exposes us to more elemental problems, including the bone-chilling moisture that so troubled us as we struggled through Scottish hedgerows.

We were lucky to have booked the Thistleneuk Bed and Breakfast for the end of our sunk-cost day. The B&B sits on Louisa Drive in Girvan, an ocean-front boulevard. Slate grey clouds scudded over the ocean and white caps frothed on the other side of a stone seawall. There was a sign by the B&B fence: "For sale." I was glad they were still in business. Short as it was, the walk from the pub to the Thisleneuk had been painful; I was still chilled to the bone. We rang the bell and waited. I couldn't keep my teeth from chattering.

"Oh, I'm so glad you're here," our host exclaimed as she opened the door. "It's getting late – we were worried." "Here, let me help," a man chimed in from behind her. He reached to take our bags. Once again, while she seemed Scottish, to my Canadian ears her husband's accent didn't seem so. We struggled through, over-filling the entrance: "You're soaking," our host said briskly, stating the obvious. Which I'm pretty sure meant: stay on the carpet.

Our hosts inquired politely after our misadventures and seemed content to hear of our discovery of the Harbour Bar and of Graziano's fish and chips. Meanwhile, I wasn't waiting for permission: I was peeling off drenched clothing. Stripping extremely wet socks and trousers off one's ankles and legs with shaking hands while crowding into a space the size of a phone booth is surprisingly difficult. I glanced at the upholstered chairs only once, getting a look from our hosts that warned me off. Our hosts observed us like parents at an elementary school drama practice.

"You must be anxious to settle in," the man commented mildly.

"Shower?" I was incapable of full sentences.

"First, let's get these wet things into the warming room." I wasn't sure what a warming room was, but by that point I had as many wet clothes off as I could while still remaining somewhat decent. I was now in my skivvies, as the man led me up flights of stairs. Ken and Christine had opted to remain on the main floor. I thought perhaps I'd made the wrong decision, until I looked out my window.

Ailsa Craig had followed us all through the day's walk. It now sat right in the middle of my third-floor view, solid and black. I tried to imagine the smugglers whose caskets were found in a cave on the island, and the tough Scottish woman who'd run a teahouse and kept goats, and the Catholics who'd found temporary respite from the religious strife and the chance to celebrate their masses. After the official banning of pilgrimage in 1581, Catholics on Ailsa Craig had covertly kept alive the memory of some of the shrines we would see in the next few days of walking (Bold 2018, 157). These were precisely the kinds of Catholics who then immigrated to Nova Scotia and whose secrecy-hardened mass habits so troubled Bishop Plessis.

When I came out of the shower, warm again and human, the sun was setting. An automated lighthouse on the island winked through the rain. Even though it was still overcast, the setting sun had fallen below the ink-dark clouds. The sunset spread a spectacular ruby glow along their undersides, shining across the sea and into my window, illuminating the silhouette of Ailsa Craig. My view couldn't have been grander.

Later, we pilgrims met in the cozy front room of Thistleneuk to compare notes. Ken was so lacerated he hadn't taken a shower for fear of making the stings worse, a decision I couldn't understand. Despite that, we were all much improved for shelter and warm, dry clothes. Ken and Christine had been to Girvan years before: they talked wistfully about how on that trip they'd strolled along the seawall for a mile or more, just enjoying the sunshine that seemed to me at that moment nearly mythical for southwest Scotland.

We wouldn't have chosen the misadventure we'd just been through. But part of walking pilgrimage has always been about just this connection of land and body, with its attendant discomforts. I was heartened to remember that the Paisley group had also gotten lost in 2013 on their inaugural re-creation of the walk (McMillan 2013, 42).

Pilgrimage brings us back to ourselves. It happens when small things that have been important all along in life, but subsumed beneath the tumult of work and schedule, recapture your attention: your feet, your lungs, the wet proofing (or not) of your jacket, the state of your breath. Walking is a kind of voluntary asceticism. Depending on how a day's journey goes, it helps us become aware of parts of ourselves forgotten in the usual routines. And it's not just the pilgrimage that's made by walking, but also the pilgrim. Because of my swollen left ankle, Christine's fatigue, and Ken's reddening welts, Scotland was making its mark on us whether we liked it or not. We were taking with us not just the plans and intentions with which we started, but especially that day, our beleaguered and complaining bodies. Pilgrims learn – sometimes precisely through difficulty – to reconnect with their bodies (Terreault 2019, 22-37).

When I looked out my window the next morning, Ailsa Craig sat solid and hopeful in a blue sea. The clothes we'd arrived in were waiting for us by the front door. Most were dry, but a few items retained some dampness. Our boots, unfortunately, were still wet. Ken's were the wettest of all, despite the newspaper the B&B owners had kindly stuffed them with overnight.

Over the eggs, bacon, haggis, sausage, and tatties of yet another full Scottish breakfast, we debated the boot problem: is it better to use dry socks in wet boots (my position, and Christine's) or continue with wet socks, since they'll soon be wet anyway (Ken's leaning)? Ken put on wet socks. I noticed that the nail on my little right toe had gone black and blue. I put a bandage over it, but I could tell my fix was too little, too late.

We decided to get a taxi to the station for the next leg of our journey. The ancient beige Vauxhall that pulled up on Louisa Drive turned out to be "Joe's Taxi," the same folks responsible for our luggage transfer that day. With his pink- and blue-flowered Hawaiian shirt, the driver was a contrast to the drab Scottish architecture. He joked about how our bags would arrive in New Luce long before we would, and how he'd pass us on the road later in the morning. At the station we had to help an ancient ticket agent do the math for our tickets by pencil on a notepad. Paying just in time, we jumped on for Barrhill.

The little ScotRail consisted of three cars. There were only two other passengers. The train didn't – or couldn't – move fast, giving us lots of time to look out over hilly country that was becoming more and more open. There were moments we slowed to a crawl to scrape through green, straight trenches of brush. The station at Barrhill was empty except for a worker behind a fence, servicing some kind of machinery. The directions we'd been given showed the route backtracking toward the village, indicating we should visit something called the "Martyr's Grave." This meant a kilometre's walk down a winding hill in the opposite direction from Whithorn. After some hesitation (we didn't want to repeat our dawdling of the first day), we descended the tarmac along stone fencing edged with purple thistle and bright yellow rockroses, the ground falling into a vast burn to our right. There was absolutely no traffic. At the entrance to the historical site, we found a sign: "Martyrs' Grave: enter at your own risk."

Despite the darkly funny sign, the murderous events it commemorated were anything but a laughing matter. "Here lys John Murchie and Daniel McJlurick" read the sign, "martyrs by bloody Drummon they were shot 1685." In the spasms of violence that plagued all of Europe in the centuries after the Reformation, Scotland was particularly hard hit. Perhaps it was that the usual religious conflicts were combined with Scottish-English political intrigues. Once it had implanted itself in Galloway, Presbyterianism could never be rooted out of southwest Scotland despite laws, occupying troops, and summary executions. Nor could Catholicism, despite equally harsh measures against it.

The land of the saints may be blessed, but in Scotland, the path to it is bloody indeed.

ON THE SUNRISE TRAIL

"I guess you could walk from here into Antigonish.
But why would you?"

(Attendant at the U-Haul depot and
gas station in Lower South River)

"Take that cinnamon bun.
If you're walking, you'll need it."

(Person at the cash register)

As far as I can tell, Taylors Road becomes a part of the Sunrise Trail after it crosses over Highway 104 and into South River, which, historically, was once called "the Settlement of Lower South River." The fact that the southern loop of Highway 4 is now designated a touristic driving route seems to me to be the government's attempt to make up for having turned this road into a tourist eddy in the first place. In any case, taking in the view from the top of the hill is worth it. Look up, and you'll see striations of pretty farmland and green forest behind the less attractive development along the road. If modern life suffers from too much distraction, pilgrimage is a cure. And this is a place to not be too distracted: the traffic on this part of the highway can be quite fast, and the shoulders not that wide.

This stretch no longer features the vast manicured lawns and neat garbage bins of Pomquet. With its chain-link fences and stub roads, it feels more dandelion than daisy, an area in such a hurry to get going that no zoning plan had a chance to catch up. According to the histories, there was once thick tree cover all through this country. In place of the massive oaks, pines, and red and white spruce that were once here, however, you'll see a well-developed trailer park community on your right, behind Smith and Fraser homes. Empty display homes line both sides of the highway, and to your left only slightly further sits the Antigonish County Industrial Park, with its steelworks and truck repair shops. Of course, industrial parks need space, too, but it's a bit jarring to see them so cheek by jowl with housing. Doubly so, when you learn that this whole area was sought after in the late 1700s precisely because it was so wooded and pretty.

If the bloody, land-hungry Kennedys of southwest Scotland have a Nova Scotian equivalent, it might just be the three Morris patriarchs: Charles Morris the first, the second, and the third. What imagination these men lacked in naming their sons, they made up for in their real estate dealings. From Boston originally, the first Morris came to Nova Scotia as a militiaman. Following his military stint along the Bay of Fundy, instead of standing down as ordered, Morris became an opportunist. He returned and wangled a position as the British crown's surveyor so he could scope out the land he would soon help depopulate. Charles Morris was instrumental in both the surveying of Halifax and the Expulsion of the Acadians. It's noteworthy that his recommendations to burn the houses, cut the dikes, and destroy the crops all took place after he'd had a chance to personally assess the Acadians' prosperous villages and farms.

Charles Morris the second assumed his father's duties as Surveyor General of Nova Scotia in time to keep the position in the family, and to lay out in his turn the lots along the North Shore at Antigonish. It was this Morris who came to the region you're walking. Even though Lower South River was not a part of the territory he surveyed, Charles Morris II liked the looks of the next valley over from Antigonish so much that he took it anyway. He surveyed two thousand acres of South River out from under the Mi'kmaq, designating it as a land grant in the names of his wife, his sister, his sister's husband, his brother, his brother's wife, and several other family members who may or may not have realized it.

As absentee landlords and developers often do, the Morris family never lived in Lower South River. Instead, they flipped the land, selling it to the Gaelic newcomers. This combination of public government office and private real estate speculation smacks of corruption to us today. But for the Morrises and the other members of the "Halifax Compact" (a group of merchants who controlled much of the colony), it was business as usual. It was the same story across Canada, always to the detriment of the Indigenous peoples: we, too, often forget how much of colonization is driven by land speculation.

In 1801 and thereafter, Scottish settlers arrived in the area from two ships, the *Nora* and later, the *Aurora* (the identity of these vessels seems somewhat confused in the historical record). The settlers were quick to set up homes and begin clearing land at Lower South River. In Nova Scotia, the establishment of certain villages can be traced directly to the arrival of overcrowded ships, whose holds contained hundreds of neighbours and relatives, emptying out whole Highland Scottish villages and creating new ones in Nova Scotia, cut from the forest.

The village that emigrated together, stayed together. Whether one was Catholic or Protestant determined the valley, and the settlement. New settlers, unable to speak the English of the new land, wished to stay in the company of their neighbours and relatives as much and as long as possible.

Many of the Scots who settled in this area arrived in Pictou in 1801 on the brig *Nora*. The ships that brought the settlers – and helped clear the Highlands – were managed by unscrupulous emigration agents who helped fill their holds with human cargo so that the ships could then return to the U.K. loaded with Maritime lumber. A Highland Scot named Hugh Denoon, based near Pictou, bears the unsavoury reputation of being chief among these brokers. He is reputed to have put six hundred people into ships that should only have held four hundred (see: https://www.capegeorgemuseum.ca/who-was-hugh-denoon/).

The *Nora* must have had a horrific voyage. Reports of passengers tell of sixty-five children dying of smallpox on the sail. The voyage from Scotland took sixteen weeks against a contrary wind. The ship was blown off course, and passengers endured the extended journey only to then face six weeks of quarantine on landing in Pictou. (Interestingly, a tryptic of this experience was painted on the back wall of St. James United Church in Antigonish, which you pass on your way to Saint Ninian Cathedral. If St. James is open, it's well worth the look.)

Among the many ships that followed the *Nora* was the *Aurora of Glasgow*, which brought more Highlanders, most of whom pushed past the Protestant environs of Pictou to arrive in Lower South River, or to move on from there to St. Andrews. The stories about the *Aurora* and the *Nora* are similar enough to possibly indicate some confusion in their telling and retelling. In one version, after a horrific journey against headwinds, and the death of many of its children by smallpox, the *Nora* arrived off the coast of Newfoundland only to be met by a British man-of-war. The military ship boarded the *Nora* and its commanding officer commandeered most of the young men with the intention of conscripting them by force into military service. It was only after strenuous negotiations and the double-checking of all the papers that the Scottish settlers were allowed to complete their voyage (MacLean 1976, 85).

In another story, it is the *Aurora*, a year later, that arrives off the coast of Newfoundland only to be spotted by a hostile ship, in this case, pirates or privateers. Captain MacKenzie, thinking quickly, orders the passengers to bring their bedding on deck and feign sickness. The pirate vessel moves alongside, takes a long look, and moves on. (Walsh's 1989 *History of Antigonish*, 34, tells this same story but gives the *Aurora* captain's name as Denoon, perhaps after the immigration agent, rather than MacKenzie).

The *Nora* and the *Glasgow Aurora*: both stories feature smallpox, threats from piracy or forced conscription, death, and crowded, unhealthy conditions during a horrifically long voyage. Perhaps the stories are confused, or perhaps they are all true. Certainly, sickness and danger from seas and from others seem to have been the common ingredients of travel by sea in the day. The fact that on his 1806 visit to the Maritimes Bishop Plessis' boat was mistaken for that of a privateer by the locals must mean that they were active at the time.

The encounter with pirates would not be the last time these Scots prayed for a miracle. After quarantine, several of the Highland families purchased lots in Lower South River at exorbitant interest rates from Morris: John McIntosh, John Fraser, William Grant, Farquer McKenzie, and Donald Chisholm. Being Catholic, they had only recently been legally able to purchase land. Neither could the Scots speak English – they all spoke Gaelic. When I was chatting with him, Fraser Dunn noted that John McIntosh and the others didn't receive their deeds for over a decade, only after they had paid the land off completely. McIntosh's great-grandson, Colin, gave Dunn the old deeds for safe keeping.

The 1976 *History of Antigonish*, Volume 1, edited by Raymond MacLean, states that this same John McIntosh led a group to Lower South River with axes and a week's supplies in the spring of 1803, following the voyage and the quarantine (86):

> "They at once set to work to cut down the huge trees. Being unused to the work, and very awkward at it, they made but little progress .... [After a week] In this state of despondency they came down to the river side and held a council to decide whether they would persevere in making homes in this huge forest. One of them suggested that before deciding they should seek for light in prayer."

According to the story, McIntosh's prayer was answered when he looked up from his supplications to see a massive bear of a Scot paddling upriver toward the group in a canoe. The man, Lauchlin (or Lauchy) McDonald, told them he had a farm downriver on the east side of what is now Antigonish Harbour. He had had so little to his name when he arrived in this land, he'd had to use a rock for a pillow. He assured them that it was still possible to make good. He took the men back to his farm, replenished their supplies and their spirits, and helped them establish themselves.

Keep walking the gradual downhill slope toward Lower South River. By the late 1800s, the area you're walking through had become a small but bustling community with a nearby rail station, a school, a cheese factory, a store, and a carriage works and blacksmith's forge. That all disappeared in the depopulation that happened throughout Antigonish County starting in the late 1800s and extended through the 1920s. Much of what you can now see of Lower South River's modest development seems to date from forty or fifty years later, in the mid-twentieth century. In addition to the industrial park and the spreading housing (commuter housing to Antigonish), there's a gas station with a U-Haul depot, a restaurant, and a two-star motel.

The Coastal Inn seems to be a favourite for work crews, judging from the number of trucks parked in its lot with their hoists and buckets lifted high in the air. There's been a hotel on this site for at least a century: the Dingle Lodge and Cabins were established in this spot in the 1920s, the first hotel in this part of the North Shore "designed for the motoring public." A photograph from the 1940s in Peggy Thompson's 2022 book, *Antigonish: A History in Pictures* (63) shows a model lighthouse alongside a stately two-storey Lodge with dual roofed porches stretching the length of the building, and seven or eight cottages alongside.

The Dingle Lodge is long gone. But there are still several worthwhile stops in South River. When you see the huge roadside sign in black and red, missing one section, announcing "Mother Webb's: you have arrived," you have! This is a local landmark of a diner.

See if you can get a seat. You won't be able to escape the graphic silhouette of Mother Webb's face. It's plastered on everything that will take a logo. But do remember to take a close look at it. Webb is not a Gaelic name. Nor is it Acadian. But to me, Mother Webb's stylized nose and chin are reminiscent of a photo of Acadian women in the fields in 1920 that I found in the book *Historic Antigonish Town and Country*. All Mother Webb would need is the Norman cap and the patterned cotton blouse.

In the lineups at the door to Mother Webb's (and be forewarned, there are often line-ups), you'll hear snatches of conversation in Nova Scotian Acadian French alongside English. Servers in Mother Webb's wear monogrammed initials and outfits that recall the heyday of the American diner in the 1950s and '60s. The motto at the restaurant is "Awesome Food – Instant Service." After being seated in front of our disposable paper placemats printed with the menu, we didn't have long to wait. You shouldn't, either.

A KING'S PACE

"Every Scottish monarch for a thousand years came to Whithorn."

(Hume 2009)

Even though our walk from Barrhill to New Luce was thirteen miles, it went by quickly. The trick was contrast: our previous afternoon had been miserable and confusing, while going to New Luce seemed idiot-proof. It required of us only that we stay on one high, single-lane country road. We had no chance, blessedly, of getting lost.

Like any welcome guest, just by showing up that morning the sun brought a change of mood. The morning was clear and pleasant, particularly satisfying when most of the day's walk was on uplands bare of trees and exposed to the elements. We were ebullient with sunshine. But Ken was hobbling badly; his wet sock decision had caused blisters.

Unlike the traffic on even the secondary highways of Antigonish County, where you certainly wouldn't walk down the middle of the road, here in rural south Ayrshire it was only every ten minutes or so a car would come through. I felt like we were kids playing road hockey. We strode down the middle of the road, yelling "car" and stepping to the side of the tarmac for a vending machine van, farm workers in trucks, and, once, a vehicle festooned with slogans advertising it as a "party rental one-stop shop." Given the lack of people in the area, it seemed to me that party rentals must have been a lonely job.

Apart from these very occasional vehicles, we were kept company by sheep and the ubiquitous wind turbines. The giant machines kept pulling my eyes to the horizon; it was like walking through a landscape created by Don Quixote with help from H.G. Wells. When I did drop my eyes, some familiar garbage made me do a double take, or rather, a double-double take: there in the Scottish ditch was a Tim Hortons' cup! In a bizarre turn, Canadian litter had somehow followed us all the way to Scotland. (We later found out there are several Timmies franchises in Glasgow.)

The open upland moors made for pleasant walking with long views, especially to the south and east. We passed a small mound of grey stone; on closer examination I discovered it was discarded slate roof tiles. In Canada, such tiles would be extremely valuable and certainly reused. Once or twice, the shape of a hill caught our attention; a quick look at the OS app revealed them as cairns, prehistoric burial mounds up to twenty feet long that have survived on the moors because of the less intensive agriculture. Like Indigenous lodge rings on the North American prairies, despite their historical significance, these cairns are almost never marked.

On February 21, 1507, King James IV's wife, Queen Margaret, had the King's first child from wedlock, a son also named James. Neither son nor mother were doing well after the birth. Fearing for the lives of both, what was a monarch to do? During the season of Lent 1507, James set off on a pilgrimage to Whithorn by foot. The King was no stranger to the trail: "A glance at the records reveals that royal pilgrimages to Whithorn began as early as the autumn of 1491 and were, at the least, annual events" (Macdougall 1997, 197).

However, this time was different. The king's pilgrimages were usually massive affairs. But this time there were no accompanying entertainments, no drummers, harpers, heralds, Italian minstrels, hunts, mistresses, or visiting diplomats. This time, James travelled with a small group. He went not by carriage but by foot. It was a pilgrimage of supplication.

Ken, hobbling, was talking about getting his hiking boots resoled; I tried to convince him that after enough miles one's feet permanently flatten and swell and it's better simply to get new footwear. We continued to disagree about the advisability of dry socks, but I suggested from my own recent foot problems (Anderson 2024) that perhaps he needed new boots altogether. One of the recorded stops of James IV on his 1507 pilgrimage was to have his shoes resoled. We had no idea where or if we could find someone along the route who could do such a thing for us. A king, of course, would have had no trouble.

St. Ninian must have heard the penitent king's prayer, at least in part. During James' pilgrim walk to Whithorn, Queen Margaret recovered. She subsequently accompanied her husband back to the shrine a few months later to give thanks for her health, but the child tragically died at the age of only one year old, in February 1508 (Macdougall 1997, 197).

Most of our day continued along the one-lane asphalt track to the east side of a meandering stream called "the Water of Luce." As promised, our flower-shirted luggage driver tootled by on his way to New Luce, giving us a thumbs-up. We passed several more half-buried Stone Age cairns and lots of sheep. The stone fences along the road were sometimes topped by barbed wire, decorated by occasional tufts of white wool marked with blue ink. Although it had begun to cloud over, the rain had held off. After a brief consultation, we stopped to rest and have some water in the grasses of a ditch just north of a small farm. There were cattle ahead and we wanted to avoid the flies that always seem to accompany livestock.

From the farm, the land funnelled into an open-throated valley. We passed a stand of trees that our OS maps indicated was part of Glenkitten Fell. We didn't realize it at the time, but on the other side of that forest was one of the treasures of that part of Scotland, the Laggangarn Standing Stones. We would have had no easy way to get to this historic site that afternoon. But perhaps later we could have tried to arrange a ride from New Luce (eight kilometres from the stones), had we done more research.

The Laggangarn Stones say a lot about the complicated relationship between ancient Scottish history, medieval Christian piety, contemporary tourism, and local life. The stones date from the late Neolithic period – think Stonehenge, but smaller. They're about four thousand years old, which dates them long before Plato and Aristotle, before the Biblical setting for Abraham and Sara, and within a few centuries of the pyramids in Egypt. Whether they were placed for religious reasons, for burials, or as a temple or lunar observation is unclear.

Just in case you think we're the only crazy age with our conspiracy theories and essential oils against vapour trails, many medieval Scots repeated bogus legends as well. Some said the stones were the remains of ancient giants who refused to accept Christianity. In fact, the stones are far older than Christianity. They also predate the druids, who also often got the credit for them, although it's possible that druids (like later

Christians) found the prehistoric sites to be useful spots to practice their rituals. Authenticity often piggybacks historical fact, and ancient symbols and places add lustre to all kinds of later ceremonies, as our own St. Ninian pilgrimages prove.

Two Laggangarn Stones are still standing, each about two metres in height. Tradition has it that these two were part of a larger circle of up to fourteen stones, seven of which were still erect in 1873. Over the centuries, most were removed, occasionally to be used as lintels in neighbouring cottages.

The name of a local farm, Kilgallioch, means "church of the standing stones." Clearly, there was once a Christian church established at the stones, likely one of the stops on the pilgrimage route to Ninian's Shrine. Throughout the ancient world it was not uncommon for Christians to co-opt existing religious sites and adapt them as sites for worship. Based on the discovery of massive slabs near Whithorn Priory, Peter Hill suggests that this may also have been true of Ninian's *Candida Casa* (2001, 26).

To add another layer to the story, about thirty years ago a local rambling and outdoor group built a bothy (a communal hikers' shelter) near the stones as a stopping place on the Southern Uplands Way, the somewhat underused coast-to-coast trail that passes through Laggangarn. One of the trustees of the bothy is the same Peter Ross with whom we were supposed to get in touch once we reached New Luce.

So different groups of peoples, over the course of nearly three millennia, have used the same site for different religious reasons. The route from Paqtnkek/Pomquet to St. Ninian of Nova Scotia has no traceable history *as a path*. Historically, the four communities we touch in some way – the Mi'kmaq of Paqtnkek, the Acadians of Pomquet, the Gaels of South River, and the English of Antigonish – were isolated from each other by language, by circumstance, by religion, and sometimes by law. Despite that, I'm sure there must have been those who shared footpaths to the cathedral, especially in the nineteenth century. But despite the relative newness of the cathedral itself, Mi'kmaki is no less ancient than Scotland. Where Ayr and Galloway have prehistoric stone cairns, Kejimkujik has petroglyphs. Where the remnants of ancient homes can be found on hummocks of damp earth in Scottish lochs, remnants of ancient homes in Nova Scotia can be found from Cape Breton to the South Shore.

However, there's at least one difference when it comes to pilgrimage: King James IV reportedly walked barefoot to Ninian of Whithorn. I would not recommend the same on the secondary highways and sidewalks that lead to Ninian of Antigonish.

A GAELIC SALMON

"I don't blame you for not giving up a honey hole ... walking, exploring the river, and finding the holes is all part of the game. I'll be sure to take your advice on that wet fly though ..."

(Post about salmon fishing the Lower South River on the website *Nova Scotia Fishing*)

Whoever at Mother Webb's gave the name "pilgrim gravy" to their signature side-dish, it probably wasn't someone walking from Pomquet to Antigonish. When you leave the restaurant, it's only about half a kilometre to the little bridge over Lower South River, which is not much time to reflect on how important this river was for moving settlers and their goods, and how much of that importance has been lost in the age of motorized transport. The shoulder of the road is slightly wider here, and the speed limit sixty kilometres an hour, not the posted eighty further on. Stay to the left of the road. There's no walk on the right. Here the road-side asphalt is crumbly and corny, but generally okay for walking.

The name Lower South River means this is the final section the South River reaches before it splits into several channels and reaches its date with the ocean at Antigonish Harbour, a short distance to your right.

The river suffers from an unimaginative name for such a lively little waterway. Where it intersects the Sunrise Trail, Lower South River becomes a tidal estuary, so it's engaged in the complex back and forth tidal negotiations all such waters constantly make between land, sea, promontory, harbour islands, currents, and shallows. This is precisely the kind of river geography of interest to fishers. It's no wonder there's an Antigonish

Rivers Association, and that they have a salmon, bass, and trout map of the Lower South River.

It's a nod back to John McIntosh and the language long spoken by the first European colonists in South River that that fish map of Lower South River is in both English and Gaelic. Since you're on the upriver side of the bridge (the side with the sidewalk), look to your left. There, if the tide is high and you know what you're looking for, you might see the feature once known to local anglers as "Sgeir Glumag," a tidal rock pool which is one of the "honey holes" referred to in the salmon fishers' message board above.

The fisher who said that he likes to walk, explore the river, and find the best fishing holes for himself is taking advantage of our natural environment in a way that I think most of us would want to encourage. Interestingly, his posts on the message board indicate a certain assumption of access to the river that I wonder about. Did he have trouble gaining access to the salmon holes along some of the riverbank? If so, did he ask landowners, or presume that someone in hip-waders carrying fishing gear would not be questioned? What if he had been Mi'kmaq? Fairly recent history not far away from South River tragically indicates that a Mi'kmaw fisher would encounter obstacles our white fisher didn't, in so optimistically "exploring the river and finding the honey holes."

Yet, before the online bulletin board of sports fishers, before the Gaelic-English map, and long before the secondary road on which you're walking over the South River, this area was yet another fishing settlement for the Mi'kmaq. One can only guess at the wealth of aquatic life that must have drawn them to the converging waterways of Antigonish Harbour: salmon, giant striped bass, Gaspereaux (a type of herring caught during their spring runs), and the massive Atlantic sturgeon, which in May and June would come upriver from the sea, and often reached lengths of fourteen or fifteen feet (Walsh 1989, 16).

There is no "presumption of access" anymore in Lower South River, or anywhere along the Nova Scotia Ninian Way for that matter, as there was in the years before Charles Morris II cast his eye over this land. The fact that there is no strictly legal path along South River for that unknown fisher, nor access for us, except along the fringe of roadways, is indicative of a loss of that accessibility. Nova Scotia has been more forward-thinking than many parts of Canada in trying to develop trail systems and encouraging hiking. But outside of provincial and national parks and certain complexes of trails systems (Haynes 2015), generally our governments have only haphazardly opened the natural world to folks on foot.

We talk about the importance of nature. We say we're interested in reducing our "nature deficits." But too often our legislation is taking us in the opposite direction. Canada tends to follow the example of the United States and to adopt ever more stringent laws against access. Landowners are posting more and more "No Trespassing Signs," despite the fact that the kinds of criminal behaviours they fear arise primarily in situations of poor enforcement of existing laws, not the need for new ones (Anderson 2018).

Because, unlike Canada, Scotland has been brave enough to adopt access laws that enshrine the right of all citizens to have access to land, even privately held land, Scots are learning by trial and error how to engage respectfully with the natural world around them. A cultural and educational shift is needed in order to prevent littering or disruption of wildlife species, but Scotland is working toward it with its "Right to Responsible Access" laws. So are several other countries. Finns, for instance, are generally taught to respect nature from kindergarten. Learning to enjoy berries, mushrooms, and views, and not disturb others, especially landowners, seems to be in Finnish DNA, but in fact their "out in nature" attitude is the result of a successful and well-coordinated educational system and resulting public culture that values *jokamiehenoikeus*, or "every person's right."

On our walk past Lower South River, we saw bottles and cans thrown into the ditches from passing cars. On our trek south from Glasgow along the Scottish seashore, we also saw a lot of trash on the beach ... a dismaying amount. Later, when we met Peter Ross, he insisted that the trash we'd seen was not Scottish. "At least," he qualified, "most of it isn't."

The prevailing ocean currents mean that refuse from Dublin and Belfast, as well as the Isle of Man, often washes into Ayrshire. "What's more," said Peter, "there's a lot that just comes from irresponsible folks on the boats, dumping their junk into the sea. You find full cans of beer when you do clean ups. That's not a beach party. That's from the ocean." It was true: on our first day's beach scramble we came across a number of full plastic bottles of Coke amongst the garbage. "Cleaning up is part of Responsible Access," says Ross, about Scotland. "It's up to local communities to put it into place."

There is no law of Responsible Access in Canada, beyond the laws that allow some access and limited camping privileges on what is called "Crown Land." Nor is there a particularly safe walking route from Pomquet Beach to Saint Ninian Cathedral. My focus on the historical has perhaps led me to understate the political: why is there not more of a public outcry for safe and accessible walking routes? How might walking routes – whether dedicated or even just well-maintained and posted shoulders on roads – allow us to experience the land on which we live more intimately and sustainably? In addition to the kinds of hikes outlined by Michael Haynes in his *Hiking Trails of Mainland Nova Scotia* (2015), what difference might even a short access path or a sidewalk along a busy street make to the Nova Scotian who has not yet been convinced of the need to safeguard some part of this wild world from degradation?

If we in Canada asked what they do right in Scotland, we'd learn from them that Responsible Access is maintained by community groups operating locally. It's already the philosophy behind groups like Hike Nova Scotia and their program Nova Scotia Walks (https://www.hikenovascotia.ca/ns-walks/). There are local paths close by the École Acadienne de Pomquet: a local outdoor living club was using them as we passed on our 2024 pilgrimage. Neighbours support neighbours getting out on the land, and local historical associations or museums such as the Antigonish Heritage Museum become centres where locals learn something about where they walk and its history. On Sunday afternoon strolls, mountain hikes, or historical walks, or even activist marches, locals learn to take in what is important, and leave nothing behind except footprints.

A society is better with some form of a "Right of Responsible Access." Maybe it's time to repair those broken old wooden bridges that are sinking into the earth on the edges of our land.

THIS GREEN DEMOCRACY

"Hunched against the Atlantic winds and distanced from the rest of Scotland by long moors and huge forestry plantations, fingers of land stretch south in a coastline of bays and peninsulas."

(Patterson 1993)

Somewhere between Barrhill and New Luce, we crossed the border from South Ayrshire into the rambling fens and tree plantations of Dumfries-Galloway. Finally, we were in the region that contains the *Candida Casa*. With one detour into the moors, our route from here paralleled the southwest coastline of the Machars of Galloway peninsula as it juts into the Solway Firth and that part of the Irish Sea separating southwest Scotland from northwest England.

The area we were walking into is the part of Dumfries-Galloway that locals call "Wigtownshire." Wigtownshire is the extreme southwest of Scotland. Depending upon how you look at the map, it resembles either a high-heeled woman's shoe as drawn by a young child, or depending on your imaginative leanings, a misshapen phallus, the tip at the Mull of Galloway, sometimes also called the Rhinns of Galloway. "Among the many evocative sites [of this area]," writes Smith, "are the carved stones at Kirkmadrine, the medieval Church of Kirkmaiden with the nearby cave and chapel of St. Medana, Chapel Patrick at Portpatrick, St. Mary's at Kilmorie, and St. Columba's Chapel at Kirkholm." These are all part of what he describes as "the remarkable religious heritage of this small but special area" (Smith 2015, 29). We passed a farmyard with the sign: "Caution: free range children and animals."

This part of Scotland tends to be somewhat warmer than areas further north, by virtue of its contact with the Gulf Stream. On a clear day – of which there are not necessarily that many – you can see Northern Ireland, the Isle of Man, and the Lake District of England, all three at once. During our final days on the Whithorn Way, it was quite common to come over a small hill and see the Irish Sea, blue and inviting in the distance.

"That's where we're going to be by the end of this," I said to Ken once. "At the Isle of Whithorn."

"You know that the Isle of Whithorn isn't actually an island, don't you?" he asked me. I didn't.

The edge of England one can see from the Isle of Whithorn is close by where Emperor Hadrian put his wall. Roman shipping moved up and down the coast from Solway's harbours, as trading vessels had for centuries even before the Roman invasion. Quite wrongly, we tend to think of the ancient world as a series of isolated spots: Jesus walked here, the Buddha there, the Egyptians here, the Gauls there, the ancient Picts further west. But in fact, there has always been commerce in goods, ideas, people, and, often, religions and diseases, across quite vast distances, even in ancient days.

By Ninian's time, whatever century you pick for him, Whithorn had long been a trading centre. Excavations at Whithorn have uncovered "amphora from the eastern Mediterranean, tableware from North Africa, cooking pots from France, and pottery from Rome" (Sharp 2006, 20). A major Roman port on the Cumbrian coast was visible from the Isle of Whithorn (Forsyth 2019, 33). To think that the Romans did *not* come across the Firth along that historic line of sight and trade stretches credulity. Which is to say that Roman-influenced Christian communities as early as the second and third centuries near Whithorn make a lot of sense as soon as one sees the actual land- and seascape.

One of the benefits of walking pilgrimage is actually seeing and experiencing the land close up. On foot, one can learn things that reading doesn't quite set into place. Just as walking in Lower South River helped me see the intimate connection of the first settlers with the tidal river, so I was starting to understand just by looking across the strait how easy it would have been for a Roman Christian community to be established in

Whithorn. This visible proximity began to erode my confident disbelief in Ninian.

After cresting some hills dotted by more wind turbines, we passed a grove of sycamores and over an old stone bridge. For a while, we'd been putting on and taking off our jackets repeatedly, every time there would be a few splatters of rain. The OS app, in its quiet way, kept advertising ancient sites we just couldn't take the time to explore: a cairn to the west of a farm we were passing, or a Neolithic cup and ring rock through the ferns at the top of a hill to our left. Occasionally, horseflies buzzing around alerted us that we were once again in sheep country, or about to encounter the small knots of cattle that would wait until we were almost upon them, then bolt awkwardly off, as if discovering their legs for the first time.

We crossed several "Texas gates," called "cattle grids" or "sheep grids" in Scotland. The gaps in the gate surface were wider than I'm used to, so wide we had to be careful not to twist an ankle ourselves. As we neared New Luce, we could see to the east the high hills that separate this region from the rest of Scotland.

We'd been told that in New Luce there would be no restaurant, nor any food. Our instructions were to call ahead and let Harry and Marlene Waugh, at Nadav's Shed, know our estimated time of arrival. We had an email from our increasingly unreliable guide informing us that they could "put something into the slow cooker" if they had a bit of notice. On the description of the Shed we'd read online, there were testimonies about laying hens, and discussions of hikers finding hard-boiled eggs on their doorstep at 6:30 in the morning.

I had assumed that "a bit of notice" meant a half-day, or the usual amount of time for a slow cooker to do its work. "Hi!" I said when we finally got to a spot that had a phone connection. "It's the Canadians. Sorry I couldn't call earlier but we had no cell access. I think we should be there about five o'clock or so."

"Well done," answered a cheery voice. "That's good, then. Well, you've probably had a nice day of it. We should be around to let you into the Shed."

I hesitated. The man hadn't said anything about food. My stomach was already grumbling. "We were told perhaps you could put something into a slow cooker for us so long as you knew when we're arriving," I went on. I paused. "One of us is a vegetarian."

The silence stretched on far too long. "But really," I added finally, anxious to break it, "we're not picky."

"You need *food*?" When it came, the voice was incredulous. "By notice I meant a week or so. We came back from town this morning. We can't go out again. The shops are closed."

Now I was the one who was flustered. "Well, uh ... hold on." I covered my cell with my hand and mouthed "NO FOOD" at Christine and Ken. "I'm sure we can work it out when we get there," I said. "Should be about five."

I still had some crumbs of leftover cheese in a plastic bag. Two Scottish National Trust rhubarb candies were deep in a damp pocket. Christine said she had a few crackers. It wasn't much, but perhaps it would get us to the next town the following morning. I was glad that Scottish breakfasts are so spectacularly generous, since it was turning out our evening meals were less than impressive. We walked on, our moods darkening to match the clouds.

At least the hut we would be staying in would be dry. That seemed a minor success in what was looking like it might be a long evening. The last few hundred metres of the day came as a surprise. I thought we had further to walk, but suddenly, the tarmac we had been tracing all day along the edges of the hills descended the open fields and led us into forest. A sign with pictograms of a bed, and – amazingly – a fork and knife announced, "New Luce." Could it be?

The skies had turned blue and sunny. Above our heads, ashes, sycamores, and maples interlocked to produce a canopy of green through which Ken and Christine walked ahead. Their figures were silhouetted against a background of brightly coloured buildings. A pub? I hoped, against hope, that what I'd heard about New Luce was wrong, that somehow the sign was right, and that just for us someone was keeping open an establishment with a shining wooden bar, bright bronze taps, cool, dark pints, and maybe a bowl of pasta.

Exiting the canopy into the village felt like entering a fairy-tale world. New Luce welcomed us with splashes of colour, a major change from the pleasant but drab buildings of Ayr and Maybole. New Luce was all spring to Girvan's grey stormy cloud. It felt like a tourist-brochure Brigadoon, its one main thoroughfare festooned with flowers – and incredibly, we its only guests.

Ken and Christine stopped to talk to someone in a solitary car stopped in the middle of the main street. As I caught up, I heard the man say to Christine: "It's because of the wind farms. It's the money THEY paid." I listened in:

"We bought the hotel when it shut down. With the pub. The shop, too. Plan to open the shop as a cooperative. We'll run it ourselves. The town, I mean. People don't necessarily always like the look of the windfarms, but they're here. And if we can get everything open again it's because their payments are financing all this."

The man jerked his thumb over at the woman who was, just then, leaning out the other side of the vehicle speaking animatedly with someone in the flowered doorway of one of the homes. "A group of citizens," he added. "The women, mostly, like my wife. They've got big plans for New Luce." He smiled proudly: "They'll do it, too."

Unfortunately for us, the planned restaurant and pub were still two months from opening, and the town's shop even further. We thanked the man and decided to find "Nadav's Shed."

"It can't be a real shed," Christine said for the third time that day. "Can it? That must just be the name. Right?"

At the end of the main street, we stopped to try to work out the terrible instructions we'd been given in Glasgow. Two rivers intersect at New Luce. Ahead of us was a stone bridge over the Cross Water. Just as we'd noticed in Ayr, Dunure, and Girvan, there were little ceramic animals and birds in the recessed windowsills of the cottages we were passing. Two yellow-breasted, blue-headed great tits and an oversized glazed frog perched in the ledge beside us. I'd just decided to call when a young, bearded man in a checked shirt poked his head out of the doorway. "Looking for Nadav's Shed?"

Clearly there weren't that many places in New Luce for folks with backpacks to go.

"Why yes."

"Americans?" He squinted, but it wasn't an unfriendly sort of squint.

"No. Sorry." I started ...

"We're Canadians!" Christine and Ken fairly tripped over each other.

"Oh, you're lucky then," the man remarked. He started to explain the directions, then interrupted himself: "Shite, I'll just show ye."

We followed him a few yards across the bridge, then left. The building sitting on the river seemed to have once been the village mill. It had a clock, and a little sign, "Faith Cottage." He pointed to a driveway and a yard immediately to our right. "See that little red building? That one, with the brown trim? That's your place." He was gone before we could properly thank him.

The address for Nadav's Shed is 7 Smithy Lane. This presumably means it was once the site of a forge. And a lane. Now, the pilgrims' stop is basically the backyard of Harry and Marlene Waugh. Nadav's turned out to be an outbuilding the size of a small apartment, with two rooms, a kitchen table, an outdoor chemical toilet, and quite a bit of space to hang hiking gear. It was warm, and it was dry. Even though there was no food, it had strong Wi-Fi, which in our day is right up there amongst pilgrim needs.

PILGRIM VIEWS

"When I walk, I sometimes greet the rabbits and the birds and the trees and the grass in the Plains Cree phrases I can remember: tânisi, wâpos! tânisi, piyêsisak! tânisi, mistikwak! tânisi, maskosiya! The rabbits bolt for cover; the birds look at me, warily, or fly away, sensing danger; the trees rustle in the wind; the grasses ripple and wave."

(Ken Wilson 2023)

Since we've been on the trail awhile, poking around moss-covered mounds that turn out to be Stone Age tombs, and Dagger Woods blunted by development, perhaps a word or two about views and even about "nature" is in order. After all, views and nature help make walking pilgrimage the surprisingly popular activity it is.

Being in Canada, one might think that Nova Scotia has more "nature" than southwest Scotland. One would be wrong. There's little of the natural world undisturbed anywhere on the planet, and neither of our Ninian walks is exempt from that fact. The parts of western Dumfries and Galloway that now feel so backwoods and eerily quiet have been inhabited, cropped, timbered, and fought over for millennia. Their present depopulation is just the latest stage in a long history. The ancient Caledonian forests that once hid Robert the Bruce's men have been replaced by vast tree farms, their Canadian-sourced evergreens unimaginatively lined up in rows like occupying soldiers.

The landscape between Pomquet Beach and Saint Ninian Cathedral must also look considerably different from the massive old-growth forest and sparkling rivers pre-Contact. Given half a minute of reflection, most of us would know that (see Grenz 2024, 150-156). But those of us who fight back the poplars and creeping dogwood from our lawns and ditches every summer may not realize just how de- and then re-treed this area is, and how completely deforested it was only a hundred years ago. Antigonish County looks nothing like it did a century ago, when general stores, fish processors, cheese factories, timber mills, and modest farms still dotted a hopeful landscape cleared first for lumber for shipbuilding and then for agrarian pursuits.

A photo taken in the first decades of the twentieth century at the Pomquet train station tells the tale (http://www.imagineantigonish.ca/pomquet-railroad-station-early-1900s/). On the platform stand three women and two men. Going to Antigonish clearly meant dressing up. Even the children who play behind, slightly out of focus, are at their best. The man on the right, in a double-breasted jacket and flat-topped straw "boater" hat, identified as Eddie Doiron, is the dandy to Simon Vincent's more working-class bowler and tie-less shirt at the left of the group. The three women – Jane Vincent, Effie Cross, and Lizzer (Doiron?) – match in their long skirts and blindingly white blouses. But it's their hats that are works of art: wide-brimmed, held by long pins, and piled high with ribbons, bows, and, likely, feathers and flowers ... the photo is grainy enough that it's hard to tell. I imagine sitting beside Jane and her rakishly angled flower arrangement while the train bumps toward Antigonish over South River, worrying about losing an eye.

Despite all this, it's the slightest sliver of horizon showing behind the group that interests me even more. What catches my attention in that photograph is nothing. That is, it's the very nothingness – the starkness – of the horizon line that's interesting.

That train station has been gone over fifty years. I've walked to the south end of our road and examined where it once stood. There's not a single angle from which you could take a photograph of that spot now where there would not be trees, or at least bushes, in the background. There has been a widespread, scrubby reforestation of this entire area, as there has been all over Nova Scotia, all over the Maritimes, and generally throughout much of eastern North America, at least where cities don't exist. Its cause? Urbanization and the abandonment of what is often now considered to be marginal farmland (Flyn 2021, 75-79).

Because we've never experienced anything else, most of us are thinking of this reforested, partially rejuvenated landscape when we say we want to "get out into nature." We are not thinking of the meadows and fields of a century ago. Nor can many of us imagine the majestic Acadian forest of sugar maples, ash, cedar, eastern hemlock, and yellow birch that once dominated Nova Scotia (Haynes 2015, 249). Conceptually, our longing for what is wild turns out to be elusive. My fondest recollections of being in nature as a kid consist of catching frogs and snakes and watching damselflies mate in the high grasses bordering a creek where the houses were never too far away, or of digging fossils at the edge of a school's baseball field where occasionally we had to watch for errant foul balls. Obviously neither of these spots were pristine wildernesses. I told my sister, Kandace, once of my memory of floating a raft on a pond in the trees behind our house. "You do remember that that was an abandoned gravel pit, don't you?" she asked.

I didn't.

As J.B. MacKinnon wrote in his 2014 *The Once and Future World*, what most of us mean when we say we love "nature" is that we love whatever nature it was we knew and experienced at some formative point in our lives. We also tend to love it as the Romantics did: when it's safely and carefully, even artfully, arranged for our aesthetic pleasure. These days, most of us enjoy our nature de-toothed and de-clawed. I felt unreasonably, but undeniably, put out when one of the bald eagles we so admire watching from our deck in Pomquet swooped in to pick off a baby duckling we had been feeling protectively parentish toward since spring. There are reliable reports from neighbours that a bobcat and at least one black bear have been seen at the north end of the gravel road that passes our house; my wife and I don't walk there alone.

The Nova Scotia Ninian Way follows a drastically altered landscape where nature can be experienced, and lovely views offer themselves up – but in just such mediated ways. The topography of the walk consists of low hills alternating with river valleys and marshy areas (by the way, in case I haven't mentioned this, during a wet year there is no such thing as "mosquito season" on the North Shore. Mosquito season is whenever there isn't snow on the ground.)

There has been so much terraforming over the past century and a half in northern Nova Scotia that the shape of the land itself betrays the human hand. The railroads and the highways were the first to raze hills and raise valleys in true Isaiah-like fashion. Many homes in rural Antigonish County, certainly in Pomquet, are built at least partially on pads of compressed gravel or levelled earth. You know that a new business is about to open on Beech Hill Road, or along old Highway 4, when the dump trucks arrive, and earth-moving machinery begins to construct a giant grey platform of crushed rock. Even from spots like Cape George (off our pilgrim route but beautiful), and Chez Deslauriers at Monk's Head, where there are abundant natural views, your vantage point has probably been solidified and braced to create the spot for that moment of sitting and enjoying the view that we identify with being "out in nature."

Contemporary walking pilgrims are pre-eminent consumers of these landscapes accentuated by human action. Once on the Harvest Moon Trail along Nova Scotia's Annapolis Valley, I passed a group of fluorescent-vested workers. I asked them what they were fixing. "The view," one responded as he pulled the cord on his chainsaw and dropped his visor. The others were already busy felling small trees. "It's beautiful here," the man shouted at me. "But you'd never know it with all this in the way!" By "this" he meant the poplars and dogwoods that had grown up, nature by any measure except aesthetics.

Along the pilgrim route to Ninian, whether in Scotland or Nova Scotia, chances are that the belvedere you look out from when you enjoy a view is man-made, the bench strategically placed, and the footing beneath you changed and perhaps shaped by human activity. All of our Nova Scotia Ninian walk falls along fairly low-lying coastal areas; it's just that sometimes you're walking up onto a slight elevation where a tableau of gently rolling hills greets your eyes, and much of the time you're at or near sea level, batting at those mosquitos.

In my researching of the saint behind our walks, a musty tome from 1964 came into my hands. It was titled *St. Ninian: Light of the Celtic North*, written by Mosa Anderson. Anderson imagines that Ninian was a Romano-Briton Cumberlander who grew up near Hadrian's Wall, of Briton parents who were comfortable provincial citizens of the Empire. For that Anderson (Mosa), like this Anderson (me), it was only natural that a local bishop would look across the strait and be sent to the small Christian communities there.

It's one of those oddities of being a pilgrimage scholar that one's research can turn out to be so much like a path: often the pilgrim-academic gets lost on side-tracks of research, following one intriguing view after another. I discovered Mosa Anderson's book while trying to learn more about Ninian, but found I was increasingly drawn to find out more about Mosa Anderson. I could find only one black and white photo of her, an obituary from the Cadbury Research Library. It shows a slim, serious woman in a military uniform and beret. Apart from Julia Muir Watt, the landscape of Ninian studies and of Whithorn walking is overwhelmingly male. In the midst of long-standing arguments about Ninian amongst Scots academics, Roman Catholic Nova Scotian bishops, and Church of Scotland ministers, an early female writer like Anderson stands out.

In 1916, Mosa Anderson was on her way back to England from Paris when she was approached to work for the *Cambridge Magazine*. The editors wanted her, in part, because of her ability to read Russian. Over the course of her life, Anderson became a political commentator and writer, and a proponent of the Women's International Movement for Peace and Freedom and the Save the Children Fund. She served as personal secretary to Charles Rodden Buxton, MP, wrote a doctoral dissertation on another member of that family, was close friends with Eglantyne Jebb (who started the Save the Children Fund) and with Bishop Harold Buxton, who was at Gibraltar throughout the Second World War (Dunstan 2018, 92). Mosa wrote several books on European politics, and (intriguingly) spent time in both Poland and Germany before and right after the Second World War, as the Russians solidified control of Eastern Europe. Her life reads a bit like a potential spy novel. She would be worth more study. Given such a life history, I'm interested in why she wrote a book about Ninian at all.

My guess is this: it's near the end of our lives we tend to think of ways to integrate all we've seen and done. Age sometimes makes us align ourselves with those who have acted similarly. Historians often write history in order to place themselves either consciously or unconsciously within it. Mosa describes Ninian in rather more detail than the limited sources will support. To my reading, her description makes the ancient bishop out to be a person much like her: an activist who was smart, politically connected and idealistic, and working behind the scenes during a time of political and social chaos and breakdown.

However optimistic Anderson may have been about reconstructing the Briton saint, it's refreshing to read a mid-twentieth century radical woman's view of the dawning of Christianity in Whithorn. I hope that someday, someone will write about Mosa Anderson the way she has about Ninian.

PETER ROSS

"Don't worry about setting an alarm.
The rooster will take care of that."
(Harry Waugh, just before bidding us goodnight)

Harry may not have been willing to drive out again for groceries for us, but he was not unsympathetic. Shortly after our arrival, he dropped by the Shed with a tin of tomato soup and the keys to one of his neighbouring cottages.

"The hens aren't laying right now, so no eggs for breakfast," he informed us. "But feel free to use the toilet in the other place if you don't like the chemical one. There's a full hob and oven over there, and a good shower, too." He didn't have to say that twice.

Keys in hand, I walked over. Like so many in southwest Scotland, the pretty little cottage was plastered in bright whitewash. A little calligraphy sign by the door read *Candida Casa* ("White" *or* "Shining" House). *Candida Casa*, in Old English, is *Hwit Aerne* ... Whithorn. Harry Waugh had given his unused little cottage the same name Bede, back in the eighth century, mentioned as belonging to Ninian's monastery.

In the twelfth century, four hundred years after Bede and perhaps six or seven hundred after Ninian, Aelred wrote in his *Life of Ninian* that Ninian had stopped in Tours (modern-day France) to spend time with St. Martin and had hired Gaulish masons there to build *Candida Casa* in "the Roman manner" (that is, with stone). Celtic monasteries at the time would have been much simpler buildings: hut-like, with thatched roofs.

It's very likely that the story of Ninian meeting Martin is medieval fiction. We know that monks from Gaul, including some adhering to the rule of St. Martin, fled to Ireland and Wales in the early 400s during a Merovingian takeover (Bradley 1993, 9). I suppose it's possible, though unlikely, that some travelled with Ninian to the already established community of Christians at Whithorn, bringing relics of the recently deceased saint. Maybe Whithorn became a shrine not only to Ninian, but also to St. Martin, sometime after Ninian's death. It seems unusual that Bede would have invented such a connection, when he seems to have had no reason for doing so (Wood 2009, 71).

But what of the "white" in Bede's term "white house"? In the 1960s, a Ninian scholar named Ralegh Radford proposed that Bede's story of *Candida Casa* was essentially accurate. Radford noted that excavations at the cemetery in Whithorn had uncovered the remains of "a tiny oratory of stones set in clay and plastered within and without with white mortar" (Radford 1967, 110). This is roughly the spot under the now missing high altar where the crypt is today. The nearest limestone deposits are twenty-two miles from Whithorn, yet there are concreted lime traces on the site, compatible with whitewashed buildings (Hill 2001, 24). (It's interesting that limestone and gypsum also feature in the walk to Nova Scotia's Ninian.) Near Whithorn was the Latinus Stone, a grave or testament marker, Christian, and dated to the 400s (Forsyth 2009).

I made myself tea with some teabags I'd been carrying from Glasgow. While Ken and Christine napped, I thought more about the Shining *Candida Casa.* One part of the pilgrimage I'd been surprised by was just how thickly the country south of Glasgow is dotted with religious remains going back to the Stone Age. The tendency seems to be that Christian communities repurposed existing pagan sites rather than inventing entirely new ones. Continuity and constant reappropriation are the rule rather than the exception. Back in the mists of time, perhaps the Shining White House had first been something else, a Pictish monument perhaps, its spot and building taken over by the Briton-Celtic monastery. Or perhaps the *Candida* first meant shining, as in "location of the saint," and it was the Anglians who, two centuries later, added the whitewash as advertising to emphasize that yes, this was where Ninian had once hung his bishop's crozier.

Years after Ninian, the historical record becomes more certain. Whithorn became Northumbrian English. The Northumbrians took charge of a physical site that was already there, but modest (Wooding 2009, 12-13). They expanded the monastery. Whithorn for many years remained under the rule of Anglian bishops (Cox, Gall, and Yeoman undated, 22-23). Later, the region was either "invaded" or "settled" (it's odd how important and contemporary that political distinction still is!) by refugees, in this case Norse-Irish, who had long before become Christian in Ireland.

The ecclesiastical structures of the Anglians collapsed under this influx of Norse refugees. But the Norse were hardly the "violent and illiterate people" about whom Patterson complains in his 1993 guidebook. Rather, the Irish-Norse, in their turn, added the rich deposit of stone carved crosses that are now in Whithorn's museum, which date to the tenth and eleventh centuries. All this happened in and around the *Candida Casa*. Following the Norse period, Galloway bishops endorsed by the ascendant Scottish royalty took control of Whithorn again, and again confirmed its saint and pilgrimage.

I was happy for Harry Waugh's local version of the *Candida Casa*, in which I could take a luxurious shower. Later, from my room at the back of Nadav's Shed I heard Christine talking to someone. I assumed Harry had come by again, perhaps with something else from his cupboard. Instead, there was a knock on the door and in walked a slim man, about five foot eight, with short grey hair and a big smile. It was Peter Ross, from Glenluce, a member of the Whithorn Way steering committee and of the Dumfries and Galloway Outdoor Trust. Peter had been alerted that three Canadians were walking the Way and had come to see how we were getting on. "Actually," we told him, "we have no food!" "I'll drive you for supplies," he immediately responded.

Peter was our pilgrim miracle. Ken's feet were suffering, and he was still dopy from nettle stings. He continued his nap while Peter drove Christine and me the five miles or so to a convenience store in Glenluce. There was no question of Peter's accent, nor his background: Scots through and through. As we sped downhill along the Water of Luce, from the back seat I thought about our next morning's departure and tried to memorize the road, and which curves might be dangerous for walkers.

There were only four or five aisles in the small grocery store where Peter dropped us. He waited outside, patiently leaning against his car while we hemmed and hummed and finally bought enough supplies for three days: macaroni and cheese, eggs, some lunch meat, a small tin of milk, and apples. Both Christine and I eyed the trail mix and nuts at the cash, then bought those, too.

Peter raised his eyebrows when he saw our bulging bags. But he said nothing. He dropped us back at Nadav's Shed, promising to meet us the next morning at Glenluce Abbey and walk with us for at least part of the day.

PARADISE BETWEEN TWO-STAR MOTELS

"Three shots meant someone had fallen down a plaster hole."

(Fraser Dunn)

Like a friend, land begins to look different once you start getting to know it. I've never needed proof of this truth. But if I did, the three kilometres or so from Lower South River toward Antigonish would provide it. As a walk, the stretch at first seems eminently forgettable. Its features are not what most of us think of as features: roads, intersections, bridges, and overpasses. Other than the river, which is behind you soon enough, you'd be forgiven for thinking this short segment is "passing through" country, where the only interesting things are where you've come from, where you're headed, and what's on the menu.

For those of us able to walk fairly easily, walking is the conscious activity closest to an unconscious one. The absence of any goal except moving forward leaves lots of unaccustomed space in our minds. That's why, even on this stretch of road, where the pavement crumbles along the shoulder and the traffic speeds pick up, there are views and thoughts to catch us by surprise. We may prefer walking in places of more obvious natural beauty, but there's something to be meditated on even in spots no one looks at for long – the "driving through" spaces. One of those reflections might be on the meaning of an ancient Briton saint to a culture and landscape like the North Shore of Nova Scotia.

Does Ninian's story, so tied to Scottish culture that it was borrowed to bolster that culture in Nova Scotia, have room for the Indigenous groups who in the past have been so negatively affected by what others call "development" (Anderson 2024)? Or has Ninian, who may well have been an early Catholic Roman-Briton, always been the saint "from away" (at its root the word "pilgrim" means "foreigner")? Does Ninian's status as an underdog mean he might become a symbol for those still finding a place in history and geography? Is he better suited as a paragon of colonialism, or resistance? When we walked the first Nova Scotia Ninian Way walk in September 2024, I handed each pilgrim a rock from Pomquet Beach with their name written on it, reminding the walkers that the saint's name took on significance with the relationships and communities it inspired, just as our names can do now.

It's about three and a half kilometres between Lower South River and your next stop. I measure it as the distance between two-star roadside motels: the Coastal Inn on the spot that once held the Dingle Inn, in Lower South River, and the Oasis Motel on route 4 into Antigonish.

This section of the Nova Scotia Ninian Way begins with a particularly noisy bit as you pass over Highway 104 for the second time, now going north. Stay on the left side since traffic moves fast here. Below you, Highway 104 is twinned. This isn't unusual. But according to the town of Antigonish's website, the highway at Antigonish was the first twinned boulevard in North America. What the website doesn't mention is the racism that accompanied this hopeful bit of development.

In the 1960s, those who planned the Trans-Canada east of Antigonish decided to run the highway right through the middle of Paqtnkek First Nation in a way that for decades cut Indigenous inhabitants off from a section of their land. In Antigonish (actually, right where a sign for the university now sits and a new and hotly debated multi-million-dollar walking path begins), the old highway was surveyed right through the middle of an area where five or six African-Canadian families were living. According to Patrick Walsh's 1989 *History of Antigonish*, when the homes of these citizens were being expropriated, a political struggle began as other Antigonish residents vocally called on the town council to not allow their Black neighbours to resettle in their neighbourhoods (265). In the end, the university's extension department helped the families resettle in a co-op housing area. Development and racism accompanied each other in Antigonish County, as they did elsewhere.

After an uphill trudge that takes you over Highway 104, keeping tight to the shoulder because of traffic, the route curves left. When you can, cross over the highway to take a look to your right and down toward South River. You'll see a Catholic cemetery sitting in a pretty spot above the water. When I asked Fraser Dunn about it, he told me that "the site was chosen because it was beside the river. Persons to be buried from the St. Andrews area were brought down the river and persons from the South Side Harbour area were brought up the river as there were no roads. All travel was by boat." After many years of neglect, in 2002 Father Vernon Boutilier arranged for the restoration of the cemetery with the help of local volunteers.

Just slightly further to your right are some unusual dirt banks, so strikingly white they almost look painted. What gives them this appearance is gypsum, the same gypsum that was already noted in the area in an aquatint etching of the harbour back in 1777 (there's a reproduction of that etching in Peggy Thompson's *Antigonish: A History in Pictures*, 12). A chemical reaction between gypsum and the limestone rock all through this area results in something called marl, a substance very high in calcium that can be used as fertilizer.

Some folks might not know the name Hugh MacPherson, but he was crucial to that observation about marl. Father "Little Doc" Hugh MacPherson, originally from Fraser's Mills, about ten kilometres south of where you're walking, was also the Reverend *Doctor* Hugh MacPherson (Ludlow 2022, 121-122 and Cameron 1996, 132, 201). It's somewhat confusing that there were two priests by the moniker Dr. Hugh MacPherson at or around St. Francis Xavier University at the same time. (For most of its history, St. FX has been run by professor priests and worker nuns, and its international, multifaith, and diverse future still seems to itch at times.) The *other* Rev. Dr. Hugh Peter MacPherson, known as the "Old Rector," was a priest with an honorary doctorate from Université Laval who served as the university's rector for thirty years starting in 1906, and was briefly in contention to be the bishop of Antigonish.

By contrast, "Little Doc Hugh" MacPherson was trained in France, taught at StFX for decades starting in 1900, and early on became an activist in rural agricultural renewal through the university. He was a priest, a professor at StFX, a social reformer, a community activist and – apparently

– the first recognized and trained soil scientist in Canada east of Ontario. From 1915 to 1919, he also ran the "Mount Cameron farm" linking diocese and university, a post which left him with a lifelong limp from an accident with a tractor (Cameron 1996, 201).

In the early twentieth century, Little Doc Hugh was doing so many things at once, it's a bit hard to get a handle on him. He was instrumental in the early days of the Antigonish Movement, a rural development initiative blending what we now call microfinancing, along with adult education, rural redevelopment, and cooperatives. Under Little Doc Hugh's leadership, the folks in the areas where you're walking organized the first co-op store in eastern Canada in 1917, which helped local cash-strapped farmers by using a barter system. There was an early co-op store run from a truck, and the rural people of this area banded together to provide for each other a very early form of medical insurance, decades before nationalized Medicare (Fiander and Cunningham 2009, 2-3).

My father managed a cooperative financial services company for many years on the prairies, and my aunts and uncles were all what we used to call "co-op people." Even now, a century after he lived and worked in Antigonish County, I recognize a kindred spirit in Little Doc Hugh MacPherson, known locally as "the father of cooperation" (Ludlow 2022, 170).

It was this MacPherson who helped introduce local farmers to the advantages of fertilizer and encouraged them to use the marl on their fields (Fiander and Cunningham 2009, 2). The dirt banks you're looking at are on private land – as it turns out, Fraser Dunn's land. When I asked him about the gypsum, Fraser told me that deposits of the white stuff extend all the way from Monk's Head to Beech Hill and Brierly Brook. He, too, is an admirer of Little Doc Hugh MacPherson.

"If it's limestone all through this area, are there caves?" I asked Fraser, happy at recalling this piece of geological trivia from some dark recess of high school boredom.

"Oh yes, there are," he responded. "And what we used to call plaster holes, too."

"Plaster holes?"

"Sinkholes," Dunn specified. "They can be quite dangerous. Our family hunted a lot, and even as kids we were always walking through the forest. We had a system because of the plaster holes. If someone fell into one while out hunting, you were to fire three shots in a row to call for help. And it happened. One day, I heard three shots. I went looking, and there was my dad. He'd been trying in vain to get out of a hole and had almost made it several times, only to fall back in. I had to throw him a rope."

Fraser went on to talk about a small body of water he called simply "mystery lake," in the bush to the north of where you're standing and looking at the dirt-banks. That lake is proof of the existence of limestone caves and channels throughout this region: although it's 150 feet above sea level, the water level in the lake goes up and down with every tide.

Keep walking toward Antigonish: you can be thankful there are no hidden plaster holes on your trail ... I think! Pass South River Stone to your left and then over a small hill. Soon you come to an area which is the mirror to what you left in Lower South River: commuter housing side by side with light industrial sites, a motel, and a few stores. However, here there's a bonus: if you're walking on a hot summer day, you can stop for a soft-serve ice cream at the Snow Queen Dairy Bar, which is a 1950s-style drive-in take-out attached to the fraying-at-the-edges, slightly post-apocalyptic-looking "Leisure World" amusement park. But don't waste your time looking for a sign saying "Leisure World" or "Snow Queen." There isn't one. Or rather, there is such a sign, but it's in town, for another Snow Queen. Which was once related to Leisure World, but now isn't.

If that sounds complicated, don't worry. You're not a local.

However, if you didn't eat at Mother Webb's, you're still in luck because the Snow Queen Drive-In is one of the few places in Nova Scotia where you can buy deep-fried clams and fries. Whole fried clams are a ubiquitous summer favourite in P.E.I. and New Brunswick, but strangely absent from Nova Scotia take-outs. The Snow Queen's fried *bar* clams are not quite the whole-bodied battered delicacies you'll find in Shediac or Charlottetown, but they do well in a pinch.

The dairy bar was taken over in the 1960s by Marie MacPherson, a war bride from the Netherlands who had married Lauchy MacPherson and raised a family with him in Antigonish. Things went well with the dairy bar. They expanded the South River location into a drive-in recreation complex and also bought a location in town and opened a Snow

Queen there. Two MacPherson boys with rhyming names bought the businesses: John, the Antigonish Snow Queen, now a family restaurant, and Don, the Leisure World location. After years of running Leisure World, Donny (as he is known locally) retired and sold the business in 2018. It was sold once again just as we walked our Nova Scotia Ninian Way in the fall of 2024. Locals are curious as to whether the new owners will "lean in" to the existing retro feel or freshen things up.

How do I know all this? Snow Queen Leisure World is the kind of place where, if you ask, the friendly staff (some of whom have worked there for many years) will pull out historic photos and tell you how things were a decade or two ago. Take some time to look around the place. It's a blast from the past.

A VALLIS LUCIS

"The truth about stories is that's all we are."

(Thomas King, 2003)

Sometime about four o'clock in the morning the rooster in the pen next to Nadav's Shed started celebrating the dawn. Hours later, we pilgrims finally acquiesced and got up as well. Harry was already out and about. We found him puttering in the yard, checking on the chicken coops, holding a baby rabbit close against his jacket. "This one's having a hard go of it," he said, stroking its downy head.

We'd all noticed that Harry moved with an unusual sureness for a senior. My room in the Shed had shelves full of scrapbooks, newspaper clippings, and medals. It looked as if the man with gardening gloves and a floppy hat, cuddling a rabbit, had been active in sport and perhaps also in the military. Preoccupied with preparing for the next day of our walk, I didn't pay that much attention to either Harry or the intriguing hints of his life until the pilgrimage was over, and I was home. Then, a quick web search turned up Harry Alexander Montgomery Waugh, the "inspirational athlete and community activist."

On arrival at Nadav's we'd told Harry all about our thirteen-mile walk. He'd nodded sympathetically at our various foot and ankle ailments. I'd have complained less had I known then what I know now: my post-walk research showed that in the mid-1990s, Harry Waugh became the first person ever to go all the way from John O'Groats in the extreme north of Scotland to Land's End, at the extreme south of England, a distance of over one thousand miles, averaging sixty miles a day – all on roller skis. At the museum in Land's End there's even a mannequin of him making the trip. As the article states:

> It took Mr. Waugh 17 days and two hours to get from one end to the other, roller-skiing an average of 60 miles each day. He managed to raise £4000 for the British Heart Foundation. He said, "I was wanting to do the trip somehow and I had thought about biking it. I coach athletics and I was looking at roller skiing as a way of cross training athletes. ... We had some interesting weather conditions because it was snowing and hailing up north and we had heatwaves down the other end." (http://www.therollerskidirectory.org.uk/pages/a002.htm).

Ignorant of our host's adventures, we made ourselves eggs and bacon in the borrowed kitchen of his *Candida Casa*, cleaned up, and said our goodbyes to the quiet seventy-four-year-old who took such good care of his rabbits, his garden, and his pilgrims. As we walked away, we all agreed that we hoped he'd keep Nadav's Shed going a while longer. Now that they've reopened the local dining room and pub, called the Kenmuir Arms, I'd like to go back to New Luce. I hope they have photos of Harry up on the wall.

Leaving New Luce, we headed south. From this point we were following a broad burn, or valley, more or less the same route as Andrew Patterson described back in '93. But only more or less: "The tarmac road from New Luce southwards to Glenluce village is not suitable for walkers," Patterson had written (3), "being narrow and winding." That was true. But it seemed we had no choice but to take the road. Slightly uphill and to the east, we'd seen a path with a sign saying "Whithorn Way," one of the first such signs we'd actually encountered. Hilariously, Peter Ross had told us, "Ignore that. It's not the right way." I wondered what we'd have done if we hadn't met him the night before.

We threaded our way through the same wooded valley that cosseted New Luce. The name Glenluce – *vallis lucis* – means valley of light. That morning, it certainly was. The morning sunlight coming through the leaves made this section emerald and magical. We were pilgrims in fairyland. The Water of Luce gurgled to our west as we passed by heavily mossed stone fences and piles of ancient, shaped rock that Patterson

(1993, 3) notes come from "an immense stone rampart that once crowned the hill."

In one overgrown clearing I noticed a pile of stone, many of the boulders strapped with metal, the whole of it looking venerably old and covered by bright green moss. Nearby, I found a sign and scrubbed off enough to read. It was a perfect example of the dilemma of being Canadian in Scotland and knowing the words, but not their meaning: "Main-water tryst," said the sign, "is a cairn-like construction that echoes the distinctive local 'bings' formed as farmers cleared stones for ploughing. Five curved strips of copper are wound around the stones – each named for a feature of the river." Standing in that clearing, dappled in light, it all sounded terribly romantic, ancient, important, and natural. But I had no idea what the sign actually meant.

I thought perhaps I might be looking at a well from the 1900s. There's an ancient well called the "Lady Well" somewhere just south of New Luce, and I assumed I might be seeing old evidence of a Victorian marking of it. But I was falling behind the others, so I rushed to catch up.

Much later, I found out that the "kettle-stones" I discovered were not old at all. They're actually part of a 2010 art installation, commissioned by local residents, supported in part once again by a grant from the windfarms, and created with artist Matt Baker (https://mattbaker.org.uk/newluce/). The stones I'd discovered mark the "Main Water" (the river) of Luce we'd been walking alongside.

My misconception – the connection with druids and water worship I'd already partially invented – was the perfect example of the problem with being an outsider in an area where the human geography is so interwoven with stories and legends. In Scotland and in Nova Scotia, myths grow like moss over artefacts. If pilgrims aren't careful, they can invent a few new ones themselves.

Even the place names we were encountering were filled with stories, and we missed far, far more than we knew. Checking my phone after a half hour's walk, the OS app would tell me that we'd passed several prehistoric cairns, some less than a kilometre off-road. The day before we'd seen a mysteriously titled bluff called "Ghost Stone Bank," and passed by "Bloody Wheel," a pool in the Main Water of Luce where two local aristocratic families had finished their feuding in mayhem and murder.

Right around Glenluce, we entered the region known as the "Machars." In Old Gaelic, *Machair* meant low-lying or flat area. The triangular region – what I think of as the Whithorn peninsula – is not as hilly as many parts of Scotland, even the immediately adjacent region to the north that we'd just passed through with all its wind turbines. But the Machars is not flat, either, as we discovered. In my uninformed geological opinion, the region of Antigonish County between Pomquet Beach and Ninian Cathedral could certainly be called "machars" as well.

In the parking lot for Glenluce Abbey, Peter Ross was waiting for us. We were in heavy rain-clothes; he was in a T-shirt and carried a small pack. He told us he would do his best to speak "standard English," as he termed it, so we Canadians could understand. But when he got excited – as he often did – he couldn't help flipping into an "Och, aye." I told him how beautiful the stone fences had been as we walked down the length of the valley. "During the time of the Clearances," Peter informed me, "in addition to the injustice of all that, they just ripped up the prehistoric hill tombs for stones. When you see the fences that led to the ejection of so many poor croppers, you may be looking at pieces of a Paleolithic grave." The lesson? Money leads to the destruction of history at least as often as its creation.

Between his low voice and his accent, at times I'd only figure out what Peter was saying a few sentences after he'd finished. His ongoing commentary was a fascinating compendium of history and politics, things like the fact that rights-of-way on the seacoast had to take into account Robert the Bruce's unusual title to his troops, that they owned the sea "as far as you can throw a spear into the surf." "Ay, Robert the Bruce," said Peter, "the Scot. Only he wasn't. Not really ...." He shook his head. I noticed he did that a lot.

Robert the Bruce, long a national hero, is credited with routing the English and re-establishing Scottish independence in the early fourteenth century (Houston and Knox 2001, 170). As we were beginning to discover, even Robert didn't necessarily "come from" southwest Scotland. His family was Norman, he originally held lands in what was then northern England, and he was actually related by marriage to the English king (whose side he was on in at least one of the earliest battles). Like Mary, Queen of Scots, and James IV, Robert the Bruce (or Robert I) is a name that comes up frequently on the Whithorn Way. Robert often made pilgrimage to Ninian's Shrine, especially near the end of his life as he prayed for healing.

The Bruce became king after murdering his chief opponent for the throne in a knife fight. Unfortunately for his relationship to the church, that fight took place in front of the high altar in the chapel at Greyfriar's monastery, Dumfries. To be a pilgrim on the Whithorn Way is to soon realize that writing a *Murder in the Monastery* historical thriller about Scotland would require choosing among the apparently endless candidates.

Robert the Bruce was another Scottish leader active in promoting Ninian. One of his biographers notes that in 1329 he made a "pilgrimage-as-recruitment-drive" to the shrine, seeking to placate an often troublesome area, and (just as Peter told us that morning) to raise troops (Penman 2014, 292). However, there was a more personal reason behind Robert's final trip to Whithorn. In the last year of his life, the Bruce spent Holy Week as a penitent at the shrine (Penman 2014, 299).

Prayers to St. Ninian were reputed to be especially helpful for healing leprosy and other skin diseases. Although there is much debate over what caused Robert the Bruce's death at age fifty-five, it appears to have manifested in some form of skin disorder, whether or not it was strictly speaking leprosy, since the medieval world lumped a number of conditions under this name (Penman 2014, 302-305).

Since at least Robert the Bruce, Ninian became linked to Scottish nationalism, which is why he was so top of mind when Bishop Plessis visited the early Catholics of Antigonish. Bede may have been the first to mention Ninian, but it was Scottish royalty that chose Ninian as patron of both country and crown, and for centuries they kept up the pilgrimage tradition. Kenneth III was a pilgrim to the shrine (Bold 2018, 156), as was every monarch after. As Patterson writes: "The Scottish royal court astutely developed as state policy the cult of Ninian" (1993, 77).

Such a link was not unusual: the St. Olaf Shrine in Norway was sponsored by the first Norwegian chiefs who attempted to become national kings, as a way of solidifying their claims to the throne and developing a national consciousness (Anderson 2019a, 63). Many Camino walkers don't know that in the early twentieth century, the resurgence of Spain's Camino de Santiago was due, at least in part, to very deliberate ideological and nationalist moves by the then-government, the fascist Franco regime (Frey 1998, 237-238). Pilgrimage may be associated in our popular mind with peacemaking, but pilgrimage as power-consolidation also has a long history (McIntosh 2017, 8).

Like other pilgrims before him, on his final pilgrimage to Whithorn, Robert stopped at Glenluce Abbey for rest and hospitality, and perhaps for special prayers for leprosy. At the abbey, there is a sign commemorating this event. We read the sign, listened to some local lore from Peter, then wandered through the remains of the cloister, the refectory, and the outbuildings. In 1560, when Catholicism was outlawed and the monasteries officially disbanded, a number of the monks were permitted to live out their lives on the abbey grounds, even as Earl Kennedy murdered one who had been foolish or frightened enough to forge a false will deeding the whole place to him.

URBAN CHANGES AND BATTING CAGES

"I'm walking the interface between the country and the city: a shallow space, with fields butting up against houses, industry and agriculture commingled. Crispy blue J Cloth towels, scraps of sky, are caught in the roadside weeds."

(Ken Wilson 2025)

There are certain rules of thumb that wise pilgrims follow, whether in southwest Scotland or northeast Nova Scotia. First, avoid busy highways as much as possible. Second, don't make eye contact with the drivers of loud trucks with flags and bumper stickers (unless it's a party supply van). Third, if they don't conflict with numbers one or two, linger in places that look a bit like they've been forgotten by time.

Hung like a hammock between hills, its back to a construction depot, the Snow Queen Leisure World on Highway 4 is one such faded glory. The place is a living museum to 1960s car culture and a time before SUVs and video screens on the back of headrests. Now, post-millennium, post-911, and post-pandemic, weeds sprout through cracks in asphalt. Faded signs bark park features – Skytrain! Bumper boats! – that haven't existed for years. The beauty of it all, however, is that kids and their slightly embarrassed mothers or fathers still get into go-karts, and their partners and parents still dutifully take photos as the go-karts pass, cheering them on.

I've always thought that go-karting is the perfect example of the structural positionality that privileged folks insist doesn't affect our standing in society. Anyone who's tried it knows that karts can go only so fast, each according to the settings on its motor's governor. That's all they'll do even when your foot is pedal to the metal: one car will always be slightly faster or slower than another. You might want to be Gilles Villeneuve or Mario Andretti. You might even have the talent – but your car won't let you. That's how structural barriers and structural racism and sexism work. They act like engine governors.

Thankfully, winning's not the point for the families who motor around the abandoned bumper boat pool, its water covered with algae and poplar saplings growing up through the hoses where the boats once battled. In season, you can buy lunch and sit at a picnic table overlooking the track. Chow down on deep-fried food while watching kids stand on their toes at the entrance to be "just tall enough" to drive on their own. Seeing them jockey and swerve around the circle is a joy. Even though (if you're betting) car #18 will always win.

I mentioned the fried clams, but that's only one possibility. The Leisure World Snow Queen brings its fish up from Digby, and Janet the cook batters it in-store. She also roasts the chicken on-site for their hot chicken sandwiches, which come smothered in gravy. The pride of the place is the Snow Queen burger, which is as tasty as they claim: the loaded version comes with everything including two signature onion rings crammed between burger and bun. I have to agree with the online reviewer who said that eating it is like "tastebud time travel." Frankly, the whole place is.

Before you continue walking, get some quarters from the folks at the drive-in's window and head a few steps downhill. For four quarters, step up to the plate in the batting cages and get eight balls either slow-pitched or fastballed at you. The pitching machines are sometimes a bit wonky. But honestly: where can you get anything for a buck anymore?

The changes in highway construction and urban planning that created this little time-warp were just the latest in a long series of such shocks in this area. Imagine the communities you've already walked through as pearls on a string. Go far enough back in time and each of them – Bayfield, Pomquet, Lower South River, St. Andrew's, William's Point, Greenwold, and Antigonish – once held their own post office, their own shops and mills and schools. One very practical reason why this was so was the language barrier between communities, and the difficulties of travel.

When the railroad came through this area in 1890, there were approximately 18,000 people in Antigonish County. Thirty years later, in 1920, the population had contracted to eight thousand. Because of the decline of the traditional industries of fishing, mining, forestry, and farming, and the adoption of national Canadian policies that favoured the west, Antigonish suffered one of the most severe settler depopulations in Canada. The railway had opened the region to the world, only to empty it out. The children of Pomquet and Lower South River fled a backwater that had few roads, no markets, and little future. (The hopeful marketing of a 1916 Antigonish Town and County pamphlet announced the area as "The Land of Plenty," Thompson 2022, 47). As has happened so often since, the children of the Atlantic region headed west, or to Boston and other big cities, following jobs, and sending money back to their families. The situation was not completely unlike that faced by so many diaspora-working Maritimers today.

These waves of depopulation and poverty, and the despondency that followed, became the spark for what, during the First World War years and after, was initially known as the Forward Movement. Basing himself out of the university, Professor "Little Doc Hugh" MacPherson was key to the development of cooperatives, the promotion of what we now call microfinancing, and the adult education led by a new extension department at StFX (Cameron 1996, 151). In turn, the social activism and university outreach it began evolved a decade or so later into the internationally known Antigonish Movement. Father Moses Coady and Father Jimmy Thompkins continued and expanded the movement for a "people's school" at the university. It was idealistic, but still practical and tough-minded, and bloomed into a movement linking education to rural revitalization. "Little Doc Hugh" MacPherson is under-recognized for the groundwork he laid for the Antigonish Movement. I note, for instance, that Wikipedia's entry on the Antigonish Movement links to separate articles on Coady and Thompkins, while none exists for MacPherson. Additionally, only now are the contributions of women such as Ida Gallant Delaney, Sister Marie Michael MacKinnon, and Sister Irene Doyle also beginning to be recognized (Delaney 1985). A podcast series about these women so crucial to the Antigonish Movement can be found at https://soundcloud.com/rneustae/sets/what-can-the-women-do-women?si=fb4ed2f62e0c49529f41443ecf5532b5.

It was a bold time that offered bold, popularly led measures. Initiatives from near where you are walking now "helped spread the development of producer, consumer, and savings and credit cooperatives throughout northeast Nova Scotia in the 1930s and '40s" (Fiander and Cunningham 2009, 3). Already in the teens of the early twentieth century, MacPherson had moved to the university, teaching many of the courses in its curriculum, and leading enthusiastic meetings in classrooms at night. Sister Marie Michael MacKinnon hosted a radio show that spread the movement's ideas, while directing the "Women and Work" program that helped women become the backbone of the revitalization, even though at the time (and for years following), women were not allowed to become Board members of the very co-ops they founded. Overall, the movement's success led one young priest at the time to gush to a friend, "We have found the lever that will move the world" (Ludlow 2015, 114).

If only they had.

PRISONERS OF GEOGRAPHY

"We're all just prisoners of geography, aren't we?"

(Peter to us, as we followed him on a trail to avoid the highway)

As we were leaving the abbey it started to rain lightly. Peter didn't seem to notice. We three Canadians struggled into various forms of protective gear. Peter stayed in his T-shirt. As he waited, he kept up a good-natured patter about local history and walking philosophy. Some folks stopped their van to say hi. Everyone, it seemed, knew Peter.

When we finally left the abbey and started walking, I asked him about his work on Scottish Access Laws. Peter was chair of the Dumfries and Galloway Outdoor Access Trust (https://www.dgoutdooraccess.org.uk/), somewhat similar to our own Hike Nova Scotia and its subsidiary program, Nova Scotia Walks (https://www.hikenovascotia.ca/ns-walks/).

I wanted to know more about the Right of Responsible Access being part of how Scots feel about their country. Any link between how people behave toward land and their beliefs about their national character interests me. For instance, in the United States, "a man's home is his castle": often, a castle armed with guns. But in Scotland, where there actually *are* castles, that kind of defensive assertion isn't common. In Canada, for too long we've had the myth that nature is our enemy, a "frontier" to be sheltered from until conquered (Northrop Frye went so far as to label this typically Canadian way of thinking "the garrison mentality"). This is part of the problem of how we settler-descendants have historically dealt with Indigenous peoples, who generally don't treat nature that way (Aldred and Anderson 2024, 2-6; Grenz 2024, 150-153). Part of the good that walking pilgrimage can do is that it gets us outside to change the stories we tell ourselves about land and how we share it.

"Are you happy with the fact that the government put all this responsibility on local groups?" I asked Peter. "It seems like a lot."

"It is," he agreed. "But going local is the only way it will work. It's a framework. Don't forget. Rules provide the general sense of it, and locally we fill in the specifics." He gave me a pamphlet. I told him about my walk in the Peaks District of England, and my research on England's "Right to Roam" (Anderson 2018). "Oh, the English are jealous of us," Peter smiled with satisfaction. "They'd love to have what we have." Then he stopped. "But it's not the same all over Scotland. Access doesn't work in Galloway the way it does, for instance, in the Highlands."

"It's not a one-size-fits-all?"

"No," Peter shook his head. "Access has to have a local reason. Otherwise, there shouldn't be any."

That statement took me aback. "You mean access isn't always good?"

"Not necessarily." Peter had set a good pace toward the village. We had to work to keep up. "Or at least, not everywhere, and not without infrastructure. That's why access has to be worked out locally. In the Highlands, access might mean there are a dozen ways up a hill. Here, we have more fenced land. Access here might mean a single path."

It surprised me that despite his years of volunteer labour for the cause, Peter didn't seem particularly dogmatic about the Right of Responsible Access. I may not have completely understood the maze of acronyms Peter tossed out, or the relationship between the various government, trust, and volunteer bodies, but I understood this: the hard-working volunteers on these Scottish committees see their civic responsibility as getting people out onto the land. But definitely not as squatters. When we told him about campers we'd discovered along the route who were creating quite a bit of litter, he shook his head. "That's the problem," he emphasized. "Camping might be part of access. But really, it's more about paths. And tracks. Anything that encourages the public to engage with history and the natural world. And it's got to have economic benefits."

Again, I was surprised. Here was someone we'd been told was the "biggest walker" in the region. "He knows everything about the paths in Galloway," our contact in Glasgow had said. "He's walked them all." And yet Peter wasn't promoting public access to land as some kind of right in and of itself, or as a spiritual heritage, or anything I'd expected. If I understood properly, he was insisting that proper public access meant making sure there's an infrastructure of trails first, before opening up land. Then it's about making sure the development of public access to the natural environment goes hand in hand with economic benefits, especially in depopulated areas. The committee's vision seemed to be that marked paths are a primary way to encourage the population toward a properly ecologically responsible and socially sustainable form of engagement with nature.

I had expected an ideologue. Peter was anything but.

The conversation never lagged while the four of us followed him into town. Our path intersected with, and then took the name of, "The Old Military Road." A beautiful, no longer used railway viaduct dating from 1858 to 1860 hangs over the south end of the village. Nearby sat a nondescript stone bridge. "It's ironic," Peter pointed. "It's the stone bridge that's a heritage site," he said. "It's ancient. But everyone comes and takes photos of the viaduct. That's just some old Victorian thing."

On entering Glenluce, Peter took us on a path that looped around the old church on its way to Main Street. "See," said Peter, "this shortcut is the only *real* historic right-of-way in the village. Rights of way are often shortcuts." I don't think Peter had heard of what urban planners call "desire lines," which are essentially the same thing, like the paths created diagonally across a greenspace to a building by the many feet that don't want to use the more circuitous sidewalk.

At Main Street, we stopped. *My* desire line at that moment went straight into the local coffee shop for tea and a bathroom break. I think Peter expected to continue, but we Canadians convinced him. I wanted to see something of Glenluce. Muir Watt's guidebook relates some wonderful ghost stories associated with the town, stories which were adopted for Sir Walter Scott's novel *The Bride of Lammermoor* (83).

It turned out that there were no ghosts, nor any Dagger Woods-style creatures, at the Glen café. It was new, bright, and cheery. We folded our wet selves into a corner table. I ordered a mushroom soup, which arrived thick and incredibly tasty. Ken had a haggis and cheese sandwich.

Peter was content with a coffee, despite our attempts to buy him a scone. As is common in the U.K., on the counter was a glass display case for desserts. I spotted a Battenberg cake which was a piece of art, its squares in every colour of the rainbow.

We bought Peter's coffee and followed him as he stepped back smartly into the misting rain. He then led us downhill past one and two-storey stone buildings with dormers, and out Bankfield Road. We passed a store window displaying an antique barometer. The others kept walking, but I was entranced by its dial, embossed with the name "David Henry, Glenluce." The thin metal arrows, two of them, were pointed at the bottom left of the dial: "stormy." I should perhaps have taken it as a portent.

Ahead of me, Ken, with his poles and neon green pack and Christine in her forest green poncho were pacing on either side of Peter, heads turned to him in animated conversation. I think they were enjoying not having to worry for the first time about our route. I know I was.

It was a treat: all we had to do was follow Peter, and we were walking in what was almost literally his backyard. Peter is one of the designers of the modern Whithorn Way. He told us how it has walkers going through a section in Glenluce which, because of the A75 motorway, has now become too dangerous. "We'll have to move that bit to go through the underpass," he said. "We want people to see the sights but stay safe."

When I suggested that it's a shame to miss a view, he shrugged mildly. "We're all just prisoners of geography, aren't we?" We'd known Peter less than twenty-four hours, and already I'd come to enjoy these little nuggets that came out of him every few minutes.

THE SOGGY WALKER

"By geographical fortune, Antigonish, even to this day, is still on the only main route for every point east of it in Nova Scotia."

(Walsh 1989)

Head west and pass the Oasis Motel and Campground and a hunting and fishing supply store. In 2024, this is where our group of fifteen walkers stopped on day one of the pilgrimage, so as to have an approximately five-kilometre stroll into the cathedral the following morning in time for their 150th-anniversary service.

Just after the motel, take the road that curves right onto South River Road. Your route will curve downward and then gradually gain elevation again. To your left is "Postech Screw Piles." The only reason I highlight this is because the need to brace everything from houses to decks into the ground with deep anchors says so much about the marshy land all along our pilgrimage to Antigonish. The section you're following at the moment is the perfect example: it essentially traces the bottom of a large triangular rise of land, a peninsula between two arms of Antigonish Bay, with William's Point (natal home to Bishop McKinnon, founder of Saint Ninian Cathedral and of the university) to the north. From the beginning of this walk, you've been following lowlands, often with water crossings, interspersed by slightly higher and dryer hummocks.

Antigonish is no exception. Colonal Timothy Hierlihy and the early Town Point settlers to the north and east of Antigonish called their settlement Dorchester in 1786. (For photos of the surveyed Town Point plan, and the cemetery stones, see Peggy Thompson, *Antigonish: A History in Pictures*

(Lunenburg: MacIntyre Purcell Publishing, 2022, 13). A century before Hierlihy, a book titled *The Description and Natural History of the Coasts of North America* named the area at the base of the bay Articougnesche (Stanley Blackwell and MacLean 2004, viii). The Mi'kmaq title, or at least an anglicized bastardization of it, was just so descriptive that over the years, it won out in popular usage, even while the Mi'kmaq themselves were pushed ever further from their traditional fishing grounds.

The town of Antigonish's website states that the name means either "place where the branches are torn off by bears eating beechnuts," which sounds odd and wonderfully specific, or something like "place of the forked rivers." I love the bear definition even while doubting it: just as I was writing this, the university sent an alert to staff and students that a black bear had been sighted on campus, along with instructions on how to behave around wildlife (a friend remarked: "No one gets gym privileges without an ID card. Not even the bear.") However, the less colourful forked river definition for Antigonish seems more likely: not only do you have multiple branches of Antigonish Bay, with the South and North rivers flowing into it, but the town sits astride three small rivers. These three also flow into Antigonish Harbour: the West River, Brierly Brook (which flows into West River), and Wright's River.

Simply put, no matter where you are in this area, there's a lot of water flowing. It was this availability of freshwater and land not bound in so strictly by the harbour that eventually led the original Hierlihy Loyalists to relocate further south and west. However, lowlands flood regularly, and even when not flooded outright, the ground is often damp in low spots.

By this point, you'll be walking along an elevated stretch of road with buildings on both sides, and the land falling away to your right. Despite the lack of lookouts, this is one of the loveliest places in the area to gaze out over Antigonish Harbour, with Mount Cameron and Sugarloaf mountains slightly to your left. As long as you can peer around the equipment rental shop, and one or two shoe and furniture stores, please do so. Then follow the narrow shoulder downhill toward the junction with Beech Hill Road. After passing it, for the first time in the pilgrimage you'll have a sidewalk, but not for long. Take the second turn to the right after Beech Hill and follow this quiet street down to the river.

The area you're in is called Greenwold, from here to where it crosses West River. Greenwold was once a community just outside the town limits of Antigonish. In 1967, when the old McAmis Bridge (built in 1886) collapsed, Antigonish, in a savvy political move, quickly made an agreement with the citizens of Greenwold to become part of the town. Having ensured that the bridge was solidly within the newly expanded boundaries, the town then informed the province that it was responsible for replacing the bridge.

When you reach the "new" McAmis Bridge, look to your left. Where the West River widens, that's the McAmis salmon and trout pool. Depending on the season and rainfall, the pool can expand over the surrounding lowlands. Ahead to your left, the Columbus Field sports area floods at particularly bad times from that pool.

If, like me, you're from a traditionally dry area, the word "freshet" may be unfamiliar. But it's an important word, and an important concept, especially in low-lying, marshy, river-fed regions that have long winters, as Antigonish does. Freshet is a word that describes a time of melting snow. The "spring freshet" or annual spring flood is usually an event to watch out for in Antigonish, whose watershed contains so much moving water as winter's snows melt. Ice jams back up the water, and a town with three rivers running through it has that much more to worry about. In 1906, the freshet was so severe that residents of the town had to break up ice jams on Main Street itself.

On November 21, 2021, it was not a freshet but a weather phenomenon known as an "atmospheric river" that caused the worst flooding in recent memory for Antigonish and area. Over one hundred millimetres of rain fell within a twenty-four-hour period. The swelling outflows were exacerbated by record high tides that didn't allow the three rivers through Antigonish to drain into the sea as they otherwise might have. A wall of water over a metre and a half deep swept through a low-lying trailer park, and in the following inundation over thirty people had to be rescued by boat. The situation worsened with power outages, road closures, and complete washouts.

The flooding problem is well known to locals – photos are still posted here and there of cars in the municipal parking just behind Main Street, off Brierly Brook, submerged by the 2021 flood. In 1967, when the province started rebuilding the McAmis Bridge, it planned the bridge with posts sunk into the river. Antigonish town councillors protested that the supports would build up ice and almost certainly cause even worse spring flooding. Political pressure resulted in the new bridge being built in one stretch with no supports.

Cross the bridge and look to your left for the shortcut path past Columbus Field. If the route doesn't feel picturesque at this point, remember that the final section into Whithorn in Scotland is not that pretty either, although it is more agricultural than the car dealerships, butcher shops, and garden supply stores ahead of you in Antigonish. Whithorn or Antigonish: take your pick. It's almost like the way to a saint always has to lead through at least some "normal" life.

CRANNOGS, CAVES, AND CASTLES

"In a part of Scotland still quite unspoiled by any great urbanisation, sites that mark ... spiritual quests throughout all the ages can still be found in abundance."

(*Sacred South-West Scotland*)

Peter Ross had told us that morning that he'd walk with us only a short distance out of Glenluce, just to get us headed in the right direction. When we reached the highway, he pointed: "In a half hour or so you'll be passing by Whitefield Loch," he told us. "When you get there, go in at the far end and have a look. You get a nice view of a crannog."

We learned that a crannog is an artificial island built by a stone- or bronze-age extended family. The prehistoric peoples made them by pushing alder trees down into the mud, then filling them in with rocks and stones until they had a base for a home out on the water, relatively safe from attack. Southwest Scotland's lakes have many of these artificial islands, some quite large and their ruins quite complex. Archaeologists can radio-carbon and ring-date the trees used in constructing these islands to determine when the ancient inhabitants built them.

Some historical fiction romanticizes this period of history. Learning about crannogs made me wonder instead how violent life must have been for folks to feel they had to build artificial islands and live on the water to enjoy a modicum of safety.

Peter made to leave. But we were so full of questions the poor man finally gave up and decided to walk with us just a little farther. We walked a short distance on the highway, then turned down a track between tall stands of fir. Peter repeated what we'd learned: that Galloway produces forty percent of Scotland's timber exports, and how it also produced most of Robert the Bruce's army. We talked about the dangers of mono-culture forestry, about salinity changes, and employment in this part of the Machars. That was the nature of the conversation: economics, history, and public policy, all at once. Few pilgrims have been so fortunate with a guide.

The rain finally made up its mind and become a proper downfall. Even Peter finally relented, opening his backpack and pulling out a light raincoat I would have considered an underlayer. "You're not in luck today," he told us. He indicated the scudding gray clouds: "This is coming from the southeast. When it comes from the west the rain may not last. From the southeast ... well, it'll sock in. You'll have a wet day of it."

I'd brought an umbrella from Nottingham which I pulled out, even though holding an umbrella didn't seem like a particularly "trekking" thing to do. Peter looked at it as if it were a living creature. "How long have you been rambling this area?" we asked him. "Ever since my wife and I moved here." He had worked in forestry many years. Peter was somewhere in his mid-seventies. Like the slightly older Harry Waugh, his age was nearly impossible to tell. Clearly, he was able to outwalk any of us, and then some.

By Whitefield Loch (Lake), the path is lined with tall beeches, maples, and oaks, a beautiful pastoral landscape, even in the rain. At the far end, as promised, Peter led us over a tiny access road toward a secluded beach. On the sand by the water was a nylon lean-to, a man fishing from under it. We exchanged pleasantries while standing in the rain. Peter pointed out two crannogs, one almost perfectly cylindrical, near our shore, and the other on the far end of the water. Patterson wonders in his 1993 guidebook whether Robert the Bruce may have stopped in this spot to bathe in the waters for his leprosy (77). It had turned into another one of those days when we certainly didn't need to bathe to get wet.

Peter looked at our maps and gave us some final instructions and moral support. I was a bit concerned. Perhaps Ken and Christine were, too. At the end of that day's walk, we were supposed to rendezvous with our night's host from what we were told would be a "truck stop" out on the moors of Challochglass (pronounced "Chill-ass," a tic which in equal parts confused and amused me). To me the "Chill-ass moors" sounded a bit like the *Princess Bride's* "Cliffs of Insanity": difficult to traverse, scary, and perhaps harbouring rodents of unusual size.

It had been easy – too easy – just following Peter. But he assured us we'd be fine, and that he would call the hotel owner in Kirkcowan to tell him to meet us at the appointed spot at five o'clock, since our phones might not work on the moors. We took a few final photos together. Then Peter was off, hands in his pockets, down the track toward Glenluce as giant oaks and beeches leaned overhead in protection against the showers.

Reluctantly, we turned southwest, just Canadians again, dark spots on a foreign map. For a while, the trail followed a paved path, with occasional fields and farms interrupting a landscape that otherwise seemed all humpy granite edged with ferns, creeping willow, and juniper. I was to find out later that we had passed several notable stone-age cairns, some as much as five thousand years old. I'd taken a picture of one for its interesting shape without realizing what it was. Ken was busy capturing images of the wildflowers, particularly the colourful lady's slipper. Boulders molded by glaciers and etched with variegated greens of moss and lichen were surrounded by grasses and low brush. The horizon opened to an undulating moor. Sheep grazed on both sides of what had become a farm track, and we made fairly good time. I checked my compass and the map compulsively.

We encountered only one vehicle and person during the rest of the day's walk. A farm truck and its driver edged over a hill toward us, spooking four rams who wound up caught between us and it, unable to go sideways because of heavy brush. There was a great deal of toing-and-froing, almost a strange dance, between us and the Scottish livestock before the animals bolted past. Somehow, they made it safely over the slotted grate into the next section of pasture, and we made it safely past the rams onto the moors.

We entered another forest plantation. Soon we were walking in the deep shadow of spruces and larches, with my app indicating another White Loch hidden just to our north. Grasses on the path got higher and higher, and our clothes more and more drenched. The path itself turned as boggy as any Antigonish marsh track; mud lined the parallel trenches of the vehicle ruts. The grasses soaked our boots and pants, and we constantly had to jump from one side to the other to avoid brackish puddles.

Cigar-sized black slugs became so common we couldn't help crushing a few underfoot. Eventually, the forest gave way to open peat, rocks, and moor as far as the eye could see. The rain socked in completely, making sky and horizon one long curtain of gray. As Peter had predicted, the drizzle was now coming head-on.

Castle Loch, with its rich history and thirteenth-century chapel, sat to our south, but we could see neither it nor the picturesque-sounding Throne of Gargrie on its far shore. Muir Watt (undated, 85) reports that one of the islands on Mochrum Loch is named Scar, deriving from the Old Norse *skarfr*, or cormorant, a small piece of linguistic evidence of the Norse presence in the last years of the first millennium.

We continued across the "Chill-ass" moors. They certainly lived up to their name. Ken forged ahead until he was a pencil on the horizon, the only vertical object in a dull brown collection of horizontal lines flooded with rain. Christine and I followed, rarely exchanging words. In such a reduced world the mind invents chimera. From the bog, my imagination called up farmers, shepherds, kings, and chieftains, the generations that walked this way.

Muir Watt writes that this area of the Mochrum Lochs is "scenic and atmospheric." It was certainly atmospheric, if only because the clouds were at ground level. Patterson also waxed poetic about this landscape back in 1993. I could imagine, but not see, the scene he was describing. Challochglass is a country, he writes, "of forestry plantations and open moor with bracken, rowan, birch, and heather vividly colouring the countryside in russets and browns .... Peat bogs are interrupted by ragged rocks against the skyline. This is wild country, hunted by merlins, buzzards, and owls, with ravens tumbling in the air, the singing of linnet and lark all around" (25).

No birds sang as we passed. They were likely under cover. But I'm sure the country would be beautiful on a sunny day.

Eventually, the mud path we'd been slogging arrived at a paved road – the first tarmac we'd seen in hours. I checked the map. We'd passed Chill-ass. This was supposed to be the "truck stop." But there was no truck. And no stop. All we could see was an intersection in the middle of a wide-open moor. Inexplicably, there was a green plastic trash bin at the crossroads, the only evidence of human activity other than the road itself.

We conferred. We were a half hour early. This must be it. But if so, what was "truck stop" supposed to mean? Intersection? There was a stone fence fifty metres or so to our east. Beyond that, a sign indicated an old quarry. No buildings, no sign of life.

It was still raining. Liberated by the open terrain, the wind was building momentum and plastering ever more moisture onto our wet bodies while we stood in a tight circle and debated the term "truck stop," which in Canada means a massive structure with petrol pumps, restaurants, toilets, showers ... and hot coffee.

Thankfully, my British phone had a signal. I called the number we'd been given for the Kirkcowan hotel. A young woman answered. "Dad just left," she told us. "He should be there soon." I asked her, politely, if she knew what time that might be. Clearly, she had no more idea than we did of where we were. "Anyway," she said, "there's no reception when he's on the road. I couldn't reach him if I tried. Sorry!" She hung up.

I was concerned about Ken. His teeth had started chattering, as mine had back in Girvan. I knew what I'd felt like, and how few reserves of energy I'd had left. I got him to walk fast with me back and forth to the stone fence several times. I hoped the exercise would raise our heartrates enough to keep us warm, while the trees provided a slight break from the rain.

Twenty minutes or so later, Christine suggested I call again. There seemed little point. Ken and I paced back and forth to the stone fence some more. Twenty minutes clicked over to a half hour. It felt longer.

Finally, almost exactly on schedule, a vehicle appeared through the rain in the distance, crawling over the dark hills. It was a measure of how disoriented we were that we had expected our host to come from the opposite direction. On arrival, the driver leaned out the window and asked with a grin if we were the Canadians – as if there were others crazy enough to be standing around outside, the only human figures in miles in an endless Galloway downpour.

COMMUNITAS AND THE "COME FROM AWAYS"

"You'll have to ask one of the locals.
I'm a come from away."
(Dr. Barry MacKenzie, director of the
Antigonish Heritage Museum)

Dave, who owns the Craighlaw Arms hotel and pub together with his wife Debbie (Debs, to the locals) and his daughter, seemed infectiously good-humoured. He laughed at our drenched state and began hoisting our bags into the boot (the trunk) of the van. It was already half-full with golden paper crowns, tassels, and other detritus. "We hosted a big hen-do (a bride-to-be's party) last night at the pub," he announced. "The place was hopping." He smiled. "But I had to kick them out because we have a retirement dinner today. Later this afternoon, in fact." Our sodden packs oozed water on top of the fake-lace veils. We thanked our lucky stars we were climbing into a vehicle with a heater.

Once again, we found ourselves in Scotland talking with someone who didn't seem to have a Scottish accent. "No, me and the family, we're from the South of England," Dave admitted, half-turning as he manhandled the van back east. "I took early retirement and some savings," he went on, "and Debs and I and the kids moved up here a few years ago. Haven't looked back."

Dave looked to be at most in his forties, not retirement age or even close. Hair slightly greying at the temples, short beard, he was full of energy, even if a bit tired around the eyes from hosting the party. We talked for the half hour or so it took to bring us to the village of

Kirkcowan, or *Cille Chomhainn* in Gaelic. Like Antigonish, the signs in this part of Scotland are often bilingual.

They don't use the term in the southwest of Scotland, but as valuable as he was in the local community, Dave was a "come from away." In fact, it was becoming increasingly obvious how many of the folks who were assisting us on the Whithorn walk fit this category.

"Come from away" means you're not *from* a place, even if you live there. Normally, it means you weren't born in the place you now live. However, it can also mean that even if you were born in a certain place, your *parents* were not born there. It's something of a sliding scale, which is where assessing someone's "come from awayness" can get interesting.

Come from away is an expression everyone in Atlantic Canada knows well; these days many folks *everywhere* know it through the hit musical of the same name. Being a come from away myself, I didn't realize the title could even apply to Maritimers who move to another part of Atlantic Canada. (I guess part of what tells folks you're a come from away is lumping all the Maritimes together.) So when Barry MacKenzie, who originally hails from the Miramichi, tells me he's a "come from away" in Antigonish, or a Newfoundlander in the novel *Some Hellish* by Nicholas Herring is called a "come from away" by the local Prince Edward Islanders, I know that someone like me, from the prairies, must be the equivalent of a space alien.

Still, I tell myself, at least I'm not from Ontario. The friendly and very helpful summer student guide at the Antigonish Museum, whose name is Matt, says he's from Moncton. When pressed, the gentle giant in his kilt admits there are "fifteen missing years" in his life he doesn't want to own up to.

Ontario, for sure.

Maybe it's the attitude behind identifying some folks as locals and others as come from aways that lies behind a tic that diaspora Maritimers and folks from Newfoundland and Labrador all seem to share. Anywhere else in the world, they all seem to dream of the day they can "move home." "Life is just so much better in the Maritimes," Sara, from New Brunswick, always told me. "And, the ocean!" – those last three words like an explanation.

Perhaps this also explains the five families whose arrival heralded the beginnings of Pomquet. An ignorant come from away such as myself might think that the poor Acadians, after being held as prisoners off the coast of Virginia, then England, and finally dumped on the west coast of France, might have been happy to be there, and consequently far away from the nasty British. Back "in the French motherland," so to speak. But then why did the Acadians scrimp and save to afford return passage to Nova Scotia as soon as they were able?

It's a question of *home*, that place that pilgrimage is always in a kind of creative tension with. Historical sketches of Acadian life sometimes focus on the hardships, which were undoubtable: wresting farmland from the sea. Moving millions of tons of stone and earth by oxen and hand to build the dikes that still hold the sea back in the Minas Basin and even stop the high tides from making all of Nova Scotia an island. It must have been back-breaking labour.

But the fact is that once they were settled in this new land, the Acadians enjoyed a freedom from political interference and from their king that subjects in France could never experience. The Acadians had good relations with the Mi'kmaq, including intermarriage and family ties. In a mere seventy-five years, the population of Acadians around Grand Pré had increased fifty-fold, due to plentiful and healthy food and good living conditions despite the hard work. In France, the infant mortality rate in the mid-eighteenth century reached seventy-five percent in some areas (LeBlanc 2020, 32). It was much lower in Acadie. Within a generation, those who were deported by the British had only ever known Acadia as their homeland. And like true Maritimers, for reasons both sentimental and practical, they wanted to go home. The five families of Pomquet did just that.

Walking pilgrimage straddles a line between this feeling of belonging to a place, and a practical knowledge that the pilgrim is always, ever, just passing through. Many pilgrimages – think of the historic Paqtnkek Mi'kmaq in procession with St. Anne on the way to their church – have always been local. But many famous pilgrims, including Brendan of Ireland in his curragh, Columbanus on his way across Europe, or Egeria, a woman who is the first named Christian pilgrim to the Holy Land, travelled to distant shrines from far away. There is something about being "from away" that gives pilgrims an observer's view of local customs and people. It also frees them from at least some local attachments so they can concentrate on the point of their pilgrimage. And then, like come from aways tend to do, pilgrims sometimes create community together with each other, the near-spontaneous gathering of those who travel together.

Since at least the mid-1970s, this process of finding spontaneous community with other travellers has been called *communitas*. The term was applied to pilgrimage by the academic couple Victor and Edith Turner. The Turners were rosily and overly idealistic about *communitas*. But it does seem that there is a kind of temporary camaraderie that happens among fellow travellers in a Spanish *albergue* on the Meseta, or when, say, your flight out of Calgary has been cancelled and you find yourself stuck for hours with strangers at a not-so-helpful help desk. I've heard more life-stories from fellow travellers in such moments than I'd like to admit. But I've also shared food, time, and advice in ways that were encouraged by the fellow travelling.

Communitas is the opposite of finally being accepted as a "local." Perhaps this is why come from aways can often be found in packs, reminiscing about how they learned to find the neighbourhood Fish Guy or understand Nova Scotia's recycling rules, or thanking God they're not from Ontario (even when they're actually from there). It's only after two generations of parents on this land that you *really* cease to be a come from away, despite the fact that, ultimately, everyone who is not Mi'kmaq qualifies for the title. Maybe the locals don't realize that there's something about this land that continues to draw us as it once did the Acadians and the Gaels. Whether from Moncton, Moose Jaw, or Mumbai, these days it's often the university that attracts folks to Antigonish County, many of whom stay and put down roots. The same seems to be true in Dumfries-Galloway.

Whoever he was historically, one thing about St. Ninian is that he probably wasn't from Whithorn. Even when they don't agree on the details – the Solway? Wales? Rome? France? – Bede's description of Ninian and the later hagiographies agree that the missionary bishop seems to have arrived from somewhere else. As turned out to be true in Antigonish, Ninian was always someone else's saint. Just another come from away.

THE CRAIGHLAW ARMS

"I don't know if you've noticed, but we're in the middle of nowhere."

(Dave, Craighlaw Arms proprietor)

Kirkcowan looked like most of the other villages we'd been through in southwest Scotland. Two-storey stone cottages in gray stucco sat side-by-each with their facades and front steps right on the street. There seemed to me to be an abundance of service vans for electrical work and plumbing. Dave pulled into a spot on the main street in front of the hotel. In contrast, it was a white-stucco building, its windows framed in green, a flowerbox in one window and a sign advertising Belhaven Best in the other.

I asked Dave about the hotel. "The wife and I were thinking of starting our own business in the south," Dave answered as he unloaded the bags. The fake bridal veils had been mashed down but were serviceable for a few hens yet. "Then we looked at our finances and realized we didn't have to start from scratch ... that a place like Kirkcowan had opportunities for all of us." He half-turned, arms wide, on the street: "Don't know if you've noticed, but we're in the middle of nowhere. The least-populated corner of the country!" Dave grinned as if he were still surprised: "So we bought the Craighlaw Arms. Now we're up to our armpits in the community. And we love it. Absolutely love it."

Two vehicles drove by. Dave gave the drivers a thumbs-up. One honked back. He turned to us and almost whispered: "But we're busy ALL the time. Have to shut the hotel down just to get a break. Victims of our own success, so to speak."

When Dave and Debs bought the Craighlaw Arms not many years before, they discovered that in true Scottish fashion, the pub wasn't just a business but a community centre. The Craighlaw Arms once operated as a coach-house. It's been in existence over two hundred years. There were signs by the bar thanking the couple for a donation of 551 pounds to a local fundraiser. As soon as we were inside the hotel, Dave disappeared. His wife showed me my room, above the pub, with a bathroom across the hall. "Don't worry," said Debs, "there's no one else up here." Unfortunately, she didn't mention that the family used that hallway as a shortcut between apartment and pub, a fact I discovered the first time I walked to the shower naked.

Even though, overall, Scotland's population is increasing, the region of Dumfries-Galloway stubbornly remains one of its emptiest pockets. The June 2019 report of the Office for National Statistics ranked the Dumfries-Galloway "council area," or region, as having the twenty-seventh lowest population density out of the country's thirty-two areas. Only the Highlands, the Shetlands, the Orkneys, and the Western Isles were less populated. Add to this the fact that the biggest town in the already depopulated area is Dumfries, far to the east of the Whithorn Way, and it skews the density rates where we were walking even lower. There are large tracts of land in the Machars with no people whatsoever. It's why we could stand for a half hour on a road in the middle of the moor and see only the one vehicle that had come to pick us up. We only met one other person who was clearly a pilgrim in our entire six days of walking. And he didn't want to talk.

You might think this would be a deterrent to a good pilgrimage. But to the three of us, it certainly wasn't. I grew up on the prairies, and Christine and Ken still live there. Much of Saskatchewan makes even rural Scotland look busy. The idea of having to work with a skeletal public transit system or scrounge for accommodation was hardly new to three folks who have walked Treaty 4 territory on the northern Great Plains (Anderson 2024).

Eventually, showered and in dry clothes, Christine, Ken, and I settled into a table in the corner of the pub. It was the size of a small living room, with a half dozen or so already filling it. Perhaps because of the close quarters, or perhaps because the word was already out, we seemed less an object of interest in Kirkcowan than we had been in the pubs in Maybole and Girvan. We soon realized it was our host who was in the kitchen cooking, while Debs and their daughter managed the bar. Two fellows beside me were having some kind of stir-fry. My head swam at the smell, not only of ginger and a spice other than salt, but also because for the first time in days, I was seeing vegetables. "I'll have what they're having," I told Debs.

Their daughter came to our table. "I'm to take you downstairs for tea," she announced. She brought us to a long table in front of a dark fireplace. There were our boots, lined up on the mantle. Once again, all three pairs had been stuffed with newspaper by our hosts.

When the meals came, mine was ginger stir-fried chicken with Thai yellow curry, over rice. It was extraordinary. It felt a bit strange to sit, just the three of us in the dining room, while upstairs in the cozy pub Scots were laughing and sharing pints. Our conversation was muted. Ken was exhausted and soon off to sleep. Christine and I sat a while, listening to the eighties' soundtrack, talking about the best places in Canada to live. It's strange how one's home can sometimes be seen in a clearer light from a distance. Then Christine climbed the stairs for bed as well. Hoping to avoid the blisters from which Ken was already suffering so badly, I made sure to restuff our three pairs of boots with fresh newspaper before turning in myself.

When eventually I tottered up to my room, two middle-aged women from the village had just arrived to sit at the bar. They looked like they were settling in as Debs washed glasses. I remembered Dave saying he had to get up at six to make sure everything was clean and to prepare our breakfasts. We'd asked if, given a chance, he'd buy a hotel and pub again. He said no. But as Ken later remarked, even while saying that, he looked like a man enjoying himself immensely.

I hung my wet gear over a line in the bathroom. The next morning, everything was dry. When we came down to the empty pub, Debs was waiting to take our orders. Eyes bleary, Dave came out of the kitchen to check how our "full Scottishes" tasted. They were great – but I wondered how much sleep the two had had. "A few hours," came the reply. "That's about it!" Dave was to drive us to our start-point of Mochrum Village and be back at the pub in time to prepare for a big family reunion that afternoon.

SAINT NINIAN UNIVERSITY ... ALMOST

"The bishop calls a meeting of the 400 families of St. Ninian's Parish on October 1, 1865, and unfolds to them his idea of erecting a large stone church 'worthy of a cathedral.'"

(Walsh 1989)

One can't really talk about Saint Ninian Cathedral in Antigonish without also talking about the university that almost took the Ninian name as well. Since its founding in 1853 in Cape Breton and its move in 1854-55 to Antigonish, the university has always been known by the name of St. Francis Xavier. But Ninian *nearly* got top honours.

If you have time, continue straight ahead to the T-intersection at the end of St. Andrew's Street / Highway 4, then take a small detour to your right to say hi to Dr. Barry MacKenzie at the Antigonish Heritage Museum, housed in the former train station. There's always something happening or about to happen at the museum, whether a ceilidh, a lecture, or the museum's "Curator's Cabinet of Curiosities" escape room.

On our inaugural group pilgrimage, we opted instead to turn left at the car dealerships and take a scenic path that winds through Columbus Field. Straight ahead was a detour through Pipers' Green, so named because it's where you can hear bagpipes being practiced even to this day. But I suggest following the path as we did, turning right at Columbus Field and exiting back onto Main Street where it intersects Elm Street. Here you can slow your pilgrimage and take in the next few blocks at leisure. Depending on whether you're walking during the school year or during summer months, what you see will be very different. Antigonish is a college town in every sense of the word. This means that the town's population very nearly doubles from September through April.

As you'll know at this point, the story of Antigonish is tightly bound with northern Nova Scotia's Catholicism. To your left, now that you're on Main Street, is a Bed and Breakfast that Dorothy Ludlow, one of our 2024 walkers, informed me was once the bishop's residence. Both the town and St. Francis Xavier University became what they are because of a succession of bishops who followed in the footsteps of Bishop Plessis. Any detailed history of Antigonish, or of St. Francis Xavier University, must include an in-depth examination of these bishops and their conflicts, foibles, rivalries, energies, and dreams. (Dorothy's son, the historian Peter Ludlow, has written two scholarly monographs about aspects of the North Shore's Catholic history.)

The history of town and gown in Antigonish also includes the sometimes radical priest-professors who literally manned the university for so many decades, and orders of dynamic and visionary sisters whose mission was to support both the university and the village ("The Marthas" and the sisters of the Congrégation de Notre-Dame). Finally, the genesis and after-effects of the internationally important economic and educational co-operative social program the Antigonish Movement marked the university for much of the early to mid-twentieth century.

Historically, the bishop to keep in mind for our pilgrim purposes is Colin F. MacKinnon. Born in 1810 in the same William's Point whose access road you passed on your way through Greenwold, Bishop MacKinnon was the first Nova Scotian-born bishop of the diocese. Perhaps his later dedication to education can be explained by the harshness of the Penal Laws against Catholics that were lifted not long before he was born, and the fact that education was so difficult to come by as a result. Technically, no Catholic could teach school in Nova Scotia for many years. Neil MacKinnon, the brother of the future bishop who would found the university, was the first Catholic to receive permission from Dalhousie, the governor of Nova Scotia, allowing him to set up a school. MacKinnon then set up a school at William's Point, the first Catholic school in the colony. Neil ended up being the teacher for his brother Colin

– which, in one sense, was the beginning of the chain of events that led to the North Shore University.

Neil must have taught his brother well. Colin was clearly ambitious: he not only founded the university, but also Saint Ninian Cathedral, building the structure before the ecclesiastical framework was even in place to sanctify it.

In retrospect, the decision to invest in a university for Antigonish seems prescient. So many places in Nova Scotia were one industry towns. Some towns had a mill. Some had mines. Others had "the yards." Antigonish never had these, but it had its own one industry: education. (Most locals would quickly point out the hospital, started by "the Marthas," has long been another important fulcrum of Antigonish community life.)

Nova Scotia is known for its working-class ballads about fishing or mining. Few Bluenosers can keep a stiff upper lip and a dry eye if Rita MacNeil's "It's a Working Man I Am" comes on the radio. It doesn't seem possible to sing a heart-tugging ballad about a university, even StFX. Somehow, post-secondary academia doesn't quite evoke the gutsy, heroic images that a shanty about the sea can conjure. But while the mills and the mines are mostly gone, now, the university goes on.

As is so often true of Canadian universities, St. Francis Xavier was first a seminary. Its pride for many of the early years was the "turning out" of priests and a number of bishops for the Catholic Church. StFX began as a school in 1853 in Arichat with a donation MacKinnon received of twenty thousand francs from the Society for the Propagation of the Faith in Paris. Despite its origins in Cape Breton, the bishop had the location in Antigonish in mind for his school from the very beginning. Two years later, he moved to Antigonish's Main Street along with his students, to a site about three blocks ahead of where you are, where the present-day Town Hall sits.

Bishop MacKinnon's stated goal was to name the new seminary "St. Ninian," so that there would have been both a cathedral and university under that banner. However, St. Francis Xavier was eventually chosen. No one knows for certain why. In hindsight, it seems likely the decision was political and economic: St. Francis Xavier was the patron saint of missions for the French group which had just donated twenty thousand francs. Always "someone else's saint," Ninian lost out on the university – but the cathedral that sits in the front and centre of the university held on to our mysterious patron's name (Walsh 1989, 66-67; Stanley-Blackwell and MacLean 2004, 150).

You may remember the Venerable Bede's comments about Ninian's *Candida Casa* – how it was an unusual structure at the time for being built of stone instead of the more common wood. Bishop MacKinnon had a similar dream for Nova Scotia's Ninian. Saint Ninian, he proposed, should be a Renaissance-style stone cathedral.

On All Saints' Day, 1865, Bishop MacKinnon brought the four hundred families of the parish together and told them of his plan to build a cathedral named Saint Ninian in Antigonish. Soon MacKinnon, together with the people of the parish, began bringing the dream to life. Work on the cathedral commenced late October 1866. In the winter of that year there was a shipwreck at nearby Morristown of a vessel carrying valuable lumber. This inspired Bishop MacKinnon to send the faithful in their sleighs to the site of the wreck to bring the lumber back to the work site. The cornerstone was laid eight months later in late June 1867, although construction continued until 1874.

With the bishop making the first and largest donation, cash flowed in to defray the costs. Additionally, parishioners of Saint Ninian were asked to pledge three days of free labour a week to the construction, except during seeding and harvest (Walsh 1989, 75). Many did. As a result, for years residents witnessed "endless caravans of horse-drawn vehicles in an unbroken chain to the site of their Cathedral" (Stanley-Blackwell and MacLean 2004, 128).

The site for the cathedral was known as Cathedral Hill, to the south and above Main Street, on the university side of Brierly Brook. The cathedral received the land from the new college. They were perhaps legally distinct entities, but in fact most of the university's first teachers were priests or nuns, as were its rectors, and this was to continue for a century. Bishop Plessis would have been pleased to know that despite the university not adopting the Ninian name, the placement of the cathedral set in literal stone the relation between Saint Ninian, the town, and the university.

The influence of religious orders on the community – in particular the nuns known as "the Marthas" – is so diverse and important that for most locals over the age of forty, all you have to do is say "the Marthas," and they know who you're talking about. The Marthas deserve their own book, and in fact they have it: James Cameron's *"And Martha Served": History of the Sisters of St. Martha, Antigonish, Nova Scotia* (Nimbus, 2000). At the same time, a pioneering role in the access of women to higher education was played by the sisters of the Congregation of Notre Dame, who founded Mount Bernard College in the nineteenth century, a woman's college which affiliated with the university in the 1890s. As a direct result, St. Francis Xavier became the first Catholic university in North America to grant degrees to women.

With so much to think about, you may want to stop a couple of blocks after your left turn, for an ice cream (right-hand side) or a visit to the Curious Cat Tea and Books (to your left), or a coffee, tea, or hot chocolate at one of the other spots along Main Street. Behind a gas station on the far end of the town's one main street is a tiny plot of land that contains the original Saint Ninian graveyard. MacKinnon's predecessor, Bishop Fraser, was once interred here. After the cathedral was finished, his remains were transferred to a vault under the building.

Further down Main Street and on the right just past the old graveyard is the Tall and Small café, run by our Pomquet neighbours, and then the new "Peace by Chocolate" storefront. The latter was started by the Hadhads – a Syrian refugee family whose chocolate factory in Damascus was destroyed by political violence. They have gone on to become a major employer and a much-lauded Canadian "immigrant success" story (Tattrie 2020). The story of their sponsored arrival in Antigonish and the heartwarming growth of their business is enshrined in books and a movie that fictionalizes their long and difficult journey to Canada, and the eventual building of their good-vibe-themed and Canadiana-themed chocolate products.

You may or may not have noticed that you passed a makeshift mosque on the north side of Main Street not long after St. James Church on the south side (St. James is named for the pilgrim saint who is patron of the Camino de Santiago: *Sant* = Saint, and *Iago* = James). Peace by Chocolate is across from Grape Leaves, a Syrian take-out restaurant. If your walk is taking place on a very hot day (and Nova Scotia's North Shore seems to be suffering more and more of those in the summer), then stop at Grape Leaves for a "Relax Refresher Juice." The combination of lemonade and blended mint leaves topped with pieces of fresh lime will solve any problems the walk has caused, and likely fix a few more, just in case.

Just as any accurate story of Antigonish's past must include ethnic groups other than the English, it seems that stories of its future will as well.

LIMINALITY

"Welcome to your pilgrim dinner!"
(Christine Briand, head of the St. James
United Church Women, Antigonish)

The word *Limin* is Latin for doorway or portal. To step out your door on a pilgrimage means to cross the *limin*, or threshold. Liminality – the state of being "in between" – is also a concept used to talk about pilgrim spaces by the pioneers of the contemporary study of pilgrimage mentioned earlier, Victor and Edith Turner. The Turners sensed that something special happened when one sets out to a shrine; they theorized about the experience using Van Gennep's 1908 work on rites of passage (Van Gennep 2004). Rather idealistically, the Turners proposed that social status becomes temporarily fluid on pilgrimage, allowing for a limited equality between people who, when not on pilgrimage, might never mix.

So, for instance, we three Canadians were accepted without question by Dave and Debs as pilgrims. In our short conversations while driving, we were able to talk honestly about some intensely personal matters, in part because we were thrown together so temporarily. Similarly, I had brief but immediately thoughtful discussions with my fellow walkers on the Nova Scotia Ninian Way, for instance sharing family news with Joy Pennick, chatting with Dianne Kristoff, or hearing about the feeling of how an Achilles injury was changing the experience for stalwart pilgrim Brent King. In both Scotland and Nova Scotia, pilgrimage brings you to a rare intimacy, perhaps because of the physical exertion, the common destination, and the liminal space you temporarily share.

After the publication of Victor and Edith Turner's *Image and Pilgrimage in Christian Culture* in 1978, pilgrimage began to evolve as a distinct area of study. Because it overlaps with tourism, adventure travel, municipal and regional economic development efforts, and through-hiking, a de facto interdisciplinary widening of the field has led inevitably to questions over what properly constitutes pilgrimage. Since the Turners, subsequent pilgrim scholars have given much more nuance to our understandings of shrines, the contested social relations which take place at them, and, perhaps especially, even the notion of what constitutes pilgrimage.

Liminality – both the word and the concept – has fallen a bit from favour as a description of what happens on pilgrimage. But the fate of St. Ninian pilgrimages past and present and even the person of Ninian himself are so well-suited to a consideration of liminality that I hope you won't mind my resurrecting the term.

In my opinion, a metaphor that describes a state of being "in-between" is still useful. Liminal, in this sense, is about being between two states; not quite outside the door, but no longer in. Or like a lintel: not quite inside the home, but no longer out. It's a place of decision and transition. Although all history is full of change, liminal periods are those times when changes seem most momentous. Personally, liminal spaces are those relational or life moments where something is changing for us, and we can't yet guess how it will all turn out.

Christine Jamieson (2019, 78) notes that even a short pilgrimage such as our Pomquet to Antigonish walk provides one of life's "destabilizing experiences, that is, experiences that break down our ordinary way of thinking about and understanding encounters with the world." That's liminality in a nutshell.

We were certainly not in our comfort zone while walking in Scotland, but that gave us a chance to get to know the people we were meeting in a way that regular tourists may not have had. On the drive to our departure point, I got a chance to ask Dave about retiring at forty, and how that came about. It turned into one of those conversations where there were some things he never specifically said, while nonetheless giving a message. "Would you like to retire from this retirement?" I asked. "The hotel and pub seem an awful lot of work," added Ken, from the back seat.

"Oh no, we love this!" Dave insisted. But as we travelled, he wondered aloud about perhaps shutting the hotel down another day a week, or maybe having their daughter take it over bit by bit.

"What else would you do, if not this?" I asked.

"I have this dream," he began, tentatively. "I'd like to go dig wells in Somalia." He sped up and pulled to the right to pass one of the tractors that can take up the whole of the one-lane roads in the area, then popped back over to the left just before an oncoming vehicle reached us. "Those people," he went on, "they really need fresh water."

Dave told us how he'd been with British forces in Africa before his retirement and the family's move to Scotland. "If I did anything else, I'd like to spend some time back in Somalia," he concluded. "Dig wells. Debs and I have talked about it, and I think she's willing. That's a good partner, willing to go with you overseas." He shook his head. We were arriving at Mochrum. "You know, we in the west took a lot out of that country." He stopped talking, as if thinking about what he'd just said. "It's time to give something back," he announced finally. Then more forcefully: "*I'd* like to give something back."

If Dave were a bit haunted, he wouldn't be the first in Kirkcowan. In the late nineteenth century, there was a story published called *The Witch of Kirkcowan.* It was about a man haunted by memories and apparitions. Galloway was among the last regions of Scotland to give up persecutions for magic, and witchcraft (Henderson 2006, 54).

Wherever we put St. Ninian on the timeline, it would have been during one of the most liminal periods in the history of the British Isles, a turning of ages and empires. When the Roman Legions were being pulled out of Britain never to return, it had been nearly four hundred years of Roman occupation. Large numbers of Celtic Britons had become Romanized and Christian. In the Roman imagination, Britain had turned from being a barbarian outpost on the far western sea to one of the most civilized and prosperous of the provinces.

By the time Ninian was reportedly bishop (even if one accepts the earliest dating), the Anglo-Saxons were beginning to make their presence felt in the east and north of the Isles. The Romans had built coastal forts for defense against this new threat. Soon, however, they could not muster sufficient troops to hold them. Since history is always lived forward but remembered backward, no one could know that Britain was in transition from its Celtic and Roman past to an Anglo-Saxon, Norse, and eventually Norman, future. I've mentioned how the fifth-century Latinus Stone discovered at Whithorn, carved in Latin but in a non-Roman area, tells of how "*Romanitas*" survived the disappearance of the Imperial troops. Whithorn stayed at least partly Roman even after the "official Romans" were gone.

This was a time of myth and legend: a liminal age. St. Patrick, who may perhaps have been a contemporary of Ninian's (MacQueen 2007, 36), was a Christian Roman kidnapped by slave-traders to Ireland, later returning as a missionary – in the popular mind, *the* missionary – to that land (Brigid of Kildare should share that honour, and the government of Ireland finally decided in 2023 to declare February 1, her feast day, as a national holiday on par with Patrick's).

Much of Patrick's history is clouded in myth and uncertainty, not because he wasn't real, but because the times were chaotic. Ninian occupies a similar time and status. The *Candida Casa* and St. Ninian's Shrine stood on what was then "the edge of the earth." Yet the area we were walking through had been Romanized, which almost certainly means that it was also, in the late-empire period, "Christianized." There is a frustratingly brief comment written by the Church Father Tertullian in the first decade of the 200s that may relate directly to Christian communities even further north than we were that day: *"Brittanorum inaccessa Romanis loca, Christo vero subdita"* ([even in] parts of Britain inaccessible to Rome [i.e. its legions], Christianity has truly triumphed) (Nordenfalk 1968, 107-108).

The irony is that even as Roman influence faded in the long-held south and east of England, it sometimes held on strongest in these border areas where Roman values, culture, goods, and even language had arrived the most recently. The region which is now Galloway was very possibly a refuge for late-Roman Christian beliefs, as nurtured in their Briton environments, and lived out in communities such as the ancient church at Whithorn (Nordenfalk 1968, 139).

As with all colonizing empires, whether the Romans were good for Scotland depends on who's asking. The opening words of W. Douglas Simpson's *Saint Ninian and the Origins of the Christian Church in Scotland*, written in 1940, are unashamedly idealistic: "Christianity was the last and greatest gift of the dying Roman Empire to the new world yet to be" (1). Contrast his sentiments to Alistair Moffat's 2005 work *Before Scotland: The Story of Scotland Before History* (226):

> "The Romans were, as usual, utterly ruthless in pursuit of their own interests, occasionally adopting genocide as imperial policy ... The reality is that the Romans came to what is now Scotland, they saw, they burned, killed, stole and occasionally conquered, and then they left a tremendous mess behind them ... Like most imperialists they arrived to make money, to gain political prestige, and to exploit the resources of their colonies at virtually any price to the conquered. And remarkably, in Britain, in Scotland, we continue to admire them for it."

In some ways, the feelings that Dave seemed to be having about his time in Africa while serving in the military are not unrelated to that quote, nor to the imperial power that the Romans practiced in Scotland, or the British in Nova Scotia.

Our conversation continued to be lively until, suddenly, we were at Mochrum's main street. Dave pulled over under a blue sign indicating the "Whithorn Way." We Canadians got out. Dave pulled out our bags from where they were again crushing the hen-party crowns and set them carefully on the road. We looked at him, and he at us. "Are you sure you know where you're going?" he asked, finally. As if it were his responsibility.

We showed him on the map. "From here to here," we said, pointing, "then only one road the rest of the way?"

"That's it." he nodded, satisfied. "Stay on the tarmac. You'll be fine." With that he hopped back into his van, checked his watch, and gunned the motor to turn around. We waved.

"Now let's not get all emotional about this," he called through the window, laughing. He waved one last time before speeding off.

BRIGADOONS

"Brigadoon [noun]: a place that is idyllic, unaffected by time, or remote from reality."
(Merriam-Webster online definitions)

Since Canadian one-cent pieces went out of production years ago, it's not likely you have pennies in your pocket while you walk down Antigonish's Main Street. But if you did, you'd be surprised to discover they still work in the parking meters. It's an example of how, here and there, hints of a simpler past hang on in this college town. If you're walking close to a crosswalk and even happen to glance at it, chances are good that in Antigonish any approaching cars will immediately slow and stop. I've had to wave stopped cars on, in a polite gestural tug-of-war with drivers. My wife admitted that on more than one occasion she has crossed a street that she wasn't intending to simply because she happened to look sideways, all the cars stopped, and by that point, she felt she had to do so.

Time hasn't stopped along Nova Scotia's north shore. But sometimes it feels like it has slowed, often in pleasing ways. People still talk to you at the line to the cashier in the grocery store – and there are still cashiers. On gravel roads in the country, drivers lift a hand in greeting as they pass. Occasionally, even the ways that Scottish identity is marked can feel somewhat like a hold-over from a romanticized past. Certain aspects of Scottish-Canadian identity – tartans, bagpipes, and clan symbols – may seem at times to be "nostalgia performances." This, despite the fact that Nova Scotia's Office of Gaelic Affairs works hard to emphasize the dynamism and evolving vitality of Gaelic culture in the province as a living heritage language.

In the 1950s, a restaurant named "The Brigadoon" welcomed diners on Antigonish's Main Street. It burned down in 1962, but you can find old photographs online and in Peggy Thompson's 2022 *Antigonish: A History in Pictures* (84 and 81). One photo shows seven Antigonish "businessmen," the managers of the banks and stores and newspapers of the day, all dressed in ties and kilts and standing in front of the diner. (The slightly more complicated ethnic make-up of the area even at the time is given away by the small "Acadian Bus Lines" sign on the sidewalk behind them.)

The newest businesses on the west end of Main Street these days are Syrian. Once you pass them, follow the sidewalk as it angles left and crosses over Brierly Brook and up toward the university. You'll soon come to Cairn Park. Stop for a bit to take in the monuments. These mark the numerically largest clans of Antigonish County. They represent the Gaelic-speaking Scots who generally settled in the rural areas, while in the town itself you would hear and speak English. Still, in some ways the clans are to Antigonish what the McIntosh brothers are to Lower South River and the five Acadian families to Pomquet. On the stones are written the names of the Chisholms, MacDonalds, Chattans, MacDougalls, Stewarts, MacLeans, and MacInneses who helped make Antigonish the booming area it was when it was incorporated in 1889. The first cairn was placed by the Chisholm clan in 1983. There are two additional cairns: one raised in honour of the Antigonish Highland Society and another for the Special Olympics.

The Antigonish Highland Society's Plaque deserves a closer examination. If you're Mi'kmaq, or perhaps even Acadian, you may find the wording of the October 1997 engraving somewhat off-putting. The plaque states:

> "In memory of the Highland pioneers who left the Isles and Highlands of auld Scotland to settle in this part of New Scotland nearly two centuries ago and who prevailed over hardships and scarcities to convert the forest primeval into the fair land that it is today" (Cairn Park signage, Antigonish).

It's unfortunate wording that sets the "forest primeval" against today's "fair land," as if the second were not the first. Mi'kmaw author Daniel N. Paul writes that in the late 1700s, the British tried to eliminate Indigenous presence by setting fire to vast sections of northern Nova Scotia's "forests primeval," destroying Mi'kmaq villages and crops. Paul also notes that the British used the exact same technique of landscape destruction against the Jacobites in the Scottish Highlands in the 1740s, with the same goal of taking over their land and displacing the people. This initial dislocation resulted in the very Gaels who would soon arrive in Nova Scotia.

It was not Highland settlers who were responsible for the starvation and death of so many Mi'kmaq, nor for the destruction of Acadian homes and the violent expulsions of the French. It was the British. And yet the complications of colonization were such that the Highlanders arrived in a land which had been "cleared" for their settlement in a pattern repeated time and again throughout Canada's history (Daschuk 2013). A government agent in Antigonish in the late eighteenth century reported that Mi'kmaq survivors in the area were in "a miserable condition" and some of them "entirely naked," while the British relief was entirely insufficient (Paul 2022, 225).

Peter MacKenzie, one of my fellow pilgrims on our group Nova Scotia Ninian pilgrimage in 2024, is very involved with the local Highland Society. I know from talking with Peter as we walked that the last thing the present-day Society wishes to promote is any denigration of Indigenous presence. Quite the opposite: these days the Gaels see the recovery of their culture and language as linked to and in some ways dependant on the priority of recognition of Mi'kmaq language, culture, and land. Since the 1990s, those of us who are not First Nations, Métis, or Inuit have learned better to watch language like "frontiers" and "unspoiled paradises" that, consciously or not, works to erase Indigenous peoples and their sovereignty.

Brigadoon was a 1947 American musical by Alan Jay Lerner and Frederick Loewe about a mystical, magical village that only appears in the Highlands for one day every one hundred years. Despite its almost detail-for-detail parallels with a well-known Bavarian folk tale of a forest village that only appears once a century (Krumpelmann 1948, 396-400), Lerner, who later wrote a book based on the musical, insisted that he did not copy nor know of Friedrich Gerstaecker's story *Germelshausen.* (In an interesting twist indicative of the complicated intertextuality of folk tales and how they move through and across cultures, some believe that

Gerstaecker's *Germelshausen* was itself inspired by a story by Edgar Allen Poe that the author read while travelling in the United States.)

The Broadway musical is the story of two Americans from New York who, while tramping the Scottish Highlands on a hunting trip, come across a mysterious village in the hills that is not on their map. Throughout the course of the play, they take part in the village's preparations for a joyous wedding, only to slowly discover that the village is "stuck in time," specifically in the year 1746, and that it only appears to the outside world once every one hundred years.

The musical gives only the vaguest reasons for the enchantment that happened on that date. The Americans are told that the local village priest or pastor prayed to God, and then "sacrificed himself" forever. Brigadoon, which the play intimates was threatened by supernatural or perhaps natural forces, disappeared to save itself from being changed. While in its centenary apparitions it is briefly visible to the outside world and outsiders can visit it, no one from the village can leave, or it will disappear forever.

There was a Hollywood movie made of *Brigadoon* in 1954 and a TV version in 1966. The play has recently been revised and updated and still plays on summer theatre circuits.

The date that Lerner and Loewe assigned Brigadoon – 1746 – would have been an interesting time for a mythical Highland village to disappear. In fact, 1746 was the year that Scots fighting as part of the Catholic Jacobite Rebellion were defeated by the British at the Battle of Culloden, near Inverness in the Highlands. It was not the only reason for the waves of Scottish exile that followed, but it was certainly a catalyst.

While it's not a part of the Nova Scotian walk to Ninian, if you had time and a car, you could drive to Knoydart, Nova Scotia, not far from Antigonish, to see the Culloden memorial cairn there. Local tradition is that three Highland Scots who survived Culloden (more than a thousand Highlanders died in the battle) later immigrated to Nova Scotia and were buried where the cairn was eventually raised, using Scottish and local stones. Peter MacKenzie is one of those who leads memorials on the site.

On the subject of coincidences concerning Brigadoon and walks to Ninian, there is not only the now-disappeared restaurant The Brigadoon on Antigonish's Main Street (will it reappear in 2050?), and the date of the Battle of Culloden and its links to a cairn nearby and to the Highland settlement of Antigonish. There is also the fact that when we started the Whithorn Way in 2019 by walking from Ayr through Alloway, the birthplace of Robbie Burns, we passed by the bridge "Brig o' Doon," the likely origin of the Broadway musical's name, via Burns' poem "Tam O'Shanter."

Brig o' Doon might physically be a spot along the Whithorn Way, but to my mind, the Nova Scotian pilgrimage route seems even more protected by enchantments from the damaging winds of time and change than the Scottish one. Certain places along the Nova Scotia Ninian Way also seem to belong to a magical past that isn't necessarily ongoing in other parts of the country. Pilgrimage by its very nature participates in this tension between past and present. Pilgrimage looks back to a saint, a miracle, an apparition, or an event, but also forward to a healing, to a community of pilgrims, or perhaps to a change of life.

Keeping that in mind, cross over from Cairn Park to the campus side of the street. Then double back, keeping your eyes on your final destination: the Cathedral of Saint Ninian, Antigonish. It's not far now.

CELTIC SCHMELTIC

"Even though it is much more difficult to find evidence for people who were not considered important by their societies, and who could not afford to leave behind writings or lasting artworks, we now understand that it is important to try anyway."

(Parks, Sheinfeld, and Warren 2022)

From where Dave dropped us in the middle of Mochrum, it was only a few paces along the Whithorn Way to the graveyard of the village's old *kirk*. I stood by the ground elder and ferns, looking out over the ancient tombstones, feeling like there was a history here I was only sensing.

That feeling was exactly right. Fragments of "carved Celtic stonework" were recovered from an earlier chapel on this site, proof that there was likely an eleventh-century church on exactly this spot (Patterson 1993, 41). At the very moment I looked out over the graveyard, two hundred yards behind me was the "Druchtag Motte," a massive, steep-sided artificial hill surrounded by a ditch, its sixty-foot flattened top the site of a twelfth-century Norman fortress (Stell 1986, 114). I'm somewhat abashed to admit I never noticed it.

Distraction is a universal problem, and it can occur even on pilgrimage. One's haste to guarantee boots and raingear, and to ascertain proper directions so as to avoid long and painful backtracks, can also blind a pilgrim to the land I've been proposing that pilgrimage so clearly opens up.

Pilgrims are advocates of "slow travel." Many of us who walk long trails believe it helps integrate us better into the natural environment. In general, I still believe that to be true. We become more knowledgeable about place through walking. By the feel of wind, rain, and sun we understand better what Indigenous writers call our *relationality* with the land (Aldred and Anderson 2024, 23-25). That's all so. Yet, at the same time, I know Camino walkers who have spent thirty days trekking the Iberian Peninsula from end to end who seemed to have had only the slightest inkling they were in Spain. The uniqueness of the place was entirely lost on them, whereas they could tell you in detail about their blisters, their comrades, and the wines they drank. It would be dishonest not to admit that Ken, Christine, and I suffered some of the same myopia. Otherwise, how could we have missed Mochrum's motte?

In general, though, walking is a far better and more nuanced way to experience a place than simply driving through. A walker is neither sheltered by a bubble of speed, nor confined to a motorway. The fantastically complicated song of a blackbird or a song sparrow, the smell of country roses, and the feel of bog beneath one's feet are all sensations hidden from a driver. There were ditches full of purple vetch, fern, wild radish, and stinging nettle as we left Mochrum's village. Poor Ken's boots were still wet and his blisters active, but we had only a shortish – nine-mile – walk that day. The grey skies of the previous days had given way to blue. Tall, puffy cumulous clouds sailed east. The sun had shown up to greet us, drying the last few puddles on the road and bringing the sounds of bees to our ears. A road-sign warned of crossing deer. In the pastoral morning light, I half-expected to see one prance across the track.

Ken has always made the point that if walking helps turn an empty or unexperienced space into an experienced place full of stories and memories, then stopping would be best of all. If slow is good, then by the same logic, he points out, some sort of staggered or sequential walking journey would be best, where one stops to learn about where they are before moving on (Wilson 2020, 6). It's hard to argue with that, which is perhaps why I'm suggesting such a slow walk to the Nova Scotia Ninian.

A less well-advertised historical feature of Mochrum is mentioned by Patterson in his guide. The quiet little village we had just left was once an important waystation for the Manxmen, smugglers from the Isle of Man. Once safely stored in the village, their contraband was held until donkey-trains of Scottish smugglers took it out again for Edinburgh and Glasgow. Sleepy little Mochrum, so peripheral now that we could stand at its centre and not fear a car, was once in the middle of ill-gotten trade between the Isle of Man and Galloway, the Solway coast of England, and Northern Ireland.

The villagers of Mochrum would be visited by government agents who would overnight in one part of the village while in another, smugglers secreted their packages from one spot to another. Robbie Burns, when he wasn't writing poetry or getting local women pregnant, was briefly one such excise officer for the government, a pseudo-policeman kept in the dark by the locals while they profited from the smugglers' trade (Patterson 1993, 49).

The first part of the morning's walk took us by green fields dotted with white clover and spotted with sheep, hemmed by the ever-present stone fences. A small herd of seven or eight cattle, alerted by the tap-tap of Ken and Christine's walking sticks, hung their heads over a fence to watch us pass, their mouths moving endlessly on the cud. I thought of Ian Bradley, whose 1993 book *The Celtic Way* reports a Hebridean song invoking the saints and angels, Mary, Brigid, and Michael, in "nibbling, chewing, and munching" (40).

The art of stone fence building seemingly never travelled to Canada with the Scottish immigrants who came to our shores. Perhaps it's the tendency of Canadian earth to freeze and heave; perhaps it's just another cultural difference. When the billionaire Irvings of New Brunswick built a private family chapel in the Scottish style on their property at Bouctouche, they had master stone-fence builders flown in from Scotland and Wales to create the mortar-less walls that now stand by the chapel grounds. From the miles of stone fence we had already traced coming south from Ayr, I could see that those which seemed to be best built were fitted at the top with vertically placed thin stones, and no concrete.

At Montreith Estates, our path intersected with the track that would take us the final stretch into Whithorn. The sun continued bright and cheery; it glinted off the White Loch of Myrton, the small lake we could see through the alders and oaks bending over to shelter the roadway. We didn't have time to look at the loch; Muir Watt writes that it contains another crannog, and that a local superstition held that if a woman or girl looked into its waters on May Day (May 1), they would see the reflection of their future husbands. There's no parallel legend of what their future husbands might witness had they looked.

Muir Watt also tells of how locals would bathe in the waters of the White Loch for their reportedly curative powers, despite local clergy warnings against the practice (90). Patterson, wearing his environmentalist hat, wrote that healing powers of the loch are now impossible to test, because of algae blooms caused by the pig manure being spread on the surrounding hills and leeching into the no-longer-so-white waters (Patterson 1993, 53).

Further on, we passed a sign for the village Clachan of Myrton. I took a photo just because of the lovely sound of the name. "Clachan" was once the word for a monastic cell. Both Patterson and Muir Watt (91) note that the shaft of the largest stone cross now in the Whithorn Museum, decorated with Irish-Norse interlacing and dating from the late 900s or early 1000s, was found near the loch. It's not surprising that we should have been coming across more and more evidence of Ninian.

Both visionary and romantic, Patterson imagined this magnificent cross once standing beside the White Loch. Interestingly, he pictured it not connected with any building, but as a lone human-made focus for the very earliest Scottish Christians to gather in prayer and for masses. As he described it: "Outdoor worship among the fellow creatures of nature was a feature of the Celtic Church which saw the whole created order as suffused with the divine, the eternal breaking into the mortal with every indrawn breath. It was only after many centuries that Norman-inspired stone vaults were raised to hem worship behind walls, so that the call of the winter geese was no longer intertwined with the liturgy" (Patterson 1993, 54).

Patterson's words here are evocative and beautiful. But they're not true. That such an organic, healthy, environmentally aware spirituality, so opposed to later Christianity, truly existed in the sixth and seventh centuries in quite the way he describes goes well beyond the evidence (Wooding 2009, 11). A bit like the "Irish Pubs" one can find from Singapore to Sao Paolo, there's *something* real behind popular notions of Celtic spirituality, but malleable and too often twisted in modern receptions. Patterson's description of ancient Celtic worship fits his environmental spirituality of the 1990s too neatly to be historically accurate.

The last decades of the twentieth century witnessed the rise, and then partial decline, of an international craze for all things Celtic. In terms of religion, this enthusiasm appeared in both new age spiritualities and revivals of so-called ancient Celtic Christianity, where the term described a certain quality of worship rather than simply the people who were engaged in it. The term "Celtic Schmeltic" was coined by Gilbert Markus to describe the unsubstantiated and quite erroneous notion that there was in ancient times, and remains today, "some Celtic essence offering vast spiritual riches for those who discover it" (Markus 1998, 380).

Donald Meek, at the time Professor of Celtic at the University of Aberdeen, felt the need to write *The Quest for Celtic Christianity* as a corrective against those who proposed (or more often, assumed) that in Ireland, Wales, and Scotland there were early, "pure," indigenous streams of Christianity that were somehow untouched by Rome, quite Protestant-like in their low-church organization and emphases on scripture, and somehow in continuity with today. Too many Celtic "experts," in Meek's view, are not familiar with any Celtic languages, do not know the regions, and are located in "usually English-based metropolitan culture" (Meek 2000, 7, 122).

Most of this was not true of Patterson. He was a Scot, and truly a committed and passionately spiritual environmentalist. Perhaps it's unfair to critique him on this one point. One only has to look closely at the animals woven into the artwork of the *Book of Kells*, or read the vivid, creation-infused prayers attributed to the Irish saints to realize that, yes, there was indeed at least a *flavour* of prayer and worship coming out of this part of the ancient world. But as Professor Tom O'Loughlin warns, "We cannot construct a detailed picture of the spirituality of the Celts, for we simply do not have enough evidence." "When any early medieval text feels warm and cosy to our religious sensibilities," O'Loughlin goes on to warn, "then we should watch out" (O'Loughlin 2000, 30, 31).

Yet there's something attractive, especially in these days, about any expression of faith that takes account of creation so effortlessly. Whether Celtic, or Anglo-Saxon, or Frankish, many of the early medieval writers saw Creation in ways similar to how Indigenous writers see it now: as part of our network of relations. For John Scotus Eriugena, for instance, "moth larvae and alpha predators, slow-growing mosses and day-old mayflies, winged pollinators and bacterial decomposers all come bubbling forth from the infinitely networking mind and heart of God" (Lane 2015, 42).

This is not so much the "romantic exoticism" or the "exotic froth" that Markus wryly observes in uncritical treatments of ancient Celts and their spirituality. Rather, it's a product of societies of all sorts that lived – or live – in more intimate contact with nature than most of us do now. Whatever seems unique to us may simply have been a natural product of how faith interacts with land: social, spiritual, and even physical. Landscape helps determine language, and through that, ways of thinking and feeling. A seafaring people do not understand water as chaotic in the same way the ancient Israelites did. I come from the wide-open prairies. For me, the Holy Spirit personified as wind makes sense. Perhaps this is how Patterson, raised on the moors, with his backpack over his shoulder and hearing the kestrel's cry, felt what he termed a "Celtic" reverence for the divine presence in nature. For the writer from Nova Scotia, it is perhaps the seascape, or the Cape Breton Highlands, or the marshes that inspire.

It must also affect a writer to spend so much time in a landscape like Wigtownshire, where Neolithic tombs, Norman mottes, and Victorian manors all jostle for space. Not long after we passed the White Loch, I had the good chance to look at the Ordnance Survey app on my phone and saw that there were "standing stones" by the trail. I looked up and could see the enclosure within a few metres of where we'd pass. "Come on," I called to Ken and Christine. "Finally we get to see one of these things!"

The Drumtroddan Stones are three to four thousand years old; they were once part of a larger stone circle. Neolithic peoples dragged the several-ton stones to this place, then set them into the earth as menhirs, so that millennia later, they're still standing. (Two of the Drumtroddan Stones have fallen; only one remains erect.) As with the many, many other standing stones in southwest Scotland, no one really knows what purpose they served, whether astrological, religious, political, or some combination (Stell 1986, 166).

The past may be foreign territory for us, but standing in that enclosure, looking south toward the ocean and east toward the Galloway Hills, it's hard not to imagine that the stones, on their natural lookout, represent what the preface to the book *Sacred South-West Scotland* says: a concern "to establish a relationship with the unseen spiritual world and acknowledge a sense of a life beyond death" (Hume 2009, ix). We wandered between the stones a short while, then decided not to go the extra half-kilometre off-track to see the cup-and-ring markings. There was a young couple just parking their car as we left, walking up the path hand-in-hand.

The balance of the afternoon was spent walking by small farms and cottages. I was pretty sure by this point that I'd lose the nail on my small toe, and my left ankle was swollen. I would have paid money to be able to walk even a while on the left side of the road, just for a change of pace from the bevelled right edge (one leg constantly very slightly higher than the other). But given the direction of traffic it was too dangerous. And I counted myself fortunate: I could see how badly Ken was hobbling, despite setting a good pace. Christine seemed resolute and cheerful as always. For a while, then, Ken fell back, and he and I chatted.

When we caught up, Christine was sitting on a large rock at an intersection, resting her feet. The map said we were at "Craig Cottages." Above Christine was a post with signs indicating "Whithorn 2" in one direction and "Glasserton 2" in another. Nearby, a man was mowing grass beside a handsomely restored stone cottage, the yard festooned with crocosmia, brilliant red against the white-washed stucco. He stopped his mower, wiped his hands on his slacks, and came over to introduce himself. Albert told us how he and his wife had holidayed for many years in a caravan park near Whithorn. After their retirement they decided they might as well purchase and stay year-round. Like so many others we'd met in Galloway, he spoke with a southern, English, accent.

"Oh, you're only a few minutes from Whithorn now," he encouraged us. We told him we'd heard that before. "No, no, this time it's true!" Al laughed. Catching a glimpse of his neighbour, he waved. "There's Ian now. Haven't seen him outside in weeks. Must be the excitement of having people pass through." Across the intersection, a thin, bearded man was weeding. "Take a look at his statues when you pass by," Albert said over his shoulder as he went back to his mower. "Ian's an artist. Does interesting stuff."

Obligingly, we slowed our pace to see the various molded-concrete busts set out alongside the road. Ian never did say hi; perhaps he wanted his statues to do the talking. Some had a generic quasi-Buddhist look;

others were downright Easter Island in inspiration. One in particular caught my attention with his bald head and huge, bulbous nose. He had a grin on his face, as if to say: "Pilgrims? I've seen *your* type before!"

121 ST. NINIAN STREET

"The building, dedicated on 13 September 1874, was a striking departure from the traditional small-scale wooden churches of rural Nova Scotia. It was a magnificent edifice with its Romanesque arches, thirty-foot (nine-metre) windows, and double colonnade of pillars with lush Corinthian capitals."

(Stanley-Blackwell and MacLean 2004)

One of the ironies of Ninian Cathedral, Antigonish, is that it's so much grander than the ruins of the original – the one-time priory in Whithorn. Another irony is that the only functioning church building now on the grounds of Ninian's site in Whithorn, Scotland, is not Catholic, but St. Ninian's Priory, which is Episcopal (Church of Scotland). By contrast, Saint Ninian Antigonish is a true cathedral, built to be the seat of the bishop of the diocese. Bishop MacKinnon's intentions were so clear, and the church so important, that it was informally called "the Cathedral" well before Antigonish was officially declared the seat of the diocese in 1886 and granted the right to have one. In this case, the people seem to have spoken before the Vatican did (Ludlow 2015, 48).

Bishop MacKinnon must have decided that a Sunday was the only proper day for a dedication, since Saint Ninian Cathedral was dedicated on Sunday, September 13, 1874, on what happened to be the "Feast of the Holy Name of Mary," rather than three days later on the feast day for St. Ninian, September 16. (Our arrival as a group for the cathedral's 150th anniversary mass took place Sunday, September 15, 2024, on what Bishop Kirkpatrick pointedly called "the *eve* of our patron saint's day.")

Sketches of the cathedral at the time of its dedication show it alone against a bare hill overlooking the town. These days, the buildings of St. Francis Xavier University surround the church on three sides. Given the proximity and the shared history, do students see it as the "university church"? That probably depends on whom you ask. One thing is sure: the tight bond between cathedral and university, and between the church's and the university's administrations has loosened markedly in the last two decades. Both the student body and the town have become less Catholic and more agnostic, ecumenical, and multifaith.

The answer may also depend on whether the students in question are looking for a parking space. Poor Saint Ninian Cathedral regularly has student vehicles parking in parishioner-only spots. The frequent funerals and weddings at Saint Ninian are preceded by extensive temporary signage begging that parking be respected for the church's needs.

This is a far cry from the time of construction. Several of the sources I consulted mentioned the 1871 bazaar, which was run as a fundraiser for the cathedral. In the place behind St. Ninian's Hall where I often park to teach, they constructed a "four-tiered amphitheatre designed to accommodate three thousand people." The bazaar was run in conjunction with the annual Highland Games, and in 1871 featured the stone put, caber toss, and Scottish hammer throw. It says something about Antigonish even now that on the Hall of Fame webpage for its Highland Games athletes (antigonishhighlandgames.ca) two of the honorees are Catholic priests.

One of the more recent, Father Doug Macdonald, at six feet, four inches tall and 285 pounds, won the world championship in caber toss five times in a row. A caber is a five- or six-metre-long pole formed from a larch tree and weighing between forty to seventy kilograms. Running with and "tossing" such a heavy and long pole involves an unusual combination of strength, agility, and balance (there's a striking photo of a 1940 caber toss in Peggy Thompson's *Antigonish: A History in Pictures* (64)). The web page remarks that Father Doug "retired after the 2004 season as a sacrifice to the Lord to focus on the priesthood."

Like many cathedrals, Saint Ninian Antigonish is set on a hill. It was, and is, quite a departure from any other church architecture in northern Nova Scotia. The main building is 170 feet long and 70 feet wide.

Its original roof was made from Scottish slate, the very type we stumbled over on our way out of New Luce. The two towers are 125 feet high, while the middle façade is a hundred feet bottom to top. The huge blocks of local sandstone and limestone from which the cathedral were built came in the 1860s and 1870s, largely from nearby North Grant and Brierly Brook, and were transported by horse and wagon or oxen and wagon, often by volunteers. There are four massive church bells, but surprisingly, the one dedicated to St. Ninian is only the second largest: the largest is for St. Joseph, while St. Columba and St. Margaret of Scotland each get a bell as well (Walsh 1989, 84).

Before you enter the cathedral, glance up to the middle of the façade. You may need binoculars for a good look, since the façade rises a hundred feet (over thirty metres) from where you stand. At the top, just below the cross, the stonemason for the cathedral, a man named McIsaac, carved the words "Tigh Dhé," or "House of God" (we were taught by two different Gaelic speakers how to pronounce this, during the 2024 group pilgrimage). To each side of the Gaelic citation there are carved shamrocks and two sprigs of thistle – the shamrocks for the master builder of the cathedral, Sylvester O'Donoghue of Wicklow, Ireland, and the thistle for the Scottish ancestry of most of the parishioners (Stanley-Blackwell and MacLean 2004, 129).

The main door of the church is an impressive wooden entrance, but I prefer to use the side door. As a pilgrim, that's the door that is most likely to be open during the day, when the faithful come to meditate or for prayer. One last thing before you enter: notice that there are three niches built into the façade, presumably for statues which have never been commissioned. When I spoke to the present rector of the cathedral not long ago, he was discussing raising money for continued art restoration inside the cathedral. Outside statues are clearly not a priority.

THE HOUSE AT THE EDGE OF THE EARTH

"Any journey can become a pilgrimage for the religiously minded."

(Falcasantos 2017)

The last few kilometres by foot into Whithorn were anticlimactic – they reminded me of the experience I had many years ago of arriving in Santiago, Spain, through the industrial parks on the outskirts of that city. Most medieval pilgrims to the Shrine of St. Ninian would not have arrived as we did in any case. They would have come from the sea and been greeted by the majestic vista of the Isle of Whithorn, four miles south and east on Wigtown Bay. There, from the waves, their first sight of their sacred destination would have been Ninian's Chapel, a lonely twelfth-century stone building standing sentry at the point. We twenty-first-century pilgrims, arriving by land, passed a series of cattle barns and a farm identified as "Bishopton" on the OS maps. Presumably these were once the lands of the Bishop of Whithorn. Where long steel cattle barns now line the road, there was once a Catholic church, but nothing remains of it (Muir Watt undated, 92). To look sideways from the road was to see long lines of bovine heads, the cattle twisting their necks sideways to gaze placidly at us, then stretching them out again through the steel rungs for hay.

Medieval seafaring pilgrims encountered other pilgrim ships from Ireland, the Isle of Man, Gaul, Scandinavia, and points further afield. We had to dodge a constant back-and-forth shuttle of Massey Ferguson and Deutz-Fahr tractors banging and bouncing past in high gear to deliver wagonfuls of loose hay. Whithorn is a sleepy place. Even in the outer village limits, there were more tractors passing on the street than cars. Here was proof positive of yet another little-known fact Peter Ross had let drop as we chased him along the path out of Glenluce. "Galloway," he told us, "is responsible for forty percent of Scotland's beef production." I wondered how much of that contribution comes from Whithorn and its former bishop's lands.

Our info sheet gave the B&B we were to stay at as the Mansefield Inn, 22 St. John Street, Whithorn. I'm not sure what I expected to see first, but it was not the sight that greeted us.

Where Google Maps told us our B&B should be, we encountered a rather unbelievable display. Two Gulf Oil gas pumps, somewhat ancient themselves, stood in front of a gaunt, dark stone church trimmed with rust-brown brick. From its ribbed and arched entrance, a bright yellow wooden kiosk emerged, looking for all the world like a garden shed with windows, extruded from the inside of the church. On the traditional Presbyterian-style turreted tower was hung a large sign with the triple triangles warning, not of predestined salvation, but of toxic chemicals.

It was as if a mid-twentieth-century petrol station had found love with an old Presbyterian Free church, and this was the postmodern offspring.

I found the whole thing delightfully odd, and more than slightly retro, and I spent more time than I should have taking photos before we discovered our actual B&B tucked in at the end of a long yard behind the petrol station. The large and gracious Mansefield House had once been the manse of St. John's Church. It had been renovated as well, but thankfully, more traditionally. "That's the first time I've seen a church converted to a gas station," I remarked to our host, who told us the church had been built in 1892 and converted to a garage in 1947. "It's not just a petrol station," she answered slightly defensively. "It has service bays on the side. It's a full-service garage."

Further toward the abbey, St. John Street (its name perhaps an echo of the St. John's Hospitallers, who once protected and helped pilgrims) turns into George Street. The street widened; we found out later that this was the medieval part of Whithorn, centred on the abbey. The homes along the main street were quiet. As elsewhere in Galloway, most are Georgian in style. They're stone, brick, or white stucco, with occasional rare splashes of colour where a homeowner has gone for a green or blue door, or a contrasting trim. We passed a Pentecostal Holiness Church operating out of a former furniture rebuilder: "Jesus Saves" under a sign reading "Stuffit Upholstery."

Then we spied a wide, blue-trimmed storefront topped by a rarity, a new sign: "The Whithorn Story." Was this the same place as the Whithorn Trust? And how did it relate to the Whithorn Priory Museum, where we knew we'd find the old stone crosses we were told we must see? The "Whithorn Story" looked inviting, not only for its welcoming glass windows, but also because it was one of the few signs of life on the street. But the steeple we'd first spotted from outside town was just around the corner. It was getting late. We decided to check the abbey first.

Two buildings down from "The Whithorn Story" was a medieval-style gatehouse, its arch topped by a heraldic crest. We walked through it into what our map called the Pend, then up the very short Bruce Street. As one would expect in Scotland, that name indicates "the" Bruce: Robert, or Robert I, the ancestor of James IV, who in 1329 made his final difficult journey to the Shrine of St. Ninian to seek a cure for the skin ailment that killed him three months later. A woman was loading gardening supplies into a car; she smiled at us as we passed. There were a few private homes, but after this many miles, our focus was the ruins of the medieval abbey straight ahead. To our right we discovered the Whithorn Priory Museum. The museum's door was closed. A little sign said: "Tour, 5 pm." It was 5:10.

Amid the graves scattered across the grounds at the top of the abbey hill ahead of us stood a grey Church of Scotland building. This one had no gas pumps. Its doors were open. It looked nineteenth century, no older. We realized this building could not be the "house at the edge of the earth." No one was about. Inside, we found a little table with a framed note. It said: "Welcome to all pilgrims. Please accept our certificate and use the stamp and ink pad provided as a memento of your visit to 'the cradle of Christianity in Scotland.'"

I wondered why that phrase was in quotation marks. There were several ink-jet printed certificates beside a stamp-pad, along with a flyer about St. Ninian, an evangelistic tract, a small pile of "Friends of the Whithorn

Way" registration forms, a devotional book and *St. Ninian's Prayer* leaflet, and hand-drawn directions to St. Ninian's Cave.

I didn't feel the need for a certificate. I left the pilgrim table undisturbed and went in to explore the church. It was pretty but felt unremarkable compared to the grand remains of the ancient priory outside. There were two notable St. Ninian stained-glass windows, which I later discovered had been given to the church by Marion (Maude) Gemmell Hutchison, daughter of the famed Scottish impressionist painter, and herself an artist (Hume 2009, 66).

When I came back to the entry, Christine and Ken handed me a certificate they had filled in for me, except for my signature. "Here," said Ken. "We think you should have this." I signed. Sometimes other people know more about us than we do. Neither of them is officially religious. I am. But I didn't ask questions: the certificate was an act of recognition and solidarity, as much *between* us as about us.

The three of us headed back to the main street to see if the "Whithorn Experience" was still open. In particular, I wanted to experience a toilet and a cup of tea, both of which were becoming real needs by this point, even after what had only been a nine-mile day.

In the tiny gift shop, we found a copy of Julia Muir Watt's book *Walk the Whithorn Way*. As so often happens on pilgrimage, we realized that the book was a resource we should have had with us from the very beginning of our walk, rather than something we only discovered at the end. We flipped through its compendium of facts, exclaiming to each other about places we'd been and things we wished we'd known. Ken bought the only copy. I asked the server/host if it might be possible to order another. "I think we may have some in the back," she answered. "Give me a few moments."

As we were enjoying our tea and cakes, a woman with reddish-blond hair, wearing a Whithorn Trust T-shirt came in, consulted with the server, and did something with the displays. It looked like my book had arrived.

The woman stopped by our table. She chatted with us about Whithorn, the abbey, and the pilgrimage route. She told us we were the first group of Canadians to make the walk. The Whithorn Welcome didn't have pilgrim certificates, but they were being designed, she said, not mentioning the certificates at the Priory Church we'd just visited. When the Whithorn

Welcome certificates were ready, she would send some to us. It was clear, both by the range of her knowledge of the Centre, and her questions of us, that she wasn't just stocking shelves. We'd bumped into none other than Julia Muir Watt, the person who had "written the book" on Whithorn and its abbey. It was Julia, because of her work with the Whithorn Trust, who was behind the drone-filmed and computer animated virtual tour of the Whithorn Way which had first inspired us to take the pilgrimage. We talked a bit about the trail and our adventures. After a short visit and a few photos with Julia, we headed back to the museum.

We were told the coat of arms we had noticed above the gatehouse was part of Whithorn's Royal Charter, granted in 1511 by the same James IV who was such an ardent pilgrim. On the voyage by foot he made in 1507, the monarch had arrived in Whigtown, north of Whithorn, only a week after leaving Edinburgh, but had refused to rest. Instead, he paid a guide fourteen shillings to take him, walking the final leg of the journey through the night, so that he could arrive for the first mass of the day (Macdougall 1997, 197).

I decided I wanted to go where James had gone that early morning so many years ago: *Candida Casa*, the shining house at the edge of the earth.

ANTIGONISH'S HIGHLAND NINIAN

"As it stands, the passage in Bede is a flashback within a flashback."

(Barrow 2004)

Step into Saint Ninian Cathedral and take a minute to let your eyes adjust. The normal human reaction to a cathedral is for the eyes to track forward and then up, toward the altar. This is by design and intent. Christian cathedral architecture was copied from large civic buildings in the Roman Empire, and awe is what such buildings were meant to inspire. For northern Nova Scotia, the inside of Saint Ninian Cathedral is extraordinary. As your eyes are drawn forward, they may rest briefly on the lush blue-greens and yellows that frame the frescoes along the ceiling. You're seeing the years of labour put into this "church in the woods" by perhaps the most famous of Canadian church artists, Ozias Leduc from Québec. More on him in a bit.

Oddly, the only painting of St. Ninian in the cathedral is not by Leduc but by an almost unknown Italian artist whom we only know as Apollonio. The painting is tucked away to your right in a corner, almost hidden behind a confessional. I was speaking with the present-day Catholic chaplain of St. Francis Xavier University, Father Donald MacGillivray, and he and the rector of St. Ninian, Rev. Danny MacLennan, both agreed that the confessional needs moving, and that, however it happens, the painting certainly needs a more significant location.

But how does one paint a figure about whom so little is historically known? Who is St. Ninian, the man behind the "flashback within a flashback"? Whoever he was, he almost certainly didn't look like the person painted by Apollonio. That artwork was commissioned by Bishop MacKinnon in 1857 for the former St. Ninian Church on Main Street and was later moved to the cathedral after it was completed (as were Bishop MacKinnon's remains). It was restored a century after its creation, in 1957, and is now the oldest artwork in Antigonish's cathedral.

I would not know what an ancient Roman-Briton person might look like. And I have only a vague, romantic notion of an ancient Irish monastic. But the visual of St. Ninian in the cathedral looks very unlike either to me. He's shown blessing – perhaps converting – a kneeling Highland chieftain, a man who is wearing what looks a bit like a blue and burgundy housecoat with a sash. Here at least, Apollonio seems to have worked at historical verisimilitude. The kilt, which is so famously associated with the Highlands, and which was worn outside The Brigadoon café by the 1950s men of Antigonish, has very little to do with ancient Highland clothing.

Paintings, like stories and hagiographies (a form of story), are meant to communicate more than facts. They contain a message, and the painting commissioned by Bishop MacKinnon is no different. Take a look at where each of the figures in Apollonio's painting stands, kneels, or sits within the frame. As you might expect, Ninian is front and centre. He takes the highest place in the painting. He's dressed as a bishop, and holds a crucifix in his left hand, while his right is palm upward, in a gesture that may mean a blessing of those gathered around him or may mean the receiving of heavenly grace. He appears to be rolling his eyes, as if saying, "What am I doing here?" It's an unfortunate and no doubt unintentional representation.

On our arrival in Antigonish after the twenty-three-kilometre trek from Pomquet Beach in 2024, we were invited to stand together at the entrance to the cathedral for a special blessing by the bishop to start the anniversary mass. Then we were given a section of seating close by the Ninian painting. During the service, it was possible to twist in our seats and watch the saint as he was being talked about.

The message given by Apollonio's positioning of the figures in the painting is clear: St. Ninian was in a position of authority over the Scots. This is a political statement as well as a spiritual and ecclesiastical one.

Whether you were Bishop Plessis in 1806 in Antigonish, with one eye on the newly conquering English in North America, or Bede in 731, in Northumberland England, with one eye on the newly conquering English in southern Scotland, Ninian was never politically neutral. Not surprisingly, pilgrimage often pulls the pilgrim one way or another as well.

ALEC'S TAXI

"Everybody knows Sandy. He's a fixture."

(Barkeep at the Harbour Inn, Garlieston)

The guide who took us around the small one-room museum to explain the stone crosses was Isla Scott. Historic Scotland, who run the place, have an excellent ambassador in her: she was as enthusiastic about the ancient stones as anyone could be, and knowledgeable enough to answer my questions about similarities with stone crosses I've encountered in Ireland. When asked about her training, she replied that it had mostly been "on the job."

Isla was particularly proud of the famous Latinus Stone, the oldest evidence of Christianity in Scotland, and one of the oldest in the British Isles. The text on the one-and-a-half-metre stone reads, in Latin: "We praise you, the Lord! Latinus, grandson (or descendant) of Barrouadus, thirty-five years of age, and his daughter, aged five, here made a sign" (Forsyth 2009, 22). The mere fact of this stone's existence confirms that people who were not monks or clerics self-identified as Latin, clearly spoke Latin, wrote Latin, and practiced some form of the Imperial religion in an area beyond Hadrian's Wall. All this, a century after Roman rule ended (Forsyth 2009, 36).

The Latinus Stone reminds us that there was no pivotal moment when bigger-than-life individuals (most of them men, since the hagiographies tend to be very masculine) fought bare-handed with monsters and "heathen." There's a lot of dramatic exaggeration in the tales of how risking life and limb brought the light of Christ to the dark isles – making such stories tempting to repeat. Good stories have a habit of spreading, despite the more prosaic evidence we now have of a late Roman Christianity that held on through the disintegration of the Imperial presence, and over the centuries, through both Celtic and Anglo-Saxon channels, gradually became local (Moffat 2005, 300-301; Wooding 2009, 16).

The next stone Isla showed us was the Petrus Stone (Stell 1986, 158-159), so-named because its carved letters spell out the inscription "The Place of Peter the Apostle" beneath a chi-rho symbol. This stone may be as much as two hundred years younger than the Latinus Stone, and likely comes from just outside the monastery on the road to the Isle of Whithorn (Radford 1967, 114). The Latinus Stone may predate Ninian, but the Petrus Stone follows him.

Ken was resting his feet and blogging about the day (his Wordpress blog is called "Reading and Walking"), but Christine accompanied me to the Ninian Shrine. There were extensive archaeological digs in Whithorn under Historic Scotland from 1972 to 1984, and by the Whithorn Trust from 1986 through to 1991 (Bold 2018, 154). In what was once the Northumbrian Abbey on this spot, the crypt we were entering would have been below ground level. In fact, Ninian's Shrine sat beneath the high altar in the nave of the abbey's chapel. When priests celebrated the mass, they were doing so right above what they believed to be the remains of their saint.

The anteroom to Ninian's Shrine was once an earlier church (Cox, Gall, and Yeoman, undated, 34). It still contains the bones of several bishops of Galloway, buried in places of honour closest to their saint. I found it touching to see these graves now, at the beginning of the twenty-first century. The saint these bishops loved and desired to be buried beside is gone. During the Reformation, Ninian's remains were removed by pious Catholics, taken to France for safekeeping, and then, unfortunately, lost. But the Anglian and Scottish bishops remain, their bones now mute witness to the theological truth that faith rarely sees what it loves so dearly.

On the far side of the bishops' remains is a small room with a gravel floor and stone and dirt walls, and a barrelled, stone ceiling. This is the partially restored crypt, which stands empty. All that indicates its importance is a modest plaque. It felt odd. Christine and I took pictures of each other in front of the plaque. Maybe it's a sign of just how post-modern I am that standing on the gravel in that quiet, empty room, celebrating a semi-mythical saint whose origins, fate, and body are all lost in time, felt just about right.

Ninian is a saint who ducks frustratingly in and out of history's shadows. He may (or may not) have been a Welsh Brythonic-speaking Romano-Briton (MacQueen 1961, 55), may or may not have trained in Rome, may or may not have been raised in a centre of late Roman Christianity near the west end of Hadrian's Wall (Meek 2000, 125), and may or may not have travelled by boat across the Solway Firth to be a bishop to some of the oldest Christian communities in Galloway (McCarthy 2009, 66-67). Ninian may (or may not) have lived in a simple, Celtic-style thatched hut monastery (Bradley 1996, 69) which may or may not have been at Whithorn and may have been (or likely wasn't) inspired by St. Martin of Tours (Wood 2009, 71-72) and by a visit Ninian may (or may not) have made to Gaul on his way back to Whithorn (Bradley 1996, 37, depending on the full traditional hagiography).

You get the picture. Whatever we can't be sure of – and there's a lot – by the end of our Scottish pilgrimage I felt I could state this, at least: Ninian existed. I believe this despite the significant scholarly opinion that even the name Ninian was a corruption of the Irish saint Finnian. It's true that a tradition of pilgrimage helps create a sacred site such as Whithorn (Cianca 2019, 17-18). It's also true that the *tradition* of pilgrimage is stronger at Whithorn than actual recollections of its saint. Yet it stretches belief that such a site might arise completely from nothing but a confusion of names. This is especially true when there is no material evidence of the kind of site disruption over a period of time that would account for the narrative to become so mistaken on such a basic point.

Dating Ninian comes down to a decision about two possible windows, the earlier during the disintegration of Roman-colonized Briton, and the second during the rise of Irish monastic influences on southwest Scotland (Wood 2009). Either we accept Bede's chronology of the late 300s or early 400s, or we understand Ninian as a more monkish saint who lived in the 500s and was part of the insular tradition, an immediate predecessor to Columba, and, according to Clancy, perhaps his teacher misremembered.

History is never neutral. Ninian's story is no exception, whether that be in its writing or in its reception. During the later Middle Ages, Ninian's memory became bound to Catholic Scottish nationalism (Turpie 2014, 4). Up until the beginning of the Reformation, royal patronage made Ninian the preeminent Scottish saint and he helped consolidate royal power (McRoberts 1968, ; Anderson 2019a). The sponsorship of the Stuart kings made the abbey wealthy and famous, and its town drew masses of pilgrims from all over the northern isles and further afield.

By the time we got back to the museum from Ninian's empty grotto, Isla was closing for the evening. We said our goodbyes and made our way back to the Mansefield House to meet the owners and arrange our rooms. Linda and Chris greeted us at the door. We were shown our rooms and showered and changed. Since there was no supper to be had in Whithorn, Linda reserved us a table at the Harbour Inn restaurant in nearby Garlieston. "Should we order a taxi?" we asked her. "Oh, I can take you!" she volunteered. Linda seemed to have a penchant for older-model, luxury cars. She unhooked the battery charger from a classic Mercedes and sped us the few miles to Garlieston.

It was the golden hour. A buttery evening sun warmed the white-flecked stones of the rock wall across from the Harbour Inn. We took photos of the purple and yellow pansies peeking out of the cracks, and of the dark sand and beached boats. The tides were high, reminiscent of the Bay of Fundy.

Tall Ken had to duck under the broad wooden beam to enter the pub. We enjoyed a good meal but were anxious to get back to Whithorn. There was still one day to go, a visit to Ninian's Cave and then a walk to the Isle of Whithorn and Ninian's Chapel. The barkeep nodded when we said we wanted to leave. "I'll just call Sandy." We waited in the sunshine outside, watching gaggles of locals who were in turn watching us.

The taxi showed up. "I'm Alec," said the driver, an older man with a ready smile. We got in. The car didn't move for a few minutes, as locals kept asking "Sandy" about his evening schedule and whether he could return at such-and-such a time to ferry them home. He never wrote anything down, just thought for a moment and answered "yeah" or "nay."

Then we were off. Alec kept up a fairly steady stream of conversation. He seemed to know the roads like the back of his hand. Christine occasionally let out little involuntary screams as Alec pushed the BMW's accelerator smoothly to the metal, speeding within inches of trees, walls, and stone fences. I hoped there were no pilgrims standing out on one of the blind curves as unwisely as I had the day before.

We were flying by one particularly impressive length of stone fencing when Alec, who had been giving a touristic introduction to the area more or less without stop, said that it had been built by French prisoners-of-war. "No one learns that history anymore."

I was confused. "Why would there be French prisoners-of-war in Scotland?"

"From the Napoleonic period," he replied, as if I were daft. While navigating another corner, he half-turned to look me up and down, an action which made Christine momentarily clutch my arm. "There were lots of Napoleon's soldiers here. And they made them build our stone fences. But they did well. People think the Scots built all our stone fences." He laughed: "Sometimes, it was the French!"

In Nova Scotia, it's the Acadians and the Scots who share history. But in Scotland, it's the French and the Scots. Some of the first Scottish kings invited French troops to help in their wars against England (Houston and Knox 2001, 173). Scotland was of use to France primarily as a counterweight and a potential military thorn in the side of England; France was of use to Scotland as a balance to England, as well, although this balance became suffocating to Protestants when French troops occupied Scotland in the 1500s. In the late 1600s and early 1700s, the French crown considered landing troops once more in Scotland, for the purposes of bringing the English to the bargaining table, restoring the Catholic House of Stuart (the Jacobites) to power, and ensuring Scottish independence (Houston and Knox 2001, 174, 318). How different Nova Scotia might have turned out had that happened.

Ken asked Alec if he'd always driven taxi. Ken hesitated on the word "taxi," since it wasn't clear that's what we were in. There was no meter, no dispatcher, and the locals, who all just seemed to know Alec, arranged rides by sidling up to the driver's side and asking if he might come pick them up.

"No," Alec replied. "The job I loved best was being a firefighter." He talked of retiring. Gales of rain sprayed against the side of the BMW. "How about Spain, or somewhere warm?" we asked Alec, gazing at the gloom. "Wouldn't you rather retire somewhere with better weather?"

"No." He downshifted smoothly for the hill near Outon. Chapel Outon may have been the "chapel on a hill" north of Whithorn that was visited by Charles IV on one of his pilgrimages to St. Ninian's Shrine (Muir Watt undated, 92). If the King were travelling now, I thought, he could do worse than Alec's BMW. "I visited the Canary Islands for twelve days once," Alec muttered. "Couldn't stand it. Got bored."

Alec, or Sandy, or whatever his name was, was certainly busy. We asked if he could drop us in the morning for our hike and then pick us up at the Isle of Whithorn the next day. Again, he didn't check phone or calendar. Just thought about ten seconds. Then nodded.

"Sure, I have several trips to make in the late afternoon. Should be fine."

NINIAN'S CAVE

"All solitary in my little cell, with not a single soul as company; that would be a pilgrimage dear to me, Before going to the meeting with death."

(Ninth-century Irish poem – Bradley 1993)

A few weeks after we departed Scotland, five hundred Roman Catholic worshippers gathered at Ninian's Cave to celebrate a pilgrim mass. This annual celebration began in 1924 when the Catholic Young Men's Society organized a train to take pilgrims to the town and the abbey. *The Galloway Gazette* reported on the event, calling it the "first post-Reformation pilgrimage to Whithorn." With the support of the Catholic bishops of Galloway, the tradition continued, with sometimes over a thousand people arriving for the mass through the 1920s and '30s (Bold 2018, 158). Starting in 1953, Bishop Joseph McGree moved the commemoration to the cave south of the village, where the saint is believed to have retreated for prayer and reflection.

When Alec/Sandy came to pick us up the next morning, there were no other pilgrims to be seen except us. "Oh, I'll take you right to the trailhead," he said, speeding the few miles down the quiet country lane, even though I'd made arrangements to meet two friends from Newcastle at the parking lot. Chris and Clare were friends I'd walked with on a previous pilgrimage. When they heard about Whithorn, they'd driven across country to join us on the final day of walking. After some confusion we managed to rendezvous with them. Finally sorted, we set off together under an umbrella of oak, maple, and ash, with ferns, bluebells, and purple milk-vetch, buzzing with insects.

Soon, the path opened onto a beach shingled with stones. At the far end there was a headland, punctuated by a spot of shadow: Ninian's Cave. We'd been told by several of the locals that sections have collapsed in the last few decades, and that the cave was once much deeper (Cox, Gall, and Yeoman, undated, 37). But the dark recesses of Ninian's Cave are still an impressive sight when the tide is up and the wind coming inland, white caps marking the sea all the way to the Isle of Man.

For most of history, humanity's highway has been the sea, not the land. The Irish Sea connected and still connects Ninian's Cave with a much wider world. In fact, Whithorn is closer to Belfast than it is to Edinburgh (Bold 2018, 154). We in the twenty-first century are so accustomed to land and air travel that we forget that what by road seems a remote part of Scotland has for most of history actually been at the very centre of water routes around the Irish Sea (Oram and Stell 1991, 3).

We took our time walking to the cave. Like everything else about the saint, the cave cannot be established with certainty to date to Ninian. But there is evidence of extremely ancient pilgrimage. Twelve centuries ago, the *Miracula Nynie Episcopi* describes how Ninian used the cave for prayers and quiet meditation. In different excavations, eight votive crosses dating to the eighth century were identified etched into the cave wall (Muir Watt undated, 99). Ancient carved crosses from the cave are on display at the museum.

For me, what was moving was seeing so much evidence of *contemporary* pilgrimage. Ninian's Cave clearly remains a shrine for many: at the entrance to the cave, present-day pilgrims have left their own crosses made of stone. Other crosses, made from twigs laced with bark, were stuffed into fissures in the rock, along with palm-sized flat stones on which people had written prayers of request or thanks, or sometimes, just names.

Set as it is beside the windswept ocean, Ninian's Cave transports one back in time. Stripped to the essentials of stone, wind, and sea, it's a perfect setting for the religious imagination. Patterson (1993, 121) waxes lyrical about the site: "At Ninian's Cave, men and women are released from the burden of regret from years past, and step as lightly into the future as John Bunyan's pilgrim once he had reached the Gate of Decision." Decades later in 2013, Catriona McMillan agreed: "The crypt is still an important enticement, but so is the wild, mythical quality of the cave. It is connected to the saint, but simultaneously represents something separate from the modern world, and in the experience of pilgrimage today, this has great appeal" (41).

Pilgrimage may have been officially banned in Scotland from 1581 through to the twentieth century, but that didn't stop pilgrims from visiting the cave. I saw one name carved into the wall dated 1718, another from 1771, and many more. After the others left, I lingered a moment, looking out over the beach. It doesn't seem unlikely that whoever he was, Ninian would have used this cave as a temporary retreat. The spot had the feel of a cloistered cell, close enough to be within the orbit of the larger monastic community, but still spartan and isolated enough for ascetic prayer.

Because of a hip problem Clare cannot walk far. She returned to her car. The rest of us crossed the shingle once more and began the climb that would lead to Whithorn Isle.

During our meeting in Glasgow with a Scot who knew the path we'd be walking, there had been an odd moment when we'd come to the part about the walk from Ninian's Cave to the Isle of Whithorn. "You don't suffer from vertigo, do you?" the man had asked with a curious smile. "No," we'd replied. He'd rubbed his hands together. "Good," he said. "On that section, the path is fairly close to some steep cliffs."

After we got up onto the highland overlooking the sea, I realized I should have answered differently. I would now say: "I don't suffer from vertigo – except on Burrow Head." That day, I absolutely *did* feel dizzy. I was terrified. I was astounded at how close the path took us to drops of hundreds of feet. Short-cropped grasses, slick with dew and buttoned with white saxifrage and yellow rockrose, hung over the lips of cliffs, nothing beneath but empty space.

"This won't be good for Ken; he suffers from a fear of heights," announced Christine, looking ashen-faced. Within minutes, I was bent over to make sure I had good footing. Christine nearly crawled on hands and knees on some parts of the trail. Ken, firmly upright, trudged along behind. "Maybe I was wrong," Christine admitted after one particularly scary stretch. "I guess it was *me* who's afraid of heights!" Fortunately, a stiff breeze was blowing inland off the sea, buttoning us firmly to the track.

We'd just passed through a short section where the path felt so close to the edge that a stumble on the slippery grass could possibly topple a careless walker down onto the rocks far below. A couple ambled toward us from the other direction, with a dog tied to the woman's waist. When we said hi, she cheerily announced, "He has to be tied up. He's a naughty dog!" She shook her finger at the wagging tail ahead of her. "We had to call the coast guard to fetch him a couple weeks ago." I still can't believe that conversation. There was no way I would have tied a dog to my waist on that part of the trail.

Once the path had turned a few metres inland, we managed to straighten ourselves and proceed through grasses dotted with yellow spearwort and tiny purple harebells. I relaxed a bit and found I could finally look out over the Solway Firth and watch the cormorants and gulls. On the promontories immediately below, we could see the remains of ancient forts, Carghidown and Castle Feather, one of which dates to the Iron Age (Muir Watt undated, 99). It was a stunning view, especially when the clouds cleared.

After that, I hung back and walked with Chris so we could catch up after almost six years of not seeing each other. Long and lanky, Chris talked about the directions his life has gone in retirement, and about his passion for the environment and his work seeking to restore the peat of the moors of Northumbria. Peat moss, he told me, is an excellent carbon sink. "How do you feel about writing about walking pilgrimages but having to fly everywhere to do it?" he asked me, gently.

Soon – too soon, now that we were comfortable again on the trail – we could see the Isle of Whithorn in the distance. We walked through a pasture, taking care not to stray too close to the back ends of the unconcerned cattle blocking our way. Clare met us at the outskirts of the village. Together we walked to the end of the spit of land, and Ninian's Chapel.

Of all the multiple endpoints for the Whithorn pilgrimage, Ninian's Chapel is arguably the most picturesque. For post-Romantic-period pilgrims like us, a windswept ocean view is exactly what one hopes for after miles of walking to a saint. Some have proposed that, in fact, this was the site of the original *Candida Casa*, the "shining house" (Maddrell 2009, 679; Simpson 1940, 71). I don't think it is. I believe the *Casa* was in Whithorn, despite the fact that Ninian's Chapel does sit, lovely and lonely, at the edge of the sea. Muir Watt puts it nicely:

> The final few miles from Whithorn via St. Ninian's Cave to the Isle of Whithorn are the coda to the Whithorn Way, just as the journey to Finisterre is the completion of the Santiago de Compostela way for many pilgrims. Facing the sea, with views of the Isle of Man, Cumbria, and distantly, Northern Ireland, certainly gives the sense of having reached the most southerly tip of Scotland (Muir Watt undated, 100).

Simpson, who in 1940 proposed that the "house at the edge of the earth" really was in the *Isle* of Whithorn, states: "The site which is the cradle of Scottish Christianity is at all times lonesome and rugged, suggesting little of its historic past, and in a storm, it is sublime in its elemental grandeur" (72). The fact that the location so perfectly fits Romantic ideals of a pilgrimage destination is one of the reasons I hesitate to accept Simpson's arguments for it. But as Muir Watt says, the spot does make a great epilogue to the pilgrimage.

There are ruins of yet another promontory fort on the extreme southern tip of the peninsula, the remains dating back to the first century CE. But it's Ninian's Chapel, a roofless, partially broken-down stone building that in its present form dates to about 1300, that immediately arrests the pilgrim's eye. We walked to the chapel, stopping just outside it at the "Witness Cairn."

The Witness Cairn is a low, stone-walled enclosure filled with clean, egg-sized rocks inscribed with prayers. It was created in May 1997 by an ecumenical group to commemorate the 1600th anniversary of Ninian's supposed arrival. There's a granite marker erected by local volunteers. It says: "You are invited to add your own stone to this cairn as a symbol of an act of witness which you have now completed or to which you now pledge" (Maddrell 2009, 680). I was struck by how many of the stones contained the names of deceased, with words like "We miss you" or "Forever in our memory." The pile of stones was several metres in diameter and over a metre deep.

We wandered briefly through the empty chapel, then sat next to the yellow St. John's wort on the low stone wall. When the on-again, off-again rain started on again, we headed back to Chris and Clare's car. Clare had brought homemade fruit cake, and from the boot she took out a container to give us for our return journey. Then we stopped by the village and St. Ninian's Tearoom for a cup of warmth and a few more minutes to talk before Clare and Chris took us back to Whithorn.

That evening, our dinner was at the Steam-Packet Inn at the Isle of Whithorn. As its name indicates, the Steam-Packet has been part of the harbour since the inn's founding in the 1800s. It witnessed the exodus of many from Galloway to Canada during the mass emigrations of the nineteenth century that also brought so many Highlanders to northern Nova Scotia (Muir Watt undated, 100).

Just inside the door of the pub, a trio of musicians were jamming on mandolin, guitar, and fiddle. We were ushered straight through and into an empty dining room whose windows open onto the harbour. We sat and looked out where travellers once moored to begin the final overland leg of their pilgrimage to the saint's remains. The view was so beautiful and barren in the grey mist that I was reminded of an Alec Colville painting.

As we sipped our pints, the dining room slowly filled. Ken ordered haggis with tatties and neeps (haggis with potato and turnip mash). The three ingredients arrived arranged in a tower topped with watercress and a savoury cream sauce. It was a Scottish masterpiece, as tasty as it was aesthetically pleasing. My meal and Christine's were wonderful and well-presented, but much less memorable.

We lingered. It was our last evening together, and we'd now covered all the possible Ninian destinations: the village with its ruined abbey, chapel, and museum; Ninian's Cave on the coast; and the Isle of Whithorn with its witness cairn and thirteenth-century Ninian's Chapel. As fellow travellers do, we began rehearsing the details of our journey. There's always something sweet in the recapitulation of trials endured and triumphs shared. We found ourselves retelling this detail of the walk or that, laughing at the memories, and shaking our heads at the mistakes. Space becomes place through experience, and meaning is carried in stories.

As we lingered over drinks, it was partly the temporary suspension of daily concerns that Christine, Ken, and I were already anticipating missing. Alec showed up to take us back to the Mansefield Inn. There, rather than heading straight to bed we stayed chatting in the sitting room.

We took turns choosing and sharing music that meant something to us. Unlike meeting other pilgrims on the Camino de Santiago or the one or two new people many of us met on the inaugural Nova Scotia Ninian Way, we had begun the Whithorn Way already friends. Yet our few days of shared experience had bonded us even more closely.

NOT FROM AROUND HERE

One third of Nova Scotians have Gaelic heritage. Gaelic language, music, and oral traditions permeate Nova Scotia's culture ... Nova Scotia is the only region outside Europe where Gaelic language, culture, and identity continue to be passed down through the generations, and where Gaelic is spoken in families and at community gatherings.

(Gaelic Nova Scotia: A Resource Guide)

Over the last two years, I've had the chance to spend some trail time with Lodaidh Séasonach-Fionghuineach, aka Lewis MacKinnon. Lewis is an avid walker and intensely interested in pilgrimage, both personally and as a tool for education and cultural awareness. He's also a poet, a fine musician, and a fluent speaker of Gaelic.

I asked him if he might be related to the same Bishop MacKinnon who established St. Francis Xavier University. "No," he replied. I was disappointed – I thought maybe I'd have some inside scoop on the bishop. "But you can be sure," Lewis went on, "that Bishop MacKinnon was a Gaelic speaker. And ...," he emphasized, "he most *certainly* would have ministered to his parishioners in Gaelic at his initial charge in St. Andrew's."

Pointing out an important historical Gaelic speaker didn't surprise me. As the head of the Office of Gaelic Affairs, Lewis never misses a chance to promote the language. But what he said next made me sit up and pay attention.

"Back in the day, there was significant pressure placed on Bishop MacKinnon by the Ultramontanist movement," Lewis said. "It worked to thoroughly 'Romanize' the Catholic Church here in eastern Nova Scotia and everywhere in the world. Ultramontanism created uniformity in worship (including language), covering the inside of churches with Roman artwork and building the Romanesque Saint Ninian Cathedral."

I reflected on the fact that pamphlets in the church emphasize the fact that the church was made with stone, drawing the parallel with St. Ninian's long-gone *Candida Casa* in Whithorn, whether or not that was part of the original impetus for the quarried limestone.

"All this resulted in Bishop MacKinnon concluding that Highland Scottish Catholics needed to shed their Gaelic language and cultural identity to advance their dire social and economic plight. Bishop MacKinnon wanted to remain in his St. Andrew's Parish – but he was directed by Rome to move to Arichat. Under pressure to 'Romanize' the region, he began to do so while his flock was still Gaelic speaking. At the time, they were even given Gaelic catechisms to address their spiritual needs." Lewis was emphatic: "From that point, however, within the confines of the sanctuary and governance of the official Church, Gaelic was out."

It turned out to be a double whammy for Nova Scotia's Gaels. The prevailing winds within the Catholic Church were encouraging them to abandon language and culture just when colonization was doing what colonization does best: pressuring Gaelic's uniqueness from the outside. As the Acadians of Nova Scotia and the Mi'kmaq also know full well, colonization works through shame to erase a community's identity and impose uniformity. Colonization's a bastard: discrimination becomes internalized, as it did by Scottish Gaels in Nova Scotia. In Lewis's words: "Whether intended or otherwise, colonial and later provincial policies removed Gaels' identity and language from the public domain and worked to prove their irrelevance. This was most evident in the exclusion of Gaelic language and cultural expression from the early public schools of Nova Scotia."

I thought we were done talking about Bishop MacKinnon, but Lewis had one more thing to say about the man with whom he shares a name but, to his knowledge, no direct relation. "Did you know a Gaelic ode was composed on Bishop MacKinnon's death?" he asked. "It was entitled

'Ó-chóin, a Rìgh! Gura mi tha muladach,' which means: 'Alas Oh Lord, I am Despondent.'"

History is complex. And sometimes ironic.

There are a million interesting things about Lewis, but one of the traits I most respect is the careful way he promotes Gaelic while making space for the other groups that have made Nova Scotia what it is today. Anyone who learned Gaelic primarily as an adult, and has become fluent, is clearly passionate about heritage and identity.

Yet in my experience he's completely unlike those – and they are too many – who see cultural identity as some kind of "zero-sum" competition, where any gains made by group A must be lost by group B, where you fight against the rights of others in order to supposedly protect your own position.

Through his office, Lewis promotes Gaelic culture and language. But you'll also find him posting about Dutch language classes, African Nova Scotian events, and Acadian festivals. He's careful to acknowledge the primacy of Mi'kmaq presence on the land he loves so dearly. In fact, when he spoke with our Nova Scotia Ninian pilgrims at the United Church supper we shared, the way he connected justice for the Mi'kmaq to the resilience and strength of Gaelic sounded, to me, almost spiritual.

In his last email to me Lewis signed off with: *Leis na beannachdan uile / With all the blessings.* It somehow felt good to be blessed in this language colonization hasn't erased.

My talks with Lewis came to mind when I sat inside Saint Ninian Cathedral and studied the frescoes lining the nave and apse, frescoes that have been painstakingly restored starting in 2012. They were first painted by Ozias Leduc from 1899 to 1904, over a period of four years. Leduc's masterpieces were unfortunately painted over in the last century by various botched "renovations" undertaken by those who did not recognize the value of the artwork: a 2020 CBC news story led with the headline: "St. Ninian's Cathedral in Antigonish, N.S., has been hiding a piece of Canadian history for decades." Michelle Gallinger, an art restoration expert, has been working with a team to recover the art from under as much as seven layers of over-painting. She does this as funds become available – if necessary, she says: "two saints at a time" (https://www.cbc.ca/news/

canada/nova-scotia/st-ninian-s-cathedral-restoration-reveals-art-history-antigonish-1.5774828).

Leduc was already famous when he was invited to Antigonish to paint art for the cathedral. Why and how he was tempted to the north shore of Nova Scotia is a mystery. The answer may be that it was a Canadian religious order who had helped pay for his trip to Paris in 1897 to study briefly there. According to conversations I've had with parishioners involved in the most recent restoration, it was a group of sisters who "called in the favour" and brought the artist to Antigonish. As a result, Saint Ninian Cathedral became the repository of some of Canada's most famous religious art, and the only church east of Quebec to feature Leduc's work.

The artist was a bit of a recluse in his hometown in rural Quebec. He was largely self-taught, apprenticing with various Italian painters in and around Montreal. His 1899 self-portrait seems, at least to me, to show the influence of Albrecht Durer, but he was also influenced by the Impressionists, and soon renowned for his own style, eventually being honoured by the Royal Canadian Academy of Arts. After his death in 1955, he was named a "person of national historic significance" in the history of Canada (Lacroix 2019).

There is much to say about Ozias Leduc, but my point as a pilgrim to Ninian is this: Ninian himself was probably never Scottish, despite the portraits of him. Nor are the later portrayals of Ninian that we find in Whithorn, and in Nova Scotia, necessarily Scottish. Leduc was from Mont-Saint-Hilaire, a town just east of Montreal. He was never a Scot, Highland or lowland, nor was Leduc Acadian.

The master builder of Saint Ninian Antigonish was Sylvester O'Donoghue, from County Wicklow in Ireland. Its architect was Adolph Levesque from Montreal. And as we've discovered, the person who first suggested the name was Bishop Plessis, back in 1812.

Lest we think that this multiplicity of paths leading to Ninian, so few of them Scottish, is only true of North America, remember that the point of origin for all we know of the saint was an English monk named Bede, writing in northeastern England. According to Bede's story, embellished in the *Miracula*, the builders of the stone church the *Candida Casa* were stoneworkers from Gaul, because building in stone was as unusual among the Celtic Britons as so many centuries later it was among the Caledonian settlers in Nova Scotia.

Ninian may be the first saint of Scotland. But he likely came from elsewhere, his story was celebrated first elsewhere, and his shrine owes much to the pilgrims from elsewhere who came to enrich it. By welcoming those who are foreigners or strangers among us, honouring what they bring, we are more in the company of St. Ninian than we think.

At least, that's the argument I made to a gathering at the Antigonish Museum in April 2024, when my speech on "The Mystery of St. Ninian" was part of their series celebrating 150 years of Saint Ninian Cathedral's existence. Judging from their reaction, I believe they found it convincing.

THE END AND THE BEGINNING

"You're early walkers from afar."

(Julia Muir Watt, post-pilgrimage email 2019)

In 1560, the Reformed parliament proclaimed the end of Catholicism as the official religion of Scotland (McMillan 2013, 4). However, its practice didn't cease, and the country briefly continued to swing back and forth between rulers and faiths. Judged by Protestants as a Catholic superstition, pilgrimage was banned altogether in 1581 (Bold 2018, 157). Over the next few decades, shrines were destroyed, abbeys torn down, and saints' body parts either lost, looted, or smuggled by Catholic believers to "safe" places where, unfortunately, as in the case of Ninian, they were lost.

After its high point in popularity under James IV, pilgrimage to the royal burgh of Whithorn ceased. Its saint and shrine disappeared from prominence – but not from the memory of the people of Galloway. Whithorn itself began a slow decline, evidence of which one can still see today. Everywhere in Protestant northern Europe, including Scotland, Christian pilgrimage went through an eclipse of several centuries. Tourism, always sheltered within pilgrimage, began to emerge as an activity in its own right (Anderson 2019b).

In the nineteenth century, in those Catholic parts of Europe where the practice had never ceased, Christian pilgrimage experienced revivals, often at scenes of Marion apparition such as Lourdes and Fatima. In many parts of the world in the twentieth century, barriers between Catholics and Protestants finally began to fall. As a result of increasing secularization and postmodernism, bringing with them some humility about one's ability to judge absolute truth, ecumenical movements took shape. Late twentieth-century Protestant churches were faced with collapsing memberships and looked with envy to both the Catholic example and the revived Camino de Santiago. They began to see pilgrimage as an opportunity for mission. The physical practice of pilgrimage was more tangible than the tired theological metaphor that "pilgrimage" had become in Protestant sermons and devotionals. It's ironic that it was only in 2017, two years before our Scottish trek, that the Church of Scotland voted to lift the long-unenforced legal prohibition on pilgrimages.

Contemporary walking pilgrimage differs from the medieval practice in at least one major way: most modern pilgrims don't walk home again. Yet pilgrimage inevitably has two directions. For our return from the Whithorn Way, we opted to take a taxi to the nearest train station and a train back to Glasgow. Our driver, like every other we had had in Ayr and the Machars, was talkative, anxious to tell us before we left whatever we might not know about this part of Galloway. He couldn't believe we hadn't visited the Kennedy castle three miles east of Stranraer. "Look," he told us, "we have enough time. I'm turning off the meter. See? I just want you to have a look at this." And with that, he drove us into the Kennedy grounds, where we gazed out at yet another White Loch, this one with a castle on an island in the middle, sitting like some fairy tale.

Despite being in the second-largest city in Galloway, the port of Stranraer had the feel of a ghost-town. Now that the terminal for the ferry to Northern Ireland has been relocated to Cairnryan, the Stranraer facilities stand forlorn. Weeds push through wide expanses of concrete near the station. An unknown travel writer named "M" took an 1809 tour of southwest Scotland. There she (I'm sure it's a she) mentions Stranraer in the most optimistic terms: "The town is so eligibly situated," she writes, "that its increase and improvement are unavoidable; the great roads to Dumfries, Ayr, and Portpatrick [are] leading through it, so that there is a constant resort of travellers" (341). We were alone for some time before a small group of others joined us on the platform for Glasgow. I wondered what "M" would have made of the place now.

"Almost unconsciously, I conjure characters out of particular places," writes Linda Cracknell of her encounters with landscapes (2014, 32). Some of the most memorable characters we met on the Whithorn Way

– Alec, the genial taxi driver; Loki's master, the gruffly winsome owner of the Maybole Arms – seemed to rise organically from the places we visited. They embodied southwest Scotland.

But equally, many of those we met didn't conform to any stereotypes of the country at all. At least, no Canadian stereotypes. The clean-cut Afghani Uber driver out of Dunure. Albert, from Cornwall, mowing his grass just outside of Whithorn. Dave, retired from the British Army and leaving the ghosts of Somalia behind in the wilds of the Machars ... in some ways, all these people were only slightly less alien to the place than we were. Southwest Scotland, and perhaps especially Galloway and the Machars, have always been a liminal place, where people from different origins met and mixed. Below the Antonine Wall, Scotland has from Roman times been a repository for immigration, as has Antigonish more recently along Nova Scotia's North Shore.

On our taxi ride from Whithorn to Stranraer, we asked our driver about the fact that so many of the people we had met seemed to be from the south, in England. He smiled and said nothing for a minute. "That's so," he admitted finally. "It's true. Folks from England." He paused again. "We call them the white settlers," he said finally. Then he laughed, slightly uncomfortably, as if knowing he was saying something he shouldn't, but couldn't help himself. It made me realize that the local Scots think of themselves as indigenous, and the newcomers as interlopers. As a North American settler-descendant, I couldn't believe my ears. To this day I'm not sure if I heard right.

The train ride back to Glasgow was uneventful. It's an odd melancholy, to retrace the steps of a walked pilgrimage in a car or train: all those days of blisters, conversation, and nettles are so easily and quickly spooled back up when witnessed from motorized transport. We laughed as we pointed at places we'd seen from angles considerably more uncomfortable than our cushioned ScotRail seats. We marvelled at the moors, wondered whether some of the Scots we saw packing their wet tents in the sunshine were squatters, and pointed at the spires we had missed in Paisley. We talked briefly about Ninian and agreed that we knew somewhat more about him for having had our eyes on the ocean along Whithorn's coasts. We were also wiser to the path's history, and to how the different groups and individuals trying to revive it continue to embody some of the uncertainty associated from the beginning with this saint and his shrine.

A SAINT OF UNCERTAIN CIRCUMSTANCE

"We walked inland from the seacoast; crossing over land rich in Mi'kmaq, Acadian, and Gaelic heritage; ending our journey by passing through the pilgrim's door; and parting with a special blessing."

(Pilgrim Brent King, Digital Postcard, September 2024)

The very lack of historical detail that makes Ninian so frustrating is the special *charism* or gift that he offers pilgrims. If faith were really just one glorious success after another, we could adopt Iona's *Columba* and be done with the Bishop of Whithorn and the Patron of Antigonish. But that's not how life works.

Most of us are weaker saints. We're thankful – until we forget to be. We trust, but then we doubt; we feel confident, but then find ourselves, surprisingly, caught on the hooks of worries and cares we know will pass tomorrow. We try to be mindful, then find that we've spent forty-five minutes ruminating on a problem that's not remotely within our power to resolve. We go through periods of exile and homecoming: sometimes literally, but perhaps also in other ways. We develop our reputations over time, and grow into our names, much as Ninian did.

The tranquility of a less popular route like the Whithorn Way and of a new path such as our walk from Pomquet Beach to Antigonish gives pilgrims space to develop as they need to, without an "ethos" into which they have to fit. There's peace in less trod paths. They embody the "silence that lives in the grass, on the underside of each blade, and in the blue space between the stones," in the words of poet Rolf Jacobsen (Kagge 2017, 34).

It was not hard to find Ninian in Antigonish, although the path to his presence in Nova Scotia is more complex than many folks realize. In Scotland, did we find the actual origins of St. Ninian? "Archaeology cannot put a name to the patron, but the burden of proof, in view of the continuity of the settlement, is surely on those who would argue that it was not 'Ninian' from the beginning," insists Jonathan Wooding (2009, 16). Despite the current scholarly consensus, I now believe the saint existed, and I think he was not a misremembered Irish monk, but a Briton sent north earlier, perhaps at the beginning of the so-called (but inaccurately named) "Dark Ages."

But we'll likely never know for sure. In a sense, Ninian stands for all of us who will be forgotten or at best misremembered by history, but who nonetheless strive to do what we can in our day. There is a profound utility to a St. Ninian. This helps explain his presence in Scotland, and why he showed up again so powerfully in northern Nova Scotia. It's also why I have come to appreciate him more and more over the years.

Back in Glasgow, Christine insisted that we stop at "Mackintosh at the Willow," an Arts and Crafts tea house designed by Mackintosh for Miss Kate Cranston, who opened the first tea room there in 1903. Every detail of the place was elegant and deliberate: the accents created by interlocking squares carved into wood, the lines of purple stained-glass balls, the door handles with flared edges, and the lamp bases whose rectangular forms match the light fixtures above – all are in the Arts and Crafts, Mackintosh style. Surrounded by this careful art, with people bustling by on the sidewalks of downtown Glasgow, my memories of the wild, cold, chaotic moors were already starting to slip.

Five years later, in September 2024, my social media was suggesting photos of Scotland for my "memories." But I was too busy to re-post them because I was finishing this other walk I had organized – a Nova Scotia Ninian Way. After our group reached the cathedral, after the mass and the ice cream social following it, I took some of "my" pilgrims back to their motel. It was the end of our inaugural Nova Scotia Ninian Way walk.

We only had to walk a few short metres to my car, waiting in the space where once thousands of the faithful watched Celtic giants toss tree trunks in the name of the Highlands. From the parking lot, it was less than twenty minutes to Pomquet by car.

In one short week – or one very long day – can a pilgrim really say that they get to know a place, even at the mindful pace of walking? In Scotland, we covered well over 140 kilometres. In Nova Scotia, it was perhaps only twenty-five kilometres all told.

In Scotland, we saw a lot of rain, beached jellyfish, sheep and cattle and dark woods, ancient tombs, barley and brambles. In Nova Scotia, I saw what my frequent commute too often makes me miss: the tidal pools where Lower South River empties into Antigonish Harbour, the great blue heron that lifted off, massive wings spread, as our group of fifteen approached Pomquet Harbour, the carved Gaelic above the cathedral entrance that fellow pilgrim Joann Chapman's example inspired me to pronounce as an exclamation, lifting my hands in the air: "Tigh Dhé!"

Walking is more intimate than driving. It's one very effective way of developing a relationship to a land, which is how you make an "anywhere" a "somewhere." It's partly by telling stories and remembering shared adventures that together we create a sense of place and a community of people. I hope that these two walks might do some of that for you, as they have for me.

Ninian's story is a narrative of exile and homecoming. The Mi'kmaq, the Acadians, and the Gaels know what that looks like: the ancient saint symbolizes so much of their history here in northeast Nova Scotia, and so many of the communities that make this place what it is.

I have a personal reason for these adventures, too, of course. Before we moved to Antigonish, Sara and I were in Dublin, Ireland. When we learned that we were moving to Antigonish, we looked at online maps of the town to see where we would be living and working. "Look, look!" I almost shouted, when we first saw it. "Can you believe it? The cathedral is named Saint Ninian!"

As someone who arrived in this place from away, I'm comforted by a saint who's also from somewhere else, and who always seems just a bit lost, both in Scotland and in Nova Scotia. When I set out on the Whithorn Way walk in 2019, I thought Ninian was likely fictitious. By the end of the walk, I discovered that, however many facts we gather, a saint's story becomes the most real when we see how well it speaks to us right now.

The *Candida Casa*, the Solway Firth, Hadrian's Wall, the Machars, Pomquet, Lower South River, Antigonish: can you imagine St. George's

Bay as the Solway, and sleepy Antigonish as *Hwit Aerne*? Official church teaching rarely admits that the purpose of a saint's story is more about shaping a future than reflecting a past. But the history a hagiography like Ninian's really cares about is the one it's creating.

Ninian is someone else's saint. But he can be ours, too, if we choose, and even more if we walk. That's how it's worked for me. This ancient, enigmatic figure turned out to be a useful patron – the saint whose open-ended story leaves it to us to fill in the details of home.

ACKNOWLEDGEMENTS

Thanks to my walking partners in Scotland: Christine Ramsay and Ken Wilson, with whom I've shared several long pilgrimages, and my partner in life and writing, Sara Parks, to whom this book is dedicated. Sara, you kept me on the path – at times quite literally – and when we finally found our way to the Nova Scotia Ninian, we found it together.

Special thanks to the brave pilgrims who followed me for the first Nova Scotia Ninian Way group walk on September 14 and 15, 2024: Joann Chapman (the first to sign on ... thank you!), Leona English, Hope Graham, Brent King, Shawna Lucas, Dorothy Ludlow, Maria Ludlow, Malcolm MacKenzie, Peter G. MacKenzie, Elizabeth Millar, Sara Parks, Sandy Pigeon, Joy Pennick, Elizabeth Skinner, and Anneke Wilken. Thanks to those who facilitated our group's pilgrimage in various ways: Paul Gagnon of the Société Acadienne Sainte-Croix, Jennifer MacDonald and the people of Ste-Croix Church, Rev. Peter Smith, Christine Briand and the St. James United Church Women for providing a pilgrim meal for us, and Lewis and Susan MacKinnon for dropping by the meal and sharing the story of Gaelic presence, culture, and language in Nova Scotia. My thanks for the welcome we pilgrims received at Saint Ninian Cathedral, especially to Dr. Barry MacKenzie for facilitating the visit, to the rector of the cathedral, Rev. Danny MacLennan, for his welcome and arrangements, and to the Most Rev. Wayne Joseph Kirkpatrick for the special blessing our ecumenical group received on arrival.

The Canada Council for the Arts gave me two Research and Creation writing grants in 2020 and 2021. While they were for a different project, it was this essential federal program that allowed me the time and space to also research the Scottish pilgrimage section of this book while living with Sara in the U.K. Canadians must work hard to preserve government funding for the arts in the face of business and political interests who wish to erode and diminish these important supports.

My time and research in Nova Scotia is funded by the Father Edo Gatto Chair, which I have the privilege of liminally holding at St. Francis Xavier University (StFX), Antigonish, Nova Scotia. I'm immensely grateful to the Gatto Committee of StFX for my term as a Chair, and to the Department of Religious Studies at StFX for housing me and welcoming me as one of the team from day one of our arrival in Antigonish. The library at StFX was incredibly helpful, and I'd like especially to thank Lorena Brothers of Special Collections and Mary Rose Laureys in the Microfilm and Music room for their help.

Thanks to the Rev. Dr. Winston Parks, former chaplain of Irving Memorial Chapel, New Brunswick, for the information concerning the stone fences and the chapel in Bouctouche, N.B.

I'd also like to express my great thanks to two local Antigonish County historians, Alfred M. Benoit of Pomquet and Fraser Dunn of South River. Alfred's advice on the local history of Pomquet, on the six founding families, and his insider's take on my community was immensely helpful. Fraser, meanwhile, was the treasure I was told he would be: not only full of maps and history, but also stories enough to enliven my search and this book.

Finally, thank you to Dr. Barry MacKenzie, who is both the director of the thriving Antigonish Heritage Museum and a down-the-corridor colleague when he wears his hat at the history department of St. Francis Xavier University. Barry – thank you for being such a God-given help, not only by putting me in touch with others who knew the area, but through your own careful reading of the manuscript. It was your invitation to speak at the museum on the topic of St. Ninian that led me down the path to this book.

SOURCES

Government, Trusts, NGO and personal websites:

Hike Nova Scotia: https://www.hikenovascotia.ca/

Nova Scotia Walks: https://www.hikenovascotia.ca/ns-walks/

Gaelic Nova Scotia: A Resource Guide: https://gaelic.novascotia.ca/sites/default/files/inline/documents/gaelic-nova-scotia-a-resource-guide.pdf

Ayrshire Green Network Consultancy Study for Ayrshire Joint Planning Unit, Forestry Commission Scotland and Scottish National Heritage (June 2011): 2.0/12.

Dumfries and Galloway Outdoor Trust: https://www.dgoutdooraccess.org.uk

Historic Environment Scotland (for information on Standing Stones, Ninian's Cave, Abbeys and much more): https://www.historicenvironment.scot/)

The Scottish Outdoor Access Code (the Right of Responsible Access): https://www.outdooraccess-scotland.scot/

The Whithorn Trust website, with information on historic and present-day Whithorn, including a "Walk the Whithorn Way" section: https://www.whithorn.com/

Walk the Whithorn Way website, with route maps available (note: not recommended for use unless with OS maps and, preferably, a smart phone with the OS app): https://walkthewhithornway.org/

2018 Mid-year population estimates of Dumfries and Galloway (Scottish Government site): https://www.nrscotland.gov.uk/files//statistics/population-estimates/mid-18/mid-year-pop-est-18-pub.pdf

Ken Wilson's blog "Reading and Walking"
https://readingandwalking.wordpress.com
Matthew R. Anderson's blog "Something Grand"
https://somethinggrand.ca
Matthew R. Anderson's pilgrimage podcast "Pilgrimage Stories from Up and Down the Staircase" https://matthewndg.podbean.com/
The Morris Family of Surveyors:
https://historicnovascotia.ca/items/show/186
"St. Ninian's Parish Cemetery" at:
https://www.stniniansparishcemetery.ca/history/
Antigonish Highland Games https://www.antigonishhighlandgames.ca
"Plessis, Joseph-Octave" in the *Dictionary of Canadian Biography*, at:
https://www.biographi.ca/en/bio/plessis_joseph_octave_6E.html

News sources:

Antigonish Aurora. "St. Ninian and the Early Scottish Church." Feb 13, 1884. p. 2. (A5-1884-110-2).
The Scotsman "Plans to Re-open West Coast Pilgrims' Way." 28 April 2011. https://scotsman.com/news/plans-to-reopen-west-coast-pilgrims-way-1678315
The Scotsman "Obituary: Andrew Patterson, parish minister and teacher." 11 Jan 2016.
https://www.scotsman.com/news/obituary-andrew-patterson-parish-minister-and-teacher-629558
The Spectator "St Columba and St Ninian." 20 Feb 1932. *The Spectator Archive*:
http://archive.spectator.co.uk/article/20th-february-1932/16/st columba-and-st-ninian
The Telegraph. "Church of Scotland asked to reverse centuries of hostility to pilgrimages.
13 April 2017. https://www.telegraph.co.uk/news/2017/04/13/ church-scotland-asked-reverse-centuries-hostility-pilgrimages/

Books and Articles:

Aldred, Ray, and Matthew R. Anderson. *Our Home and Treaty Land: Revised and Expanded Edition.* Altona, MB: FriesenPress, 2024.

Anderson, Matthew R. *The Good Walk: Creating New Paths on Traditional Prairie Trails.* Regina, SK: University of Regina Press, 2024.

Anderson, Matthew R. "Walking to be Some Body: Desire and Diaspora on the St. Olaf Way." *International Journal of Religious Tourism and Pilgrimage.* 7, 1, 7 (2019a).

Anderson, Matthew R. "Luther and the Trajectories of Western Pilgrimage." *International Journal of Religious Tourism and Pilgrimage.* 7, 1, 6 (2019b).

Anderson, Matthew R. "Why Canadians Need the Right to Roam." 29 July 2018. *The Conversation Canada.*

Anderson, Mosa. *St. Ninian: Light of the Celtic North.* Faith Press, 1964.

Barrow, Geoffrey. *Saint Ninian and Pictomania.* The Twelfth Whithorn Lecture, 20 September 2003. Friends of the Whithorn Trust, 2004.

Bede, *The Ecclesiastical History of the English People.* Eds. Judith McClure and Roger Collins. Oxford: Oxford University Press, 1994.

Bold, Valentina. "Chapter 12: The Whithorn Way: Twenty-First Century Pilgrimage in Scotland." *At the Interface / Probing the Boundaries* 109 (Oct 2018): 150-161.

Bradley, Ian C. "Scotland's First Minister." *History Today* 63, 7 (2013): 11-17.

Bradley, Ian C. *Columba: Pilgrim and Penitent.* Glasgow: Wild Goose, 1996.

Bradley, Ian C. *The Celtic Way.* London: Darton, Longman and Todd, 1993.

Brown, Keith M. "A House Divided: Family and Feud in Carrick under John Kennedy, Fifth Earl of Cassillis." *The Scottish Historical Review* 75, 200 (1996): 168-196.

Cameron, James. *For the People: A History of St Francis Xavier University.* 1st ed. Montreal, QC: McGill-Queen's University Press, 1996.

Cameron, James. *"And Martha Served": History of the Sisters of St. Martha, Antigonish, Nova Scotia.* Halifax, NS: Nimbus, 2000.

Cianca, Jenn. "Written by the Body: Early Christian Pilgrims as Sacred Placemakers." *International Journal of Religious Tourism and Pilgrimage* 7, 1 (2019): 11-21.

Clancy, Thomas. "The Real St Ninian." *Innes Review* 52, 1 (2001): 1-28.

Cox, Adrian, Sally Gall, Peter Yeoman. *Whithorn Priory and St Ninian's Chapel and Cave. Official Souvenir Guide.* Historic Scotland. Undated.

Cracknell, *Doubling Back: Ten paths trodden in memory.* Glasgow: Freight, 2014.

Daschuk, James. *Clearing the Plains: Disease, Politics of Starvation, and the Loss of Aboriginal Life.* Regina, SK: University of Regina Press, 2013.

Delaney, Ida. *By Their Own Hands: A Fieldworker's Account of the Antigonish Movement.* Hantsport, NS: Lancelot Press, 1985.

Dunstan, Petà. *Campaigning for Life: A Biography of Dorothy Francis Buxton.* Cambridge, UK: Lutterworth Press, 2018.

Eckardt, Hella, Gundula Müldner, and Mary Lewis. "People on the Move in Roman Britain." *World Archaeology* 46, 4 (2014): 534-50.

Falcasantos, Rebecca Stephens. "Wandering Wombs, Inspired Intellects: Christian Religious Travel in Late Antiquity." *Journal of Early Christian Studies* 25, 1 (2017): 89-117.

Fiander, Kate, and Gord Cunningham, "By Their Own Hands: 200 Years of Building Community in St. Andrew's Nova Scotia," *Coady International Institute, Occasional Papers Series,* 7 (May 2009), 3.

Flyn, Cal. *Islands of Abandonment: Life in the Post-Human Landscape.* Glasgow: William Collins, 2021.

Forsyth, Katherine. "The Latinus Stone: Whithorn's Earliest Christian Monument." Pages 19-41 in Jane Murray, ed. *St Ninian and the Earliest Christianity in Scotland: Papers from the conference held by The Friends of the Whithorn Trust in Whithorn on September 15th 2007.* BAR British Series; 483. Oxford: Archaeopress, 2009.

Frey, Nancy Louise. *Pilgrim Stories on and off the Road to Santiago.* Oakland, CA: University of California Press, 1998.

Gordon, Ariel. *Fungal: Foraging in the Urban Forest.* Hamilton, ON: Wolsak & Wynn, 2024.

Grenz, Jennifer. *Medicine Wheel for the Planet: A Journey Toward Personal and Ecological Healing.* Toronto, ON: Knopf, 2024.

Gribben, Crawford. "John Knox, Reformation History and National Self-Fashioning." *Reformation & Renaissance Review* 8, 1 (2006): 48-66.

Haynes, Michael. *Hiking Trails of Mainland Nova Scotia. 9th Edition.* Fredericton, NB: Goose Lane, 2015.

Henderson, Lizanne. "The Survival of Witchcraft Prosecutions and Witch Belief in South-West Scotland." *The Scottish Historical Review* 85:1 (2006): 52-74.

Hill, Peter. "Whithorn, Latinus, and the Origins of Christianity in Northern Britain." Pages 23-32 in Helena Hamerow and Arthur MacGregor, eds. *Image and Power in the Archaeology of Early Medieval Britain: Essays in Honour of Rosemary Cramp.* Oxford, UK: Oxbow Books, 2001.

Houston, R.A. and W.W. J. Knox. *The New Penguin History of Scotland: From the Earliest Times to the Present Day.* London, UK: Penguin, 2001.

Hume, John R. ed. *Sacred South-West Scotland.* Sacred Places. Edinburgh: Saint Andrew Press, 2009.

Jamieson, Christine. "Pilgrimage, Existence, and Psychic Distress: An Exploration of the Bodily and Psychic Phenomenon of Pilgrimage." *International Journal of Religious Tourism and Pilgrimage.* 7, 1 (2019): 77-84.

Johnston, A.A. *A History of the Catholic Church in Eastern Nova Scotia. Vol II.* Antigonish, NS: St. Francis Xavier University Press, 1960.

Kagge, Erling. *Silence: in the Age of Noise.* New York: Pantheon, 2017.

King, Thomas. *The Truth about Stories: A Native Narrative.* Toronto: House of Anansi Press, 2003.

Krawec, Patty. *Becoming Kin: An Indigenous Call to Unforgetting the Past and Reimagining our Future.* Abergavenny, UK: Broadleaf Books, 2022.

Krumpelmann, John T. "Gerstaecker's 'Germelshausen' and Lerner's 'Brigadoon.'" *Monatshefte* (Madison, Wis.: 1946) 40, no. 7 (1948): 396-400.

Lacroix, Laurier, Ozias Leduc, and Art Canada Institute. *Ozias Leduc: Life & Work.* Translated by Doris Cowan and Michael Frederick Rattray. Toronto, ON: Art Canada Institute/Institut de l'art canadien, 2019.

Landry, Simon Louis, and Mary Ida Landry. *Simon Louis Landry Speaks of Life in Pomquet.* Pomquet Press, 1990.

Lane, Beldon C. *Backpacking with the Saints: Wilderness Hiking as Spiritual Practice.* Oxford: Oxford University Press, 2015.

Lawson, Roderick. *Crossraguel Abbey: A History and a Description.* Paisley: J. and R. Parlane, 1883.

Leblanc, Tyler. *Acadian Driftwood: One Family and the Great Expulsion.* Fredericton, NB: Goose Lane Editions, 2020.

Leonard, Margaret Jane. *My Family History: A Historical and Genealogical Account of the Acadian Families Benoit, DeCoste, Boudreau and Deon.* Antigonish, NS: St. Francis Xavier University. StFX Digital Collections, 2007.

Ludlow, Peter. *The Canny Scot: Archbishop James Morrison of Antigonish.* Montreal, QC: McGill-Queen's University Press, 2015.

Ludlow, Peter. *Disciples of Antigonish: Catholics in Nova Scotia 1880-1960.* Montreal, QC: McGill-Queen's University Press, 2022.

M. "Sketch of a Short Excursion Lately Taken in the West of Scotland." *The Belfast Monthly Magazine* 2, 10 (1809): 341-45.

MacLean, Raymond A. *History of Antigonish.* Antigonish, NS: The Casket Printing & Publishing Co. Ltd., 1976.

Macdougall, Norman. *James IV: The Stewart Dynasty in Scotland.* Edinburgh: John Donald, 1997.

MacGillivray, Charles Joseph. *Timothy Hierlihy and His Times: The Story of the Founder of Antigonish N.S.* Antigonish, NS: Casket Print Co., 1935.

MacIntyre, Linden. *The Bishop's Man.* Toronto, ON: Random House Canada, 2009.

MacKinnon, J. B. *The Once and Future World: Nature As It Was, As It Is, and As It Could Be.* Toronto, ON: Vintage Canada, 2014.

MacQueen, John. *Ninian and the Picts.* Whithorn Lecture No. 15. Friends of the Whithorn Trust, 2007.

MacQueen, John. *St. Nynia: a study of literary and linguistic evidence.* Edinburgh: Oliver and Boyd, 1961.

Maddrell Avril. "A Place for Grief and Belief: the Witness Cairn, Isle of Whithorn, Galloway, Scotland." *Social & Cultural Geography,* 10:6 (Sept 2009): 675-693.

Maitland, Sara. "Let's learn to live with our "immigrant" wildflowers – one part of nature's rich tapestry." *BBC Countryfile Magazine* 152 (June 2019): 17.

Margry, Peter Jan. "Secular Pilgrimage: A Contradiction in Terms?" Pages 13-46 in Peter Jan Margry, ed. *Shrines and Pilgrimage in the Modern World: New Itineraries into the Sacred.* Amsterdam: Amsterdam University Press, 2008.

Markus, Gilbert. "Celtic Schmeltic (1)." *Spirituality* 4, 21 (Nov–Dec 1998): 379-383.

Markus, Gilbert. "Celtic Schmeltic (2)." *Spirituality* 5, 22 (Jan–Feb 1999): 57-61.

Marsh, James H. "Acadian Expulsion (the Great Upheaval)." *The Canadian Encyclopedia. Historica Canada.* Article published September 04, 2013; Last Edited July 15, 2015.

McCarthy, Mike. "Christianity in Northern Britain in the Late Roman Period: A Critical Assessment." Pages 57-70 in Jane Murray, ed. *St Ninian and the Earliest Christianity in Scotland: Papers from the conference held by The Friends of the Whithorn Trust in Whithorn on September 15th 2007.* BAR British Series; 483. Oxford: Archaeopress, 2009).

McGoogan, Ken. *How the Scots Invented Canada.* Toronto, ON: Harper-Collins, 2011.

McIntosh, Ian S. "Pilgrimages and Peace-Building on the Global Stage." Pages 3-18 in Ian S. McIntosh and Lesley D. Harman, eds. *The Many Voices of Pilgrimage and Reconciliation.* CABI Press, 2017.

McMillan, Catriona. *The Whithorn Pilgrimage: A Report. Third Sector Internship Report: Solway Centre, University of Glasgow,* 2013. Unpublished.

McRoberts, David. "The Scottish church and nationalism in the fifteenth century," *Innes Review* 9 (1968) 3-14.

Meek, Donald E. *The Quest for Celtic Christianity.* Haddington, UK: Handsel Press, 2000.

Methot, Suzanne. *Legacy: Trauma, Story, and Indigenous Healing.* Toronto: ECW, 2019.

Moffat, Alistair. *Before Scotland: The Story of Scotland Before History.* London: Thames & Hudson, 2005.

Murray, Jane. *St Ninian and the Earliest Christianity in Scotland: Papers from the Conference Held by the Friends of the Whithorn Trust in Whithorn on September 15th 2007.* BAR British Series; 483. Oxford: Archaeopress, 2009.

Murray, Peter J. "The Lay Administrators of Church Lands in the Fifteenth and Sixteenth Centuries." *The Scottish Historical Review* 74, 197 (1995): 26-44.

Nordenfalk, Carl. "An Illustrated Diatessaron." *The Art Bulletin* 50, 2 (1968): 119-40.

O'Loughlin, Thomas. *Journeys on the Edges: The Celtic Tradition.* London: Darton, Longman and Todd, 2000.

Oram, Richard D. and Geoffrey P. Stell. *Galloway: Land and Lordship*. Newton Stewart: The Scottish Society for Northern Studies, 1991.

Owen, David L. "Rocks on Ice." *The New Yorker*, 2018.

Parks, Sara, Shayna Sheinfeld, and Meredith J. C Warren. *Jewish and Christian Women in the Ancient Mediterranean*. Abingdon, Oxon; Routledge, 2022.

Patterson, Andrew. *A Way to Whithorn*. Edinburgh: Saint Andrew Press, 1993.

Paul, Daniel N. *We Were Not the Savages: Collision between European and Native American Civilizations*. 4th Edition. Halifax, NS: Fernwood Publishing, 2022.

Penman, Michael A. *Robert the Bruce King of Scots*. New Haven, CT: Yale University Press, 2014.

Radford, C. A. Ralegh. "The Early Church in Strathclyde and Galloway." *Medieval Archaeology* 11, 1 (1967): 105-26.

Rice, Waubgeshig. *Moon of the Crusted Snow*. Toronto: ECW Press, 2018.

Sharp, Iris. "From Whithorn to Wigtown." *British Heritage* 27, 1 (March 2006): 18-24, here 20.

Simpson, W. Douglas. *Saint Ninian and the Origins of the Christian Church in Scotland*. Edinburgh: Oliver and Boyd, 1940.

Smith, Donald. *Pilgrim Guide to Scotland*. Edinburgh: Saint Andrew Press, 2015.

Stell, Geoffrey. *Exploring Scotland's Heritage: Dumfries and Galloway*. The Royal Commission on the Ancient and Historical Monuments of Scotland, 1986.

Stanley-Blackwell, Laurie C.C. and Raymond A. MacLean, *Historic Antigonish Town and Country: Images of our Past*. Halifax, NS: Nimbus, 2004.

Tattrie, Jon. *Peace by Chocolate: The Hadhad Family's Remarkable Journey from Syria to Canada*. Fredericton, NB: Goose Lane Editions, 2020.

Terreault, Sara. "The Eschatological Body: Fleeing the Centre in Pre-Modern Insular Christianity and Post-Modern Secularity." *International Journal of Religious Tourism and Pilgrimage*. 7, 1 (2019): 22-37.

Thompson, Peggy. *Antigonish: A History in Pictures*. Cloverville, NS: MacIntyre Purcell Publishing, 2022.

Towill, Edwin Sprott. *The Saints of Scotland*. Edinburgh: Saint Andrew Press, 1983.

Turner, Victor and Edith Turner. *Image and Pilgrimage in Christian Culture.* New York: Columbia University Press, 1978.

Turpie, Tom. "Our Friend in the North: The Origins, Evolution and Appeal of the Cult of St Duthac of Tain in the Later Middle Ages." *Scottish Historical Review* 93, 1 (2014): 1-28.

Upton, L.F.S. "Indian Policy in Colonial Nova Scotia 1783-1871." *Acadiensis* 5, 1 (Oct. 1975), 3-31.

Van Gennep, Arnold. *The Rites of Passage.* First Ed. 1908. First English Ed. 1960. London: Routledge, 2004.

Walsh, Patrick F. *History of Antigonish.* Antigonish, NS: Casket Printing Co., 1989.

Warren, Meredith. "Invisibility, Erasure, and a Jewish Tombstone in Roman Britain." *Journal of Ancient Judaism* 14, 1 (2022): 1-20.

Watt, Julia Muir. *Walk the Whithorn Way. The Whithorn Trust Companion Guide to Pilgrim Heritage along the Westerly Route to Whithorn.* Whithorn Trust, undated.

Wilson, Ken. *Walking the Bypass: Notes on Place From the Side of the Road.* Regina, SK: University of Regina Press, 2025.

Wilson, Ken. "Populus." *Queen's Quarterly* 130, 1 (2023): 146-159.

Wilson, Ken. "Place and Space in Walking Pilgrimage." *International Journal of Religious Tourism and Pilgrimage* 8, 1, Article 3 (2020): 1-10.

Wood, Ian. "Britain and the Continent in the Fifth and Sixth Centuries: The Evidence of Ninian." Pages 71-82 in Jane Murray, ed. *St Ninian and the Earliest Christianity in Scotland: Papers from the conference held by The Friends of the Whithorn Trust in Whithorn on September 15th 2007.* BAR British Series; 483. Oxford: Archaeopress, 2009.

Wooding, Jonathan M. "St Ninian: Archaeology and the Dossier of the Saint." Pages 9-18 in Jane Murray, ed. *St Ninian and the Earliest Christianity in Scotland: Papers from the conference held by The Friends of the Whithorn Trust in Whithorn on September 15th 2007.* BAR British Series; 483. Oxford: Archaeopress, 2009.

ABOUT THE AUTHOR

Originally from Saskatchewan (Treaty 4 territory) and arriving in Nova Scotia via Montreal, England, and Ireland, Matthew R. Anderson is Gatto Chair of Christian Studies at Saint Francis Xavier University, Antigonish, Nova Scotia. He has walked ancient pilgrimage paths and inaugurated new ones in Spain, Austria, Norway, Scotland, England, Ireland, Iceland, Quebec, western Canada, and the Maritimes. He teaches, researches, and writes about history and pilgrimage.

Matthew's 2024 bestseller, *The Good Walk*, tells of the long treks he initiated with others across the Prairies to help recover traditional First Nation, Métis, and settler trails. His podcast is "Pilgrimage Stories from Up and Down the Staircase" and his walking blog is somethinggrand.ca. Matthew lives with his wife Dr. Sara Parks in Pomquet, Nova Scotia. *Someone Else's Saint* is his sixth book.

OTHER BOOKS BY MATTHEW R. ANDERSON

The Good Walk: Creating New Paths on Traditional Prairie Trails.
Regina, SK: University of Regina Press, 2024.

Our Home and Treaty Land: Revised and Expanded Edition.
Co-authored with Ray Aldred. Altona, MB: FriesenPress, 2024.

Prophets of Love: The Unlikely Kinship of Leonard Cohen and the Apostle Paul.
Montreal, QC: McGill-Queen's University Press, 2023.

Apocalypse et gin tonic: 10 cocktails pour explorer la bible
(French translation of *Pairings.*) Montreal, QC: Éditions Novalis, 2022.

Pairings: The Bible and Booze.
Montreal, QC: Novalis, 2021.